BOUNDARY ISSUES AND DUAL RELATIONSHIPS IN THE HUMAN SERVICES

BOUNDARY ISSUES AND DUAL RELATIONSHIPS IN THE HUMAN SERVICES

SECOND EDITION

Frederic G. Reamer

COLUMBIA UNIVERSITY PRESS   NEW YORK

COLUMBIA UNIVERSITY PRESS
Publishers Since 1893
New York   Chichester, West Sussex

cup.columbia.edu

Library of Congress Cataloging-in-Publication Data

Reamer, Frederic G., 1953–
   Boundary issues and dual relationships in the human services / Frederic G. Reamer. — 2nd ed.
     p. cm.
   Rev. ed. of: Tangled relationships. c2001.
   Includes bibliographical references and index.
   ISBN 978-0-231-15700-1 (cloth : alk. paper) — ISBN 978-0-231-15701-8
(pbk. : alk. paper) — ISBN 978-0-231-52768-2 (ebook)
   1. Social workers—Professional relationships. 2. Human services personnel—Professional
relationships. 3. Counselor and client. 4. Social service. I. Reamer, Frederic G.,
1953– Tangled relationships. II. Title.

   HV40.35.R43 2012
   361.3'2—dc23

2012001129

Columbia University Press books are printed on permanent
   and durable acid-free paper.

This book is printed on paper with recycled content.

Printed in the United States of America
c 10 9 8 7 6 5 4 3 2 1
p 10 9 8 7 6 5 4 3 2

Cover photo by Blue and White. © Getty Images

CONTENTS

PREFACE

IN RECENT YEARS the topic of boundary issues—both simple and complex—has become a staple in conversations among human service professionals. Boundary issues range from egregious cases of sexual misconduct to much more subtle and nuanced questions related to, for example, practitioner self-disclosure to clients and boundary management in small and rural communities.

Boundary issues occur when professionals—including social workers, psychologists, mental health counselors, marriage and family therapists, addictions specialists, pastoral counselors, psychiatrists, and psychiatric nurses—enter into more than one relationship with clients (and, in some instances, colleagues), whether professional, social, or business. Not until the 1990s did a critical mass of literature on the subject begin to emerge, although the broader field of professional ethics emerged as a bona fide specialty in the 1970s. This is a significant development in the evolution of the professional ethics field. Exploration of boundary issues also is the most recent development in my own evolving concern with professional ethics.

I first explored issues of professional ethics in the mid-1970s, at about the time the broader field of professional ethics (also known as applied and practical ethics) was just emerging. My inquiry started when I began to appreciate the complex ways in which human service professionals—including clinicians, administrators, managers, community advocates, policy makers, and researchers—encounter daunting ethical dilemmas that require difficult decisions. At the time I did not fully grasp how my nascent interest in this subject reflected a much larger phenomenon: the emergence of a new, discrete academic field focused on professional ethics. With the benefit that only hindsight can provide, I now understand how significant that period was. What began as a fledgling interest among a relatively small coterie of scholars and practitioners has evolved into an intellectually rich, widely respected field with its own conceptual frameworks, body of knowledge, vocabulary, and academic imprimatur. Professional ethics truly has come of age and is now embedded deeply in professional education and discourse.

At the same time my own understanding of ethical issues has evolved, leading to my current interest in boundary issues—particularly those in which human service professionals become involved in "dual relationships" with clients and, at times, colleagues. Up through the late 1980s my work in the professional ethics arena focused mainly on the nature of diverse ethical dilemmas encountered by practitioners, ethical decision-making models, and the practical implications of ethical theory. During this period my colleagues and I paid relatively little attention to complex boundary issues; the general subject hardly was a major focus of attention.

By the early 1990s my own interests had broadened to include issues pertaining to what I now call ethics risk management, including concepts and strategies that human service professionals can use to protect clients' rights, first and foremost, and prevent ethical complaints and lawsuits that allege ethics-related negligence or malpractice committed by professionals. This interest stemmed in part from my expanding service as an ethics consultant and expert witness (to use the court's term) in a large number of lawsuits and licensing board cases around the United States involving human service professionals. Also, my emerging interest in risk-management issues has been influenced by my position as chair of a statewide committee responsible for managing ethics complaints filed against social workers. Further, a significant portion of the court cases and ethics complaints in which I have been involved as a consultant or expert witness have concerned the kinds of boundary issues that I examine in this book. In addition, my experience as chair of the national committee that wrote the current *Code of Ethics* of the National Association of Social Workers deepened my understanding of the complicated challenges involved in cultivating ethical standards and providing sound guidance pertaining to boundary issues.

What I have learned over the years is that, without question, boundary and dual relationship issues are among the most challenging ethical dilemmas in the human services. Some dual relationships, such as sexual relationships with clients, need to be prevented. Other dual relationships are inevitable and need to be managed carefully—for example, when professionals who work and live in a rural area or on a military base encounter clients outside the clinical office.

Human service professionals have struggled with some boundary issues ever since the field was created, for example, managing social interactions with former clients, self-disclosures to clients, and responding to clients' gifts. However, other boundary issues are of much more recent origin—such as practitioners' use of social media sites and other Internet services in their relationships with clients—and could not possibly have been imagined by earlier generations of practitioners. Our collective understanding of these issues—the diverse forms they take, their consequences, and implications—has matured greatly in recent years. This book represents my effort to organize and reflect on these complex issues and to suggest how human service professionals who face them can best protect clients and themselves.

This book contains considerable case material. In most instances I disguise case-related details to protect the privacy of the parties involved. Some cases are a matter of public record.

BOUNDARY ISSUES AND DUAL RELATIONSHIPS IN THE HUMAN SERVICES

choice, matching, fill-in-the-blank/short answer,
differences in test-taking ability amongst
avenues of assessment. *Note: anyone needing
instructor PRIOR to exam day unless previously

and critical thinking in order to complete projects
ons. These presentations will be graded on content
ated, this is not a speech course therefore delivery

e, matching, and fill-in-the-blank questions. They
yone needing assistance with tests or quizzes must
ss previously arranged through the counseling

1

BOUNDARY ISSUES AND DUAL RELATIONSHIPS

Key Concepts

CONSIDER THE FOLLOWING case scenarios and imagine yourself as the human service professional. How would you handle the boundary issues in these circumstances?

■ Tanya M., a counselor employed in a community mental health center, provides services to clients with chronic mental illness. One of her clients, who is being treated for bipolar disorder, has been abusing alcohol and cocaine. Tanya encouraged the client to begin attending twelve-step meetings. The client decides to attend a local meeting that she chose from a list of area meetings. At the meeting the client encountered Tanya, who has been in recovery for nearly nine years. Tanya was surprised to see her client at the meeting and had to decide whether to stay in the meeting and whether to speak at the meeting in front of her client.

■ Belinda K. was a case manager at a family service agency. She developed a good working relationship with a client, Theresa B., who was referred to the agency after she was released from prison on parole. Theresa deeply appreciated the help she received from Belinda and decided to give Belinda a gift—a bracelet worth about twenty dollars. Belinda had to decide whether to keep the gift. One concern she had was that Theresa would be offended if Belinda returned the gift. However, Belinda's agency had a policy that prohibited staff from accepting gifts from clients.

■ Stephen M. was a counselor in private practice. One of his clients, Daphne F., a religious woman, asked Stephen to please spend time with her reading passages from the Bible. Stephen was not particularly religious but thought it might be therapeutically helpful to Daphne to read the Bible with her. Stephen wasn't sure whether it would be appropriate for him to read the Bible with Daphne.

■ Phoebe W. was a social worker at an outpatient counseling program for adolescents. One of Phoebe's clients, Anna, sixteen, struggled with issues of depression and marijuana abuse. Over time Phoebe and Anna developed a strong therapeutic alliance. During one clinical session Anna asked Phoebe whether she had smoked marijuana as a teenager and whether Phoebe had ever gotten high. Phoebe was unsure whether to respond candidly about her own drug use as a teenager. In addition, Anna asked Phoebe to "friend" her on Facebook.

■ Phil C. was a counselor in a group private practice. Phil provided counseling services to a young man, Dwayne L., who was struggling with anxiety. Dwayne worked hard in treatment and terminated after about seven months. Phil and Dwayne had an excellent therapeutic relationship. Nearly seven years later Phil and Dwayne encountered each other, entirely by coincidence, at a mutual acquaintance's holiday party. Phil and Dwayne thoroughly enjoyed reconnecting. Phil and Dwayne enjoyed each other's company so much that they talked about getting together again socially. A couple of colleagues in Phil's peer consultation group expressed concern about his entering into a relationship with a former client.

In recent years human service professionals have developed an increasingly mature grasp of ethical issues in general and, more specifically, boundary issues (Reamer 2006c). The professional literature has expanded markedly with respect to identifying ethical conflicts and dilemmas in practice; developing conceptual frameworks and protocols for ethical decision making when professional duties conflict; and formulating risk-management strategies to avoid ethics-related negligence and ethical misconduct (Barnett and Johnson 2008; Barsky 2009; Bernstein and Hartsell 2008; Bersoff 2008; Congress 1999; Corey, Corey, and Callanan 2010; Gray and Webb 2010; Koocher and Keith-Spiegler 2008; Loewenberg, Dolgoff, and Harrington 2008; Nagy 2010; Pope and Vasquez 2010; Reamer 2003a, 2006a–b, 2009a; Wilcoxon, Remley, and Gladding 2011).

Clearly, ethical issues related to professional boundaries are among the most problematic and challenging. Briefly, boundary issues arise when human service professionals encounter actual or potential conflicts between their professional duties and their social, sexual, religious, collegial, or business relationships (DeJulio and Berkman 2003; Gutheil and Gabbard 1993; Reamer 2008a–b, 2009a–c; St. Germaine 1993, 1996; Syme 2003; Zur 2007). As I will explore more fully later, not all boundary issues are problematic or unethical, but many are. My principal goal is to explore the range of boundary issues in the human services, develop criteria to help professionals distinguish between boundary issues that are and are not problematic, and present guidelines to help practitioners manage boundary issues and risks that arise in professional work.

BOUNDARY ISSUES IN THE HUMAN SERVICES

Human service professionals—be they clinicians (social workers, psychologists, mental health counselors, psychiatrists, marriage and family therapists, psychiatric nurses, pastoral counselors), case managers, administrators, community organizers, policy makers, supervisors, researchers, or educators—often encounter circumstances that pose actual or potential boundary issues. Boundary issues occur when practitioners face potential conflicts of interest stemming from what have become known as dual or multiple relationships. According to Kagle and Giebelhausen, "A professional enters into a dual relationship whenever he or she assumes a second role with a client, becoming social worker and friend, employer, teacher, business associate, family member, or sex partner. A practitioner can engage in a dual relationship whether the second relationship begins before, during, or after the social work relationship" (1994:213). Dual relationships occur primarily between human service professionals and their current or former clients, between professionals and their clients' relatives or acquaintances, and between professionals and their colleagues (including supervisees, trainees, and students).

Historically, human service professionals have not generated clear guidelines regarding boundaries for use in practice. This is partly because the broader subject of professional ethics—to which the topic of boundaries is closely tied—did not begin to receive serious attention in the scholarly and professional literature until the early 1980s. In addition, the human services field, starting with Freud, is rife with mixed messages related to boundaries and dual relationships (Gutheil and Gabbard 1993). Freud sent patients postcards, lent them books, gave them gifts, corrected them when they spoke inaccurately about his family members, provided some with considerable financial support, and on at least one occasion gave a patient a meal (Gutheil and Gabbard 1993; Lipton 1977; Syme 2003). According to Gutheil and Gabbard,

The line between professional and personal relationships in Freud's ana-lytic practice was difficult to pinpoint. During vacations he would analyze Ferenczi while walking through the countryside. In one of his letter to Ferenczi, which were often addressed "Dear Son," he indicated that during his holiday he planned to analyze him in two sessions a day but also invited him to share at least one meal with him each day (unpublished manuscript by A. Hoffer). For Freud the analytic relationship could be circumscribed by the time boundaries of the analytic sessions, and other relationships were possible outside the analytic hours. The most striking illustration of this conception of boundaries is Freud's analysis of his own daughter, Anna.

(1993:189)

These various manifestations of blurred boundaries occurred despite Freud's explicit and strongly worded observations about the inappropriateness of ther-apists' love relationships with patients: "The love-relationship actually de-stroys the influence of the analytic treatment on the patient; a combination of the two would be an inconceivable thing" (Freud 1963, cited in Smith and Fitzpatrick 1995).

Several other luminaries have provided intriguing mixed messages re-garding boundaries. When Melanie Klein was analyzing Clifford Scott, she encouraged him to follow her to the Black Forest for her vacation. During each day of the vacation, Klein analyzed Scott for two hours while he reclined on the bed in Klein's hotel room (Grosskurth 1986; Gutheil and Gabbard 1993). Klein also analyzed her own children (Syme 2003). D. W. Winnicott (1949) reported housing young patients as part of his treatment of them. Ac-cording to Margaret Little's (1990) first-person account of her analysis with Winnicott, he held her hands clasped between his for many hours as she lay on the couch. Little also reports that Winnicott told her about another patient of his who had committed suicide and disclosed significant detail about his countertransference reactions to the patient. Winnicott also ap-parently routinely concluded sessions with coffee and biscuits. Carl Jung reportedly had close and loving relationships with two of his patients who later became his students (Syme 2003).

Further complicating efforts to develop definitive guidelines regarding proper boundaries is the contention by a relatively small number of critics that the human service professions have mishandled their efforts to generate boundary-related guidelines and that current prohibitions are too simplistic. In one of the earlier critiques Ebert, for example, argues that "the concept of dual relationship prohibitions has limited value in that it creates confusion and leads to unfair results in ethics and licensing actions. It serves little purpose because it does not assist psychologists in analyzing situations. Neither does it provide much help in assisting psychologists in deciding how to act in a particular situation, such that the client's best interest in considered" (1997:137). Ebert asserts that many dual relationship prohibitions enforced by the American Psychological Association during that era—especially those related to nonsexual relationships—violate practitioners' constitutional and privacy rights and are overly vague.

The contemporary human service literature contains relatively few indepth discussions of boundary issues and guidelines. Understandably, much of the available literature focuses on dual relationships that are exploitative in nature, such as the sexual involvement of clinicians with their clients (Celenza 2007; Gabriel 2005; Gerson and Fox 1999; Gutheil and Brodsky 2008; Herlihy and Corey 2006; Olarte 1997; K. Pope 1991; Simon 1999; Syme 2003). Certainly, these are important and compelling issues. However, many boundary and dual relationship issues in the human services are much more subtle than these egregious forms of ethical misconduct (Lamb, Catanzaro, and Moorman 2004; Lazarus and Zur 2002; Moleski and Kiselica 2005; Younggren and Gottlieb 2004). A pioneering empirical survey of a statewide sample of clinicians uncovered substantial disagreement concerning the appropriateness of such behaviors as developing friendships with clients, participating in social activities with clients, serving on community boards with clients, providing clients with one's home telephone number, accepting goods and services from clients instead of money, and discussing one's religious beliefs with clients (Jayaratne, Croxton, and Mattison 1997; also see Borys and Pope 1989; Pope, Tabachnick, and Keith-Spiegel 1988; Strom-Gottfried 1999). As Corey and Herlihy note,

> The pendulum of controversy over dual relationships, which has produced extreme reactions on both sides, has slowed and now swings in a narrower arc. It is clear that not all dual relationships can be avoided, and it is equally clear that some types of dual relationships (such as sexual intimacies with clients) should always be avoided. In the middle range, it would be fruitful for professionals to continue to work to clarify the distinctions between dual relationships that we should try to avoid and those into which we might enter, with appropriate precautions.
>
> (1997:190)

To achieve a more finely tuned understanding of boundary issues, we must broaden our analysis and examine dual relationships through several conceptual lenses. First, human service professionals should distinguish between boundary violations and boundary crossings (Gutheil and Gabbard 1993). A boundary violation occurs when a practitioner engages in a dual relationship with a client or colleague that is exploitative, manipulative, deceptive, or coercive (Glass 2003; Gutheil and Simon 2002; Johnston and Farber 1996). Examples include practitioners who become sexually involved with clients, recruit and collude with clients to fraudulently bill insurance companies, or influence terminally ill clients to include their therapist in their will.

One key feature of boundary violations is a conflict of interest that harms clients or colleagues (Anderson and Kitchener 1998; Baer and Murdock 1995; Celenza 2007; Epstein 1994; Gabbard 1996; Gutheil and Brodsky 2008; Kitchener 1988; Kutchins 1991; Peterson 1992; K. Pope 1988, 1991; Syme 2003). Conflicts of interest occur when professionals find themselves in a relationship that could prejudice or give the appearance of prejudicing their decision making. In more legalistic language, conflicts of interest occur when professionals are in "a situation in which regard for one duty leads to disregard of another or might reasonably be expected to do so" (Gifis 1991:88). Thus a human service professional who provides services to a client with whom he would like to develop a sexual relationship faces a conflict of interest; the professional's personal interests clash with his professional duty to avoid harming the client. Similarly, a practitioner who invests money in a client's business is embedded in a conflict of interest; the professional's financial interests clash with her duty to the client (for example, if the professional's relationship with the client becomes strained because they disagree about some aspect of their shared business venture).

The codes of ethics of several human service professions explicitly address the concept of conflict of interest. A prominent example is the National Association of Social Workers' (NASW) *Code of Ethics* (2008):

> Social workers should be alert to and avoid conflicts of interest that interfere with the exercise of professional discretion and impartial judgment. Social workers should inform clients when a real or potential conflict of interest arises and take reasonable steps to resolve the issue in a manner that makes the clients' interests primary and protects clients' interests to the greatest extent possible. In some cases, protecting clients' interests may

require termination of the professional relationship with proper referral of the client.

(standard 1.06[a])

The NASW code goes on to say that "social workers should not engage in dual or multiple relationships with clients or former clients in which there is a risk of exploitation or potential harm to the client" (standard 1.06[c]).

The *American Association for Marriage and Family Therapy Code of Ethics* (2001) conveys similar guidance with regard to this profession's narrower focus on counseling relationships:

> Marriage and family therapists are aware of their influential positions with respect to clients, and they avoid exploiting the trust and dependency of such persons. Therapists, therefore, make every effort to avoid conditions and multiple relationships with clients that could impair professional judgment or increase the risk of exploitation. Such relationships include, but are not limited to, business or close personal relationships with a client or the client's immediate family. When the risk of impairment or exploitation exists due to conditions or multiple roles, therapists take appropriate precautions.
>
> (standard 1.3)

Some conflicts of interest involve what lawyers call *undue influence*. Undue influence occurs when a human service professional inappropriately pressures or exercises authority over a susceptible client in a manner that benefits the practitioner and may not be in the client's best interest. In legal parlance undue influence involves the "exertion of improper influence and submission to the domination of the influencing party. . . . In such a case, the influencing party is said to have an unfair advantage over the other based, among other things, on real or apparent authority, knowledge of necessity or distress, or a fiduciary or confidential relationship" (Gifis 1991:508). The American Medical Association's *Principles of Medical Ethics with Annotations Especially Applicable to Psychiatrists* (2009) specifically addresses the concept of undue influence: "The psychiatrist should diligently guard against exploiting information furnished by the patient and should not use the unique position of power afforded him/her by the psychotherapeutic situation to influence the patient in any way not directly relevant to the treatment goals" (sec. 3, annotation 2).

In contrast to boundary violations, a boundary crossing occurs when a human service professional is involved in a dual relationship with a client or colleague in a manner that is not exploitative, manipulative, deceptive, or coercive. Boundary crossings are not inherently unethical; they often involve boundary bending as opposed to boundary breaking. In principle the consequences of boundary crossings may be harmful, salutary, or neutral (Gutheil and Gabbard 1993). Boundary crossings are harmful when the dual relationship has negative consequences for the practitioner's client or colleague and, potentially, the practitioner. For example, a professional who discloses to a client personal, intimate details about his own life, ostensibly to be helpful to the client, ultimately may confuse the client and compromise the client's mental health because of complicated transference issues produced by the practitioner's self-disclosure. An educator or internship supervisor in the human services who accepts a student's dinner invitation may inadvertently harm the student by confusing him about the nature of the relationship.

Alternatively, some boundary crossings may be helpful to clients and colleagues (Zur 2007). Some professionals argue that, handled judiciously, a practitioner's modest self-disclosure, or decision to accept an invitation to attend a client's graduation ceremony, may prove, in some special circumstances, to be therapeutically useful to a client (Anderson and Mandell 1989; Chapman 1997). A practitioner who coincidentally worships at the same church, mosque, or synagogue as one of his clients may help the client normalize the professional-client relationship. Yet other boundary crossings produce mixed results. A practitioner's self-disclosure about personal challenges may be both helpful and harmful to the same client—helpful in that the client feels more connected to the practitioner and harmful in that the self-disclosure undermines the client's confidence in the practitioner. The human service administrator who hires a former client initially may elevate the former client's self-esteem, but boundary problems will arise if the employee subsequently wants to resume his status as an active client in order to address some new issues that have emerged in his life.

Practitioners should also be aware of the conceptual distinction in the terms *impropriety* and *appearance of impropriety*. An impropriety occurs when a practitioner violates a client's boundaries or engages in inappropriate dual relationships in a manner that violates prevailing ethical standards. Conducting a sexual relationship with a client and borrowing money from a client are clear examples of impropriety. In contrast, an appearance of impropriety occurs when a practitioner engages in conduct that appears to be improper but in fact may not be. Nonetheless, even the appearance of impropriety may be ethically problematic and harmful.

Let me illustrate this with a personal example. A number of years ago I had a leave of absence from my academic position and served as a senior policy adviser to the governor in my state. In that position I helped formulate public policy related to a number of human services issues. I worked directly with the governor when important issues arose, such as when relevant bills were pending in the state legislature. After several years I resigned that position to return to my academic duties; shortly thereafter the governor concluded his term in office. The new governor then appointed me to the state parole board, which entails conducting hearings for prison inmates eligible for parole. After I began serving in that position, the former governor—my former employer—was indicted and charged in criminal court with committing offenses while in office (among other issues, this complex case involved financial transactions between the governor, his political campaign staff, and building contractors and other parties who sought state contracts). The former governor was subsequently convicted and sentenced to prison. When he became eligible for parole and was scheduled to appear before me, I had to decide whether to participate in his hearing or recuse myself. I knew in my heart that I would be able to render a fair decision; the former governor was not a personal friend, and I had no knowledge of the events that led to his criminal court conviction. However, I also knew that I needed to be sensitive to the *appearance* of impropriety. I could not expect the general public to believe that I could be impartial, in light of my relationship with the man when he had been in office. No matter how certain I was of my ability to be fair and impartial, I had to concede that, at the very least, it would appear that I was involved in an inappropriate dual relationship. Because of the likely appearance of impropriety, I decided to recuse myself. Thus, although engaging in behaviors that only appear to be improper may not be unethical, human service practitioners should be sensitive to the effect that such appearances may have on their reputation and the integrity of their profession.

EMERGING BOUNDARY CHALLENGES: SOCIAL MEDIA AND ELECTRONIC COMMUNICATIONS

Some boundary issues in the human services have existed since the invention of the helping professions themselves. Examples include sexual attraction between clinician and client, practitioner self-disclosure, and the management of dual relationships in small communities. However, other boundary issues are of much more recent vintage, especially those involving practitioners' use of social media and various electronic communications and interventions. As I will explore more fully, the advent of Facebook, Twitter, email, cell and smartphones, videoconferencing, and web-based therapies has triggered a wide range of challenging boundary issues that did not exist when many contemporary practitioners concluded their formal education. Practitioners who use Facebook must decide whether to accept clients' requests for "friend" status. Similarly, practitioners must decide whether they are willing to exchange email and text messages with clients and, if so, under what circumstances; share their cell phone numbers with clients; offer clinical services by means of videoconferencing or other cybertherapy options, such as those that allow clients to represent themselves using graphical avatars rather than real-life images.

These novel electronic media have forced practitioners to think in entirely new and challenging ways about the nature of professional boundaries. Self-disclosure issues are no longer limited to practitioners' in-office sharing of information with clients about aspects of their personal lives. Practitioners' strategies for setting limits with regard to clients' access to them are no longer limited to office and landline telephone availability. Widespread use of email, text messaging, and cell phones has greatly expanded practitioners' availability, thus requiring them to think differently about boundary management. As Zur notes,

> The technological explosion toward the end of the 20th century, with its widespread use of cell phones, e-mails, and more recently, Instant Messaging (IM), chat rooms, video teleconferencing (VTC), text messaging, blogging, and photo-cell technology, has changed the way that billions of people communicate, make purchases, gather information, learn, meet, socialize, date, and form and sustain intimate relationships. Like global, national, and cultural boundaries, therapeutic boundaries are rapidly changing as a result. . . .
>
> Telehealth and online therapy practices challenge boundaries both around and within the therapeutic relationship. Telehealth or online therapy transcends the physical boundaries of the office as phone or Internet-based therapies take place in the elusive setting we often refer to as cyberspace. Nevertheless, telehealth is subject to exactly the same federal and state regulations, codes of ethics, and professional guidelines that define the fiduciary relationship in face-to-face and office-based therapy.
>
> (2007:133, 136)

A TYPOLOGY OF BOUNDARY ISSUES AND DUAL RELATIONSHIPS: A SYNOPSIS

Given the great range of both long-standing and novel boundary issues in the human services, practitioners need a conceptual framework to help them identify and manage dual relationships they encounter. What follows is a brief overview of a typology of boundary issues; I based it on several data sources: insurance industry statistics summarizing malpractice and negligence claims; empirical surveys of human service professionals about boundary issues; legal literature and court opinions in litigation involving boundaries; and my experience as chair of a statewide ethics committee and expert witness in a large number of legal cases throughout the U.S. involving boundary issues. Following this brief overview I will explore the elements of this typology in greater depth.

Boundary issues in the human services fall into five conceptual categories: intimate relationships, pursuit of personal benefit, how professionals respond to their own emotional needs, altruistic gestures, and responses to unanticipated circumstances.

INTIMATE RELATIONSHIPS

Many dual relationships in the human services involve some form of intimacy. Typically, these relationships entail a sexual relationship or physical contact, although they may also entail other, more subtle, intimate gestures, such as gift giving, friendship, and affectionate communication.

Sexual relationships. A distressingly significant portion of intimate dual relationships involves sexual contact (Akamatsu 1988; Bouhoutsos 1985; Coleman and Schaefer 1986; Celenza 2007; Committee on Women 1989; Feldman-Summers and Jones 1984; Gabbard 1989; Gechtman 1989; Gutheil and Brodsky 2008; Pope and Bouhoutsos 1986; Reamer 1992; Sell, Gottlieb, and Schoenfeld 1986; Strom-Gottfried 1999; Syme 2003). Human service professionals agree that sexual relationships between clinicians and current clients are inappropriate but are not so unanimous regarding sexual relationships with former clients.

Professionals must also be aware of other potentially problematic sexual relationships that may involve a client indirectly. For example, current ethical standards in most human service professions prohibit sexual relationships between practitioners and a client's relatives or other individuals with whom a client maintains a close personal relationship. Typical is the NASW *Code of Ethics* (2008) standard on this issue:

> Social workers should not engage in sexual activities or sexual contact with clients' relatives or other individuals with whom clients maintain a close personal relationship when there is a risk of exploitation or potential harm to the client. Sexual activity or sexual contact with clients' relatives or other individuals with whom clients maintain a personal relationship has the potential to be harmful to the client and may make it difficult for the social worker and client to maintain appropriate professional boundaries. Social workers—not their clients, their clients' relatives, or other individuals with whom the client maintains a personal relationship—assume the full burden for setting clear, appropriate, and culturally sensitive boundaries.
>
> (standard 1.09[b])

Other potentially problematic sexual relationships can occur between educators, supervisors, or trainers in the human service professions and their students, supervisees, or trainees.

Physical contact. Not all physical contact between a practitioner and a client is explicitly sexual in nature. Physical contact in a number of circumstances may be asexual and appropriate—for example, a brief hug at the termination of long-term treatment or placing an arm around a client in a residential program who just received bad family news and is distraught. Such brief, limited physical contact may not be harmful; many clients would find such physical contact comforting and therapeutic, although other clients may be upset by it (perhaps because of their personal trauma history or their cultural or ethnic norms related to touching).

Some forms of physical contact have greater potential for psychological harm. In these circumstances physical touch may exacerbate a client's transference in destructive ways and may suggest that the practitioner is interested in more than a professional relationship. For example, a clinician provided counseling to a twenty-eight-year-old woman who had been sexually abused as a child. As an adult the client sought counseling to help her understand the effects of the early victimization, especially those pertaining to her intimate relationships. As part of the therapy the practitioner, aiming to comfort the client, would occasionally dim the office lights, turn on soft music, and sit on the floor while cradling and talking with the client. The client was thus retraumatized because this physical contact with the clinician exacerbated the client's confusion about intimacy and boundaries with important people in her life.

The NASW *Code of Ethics* (2008) is one of the few professional ethics codes that includes a standard pertaining specifically to the concept of physical touch: "Social workers should not engage in physical contact with clients when there is a possibility of psychological harm to the client as a result of the contact (such as cradling or caressing clients). Social workers who engage in appropriate physical contact with clients are responsible for setting clear, appropriate, and culturally sensitive boundaries that govern such physical contact" (standard 1.09[d]).

Counseling a former lover. Providing clinical services to someone with whom a practitioner was once intimately, romantically, or sexually involved also constitutes a dual relationship. The relationship history is likely to make it difficult for the practitioner and the client to interact with each other solely as professional and client; inevitably, the dynamics of the prior relationship will influence the professional-client relationship—how the parties view and respond to each other—perhaps in ways that are detrimental to the client's best interests. According to the American Psychological Association's *Ethical Principles of Psychologists and Code of Conduct* (2010), "Psychologists do not accept as therapy clients/patients persons with whom they have engaged in sexual intimacies" (standard 10.07).

Intimate gestures and friendships. Boundary issues can also emerge when practitioners and clients engage in other intimate gestures, such as gift giving and expressions of friendship (including sending affectionate notes, for example, on the practitioner's personal stationery). It is not unusual for a client to give a clinician or case manager a modest gift. Certainly, in many instances a client's gift represents nothing more than an appreciative gesture. In some instances, however, a client's gift may carry great meaning. For example, the gift may reflect the client's fantasies about a friendship or more intimate relationship with the practitioner. Thus it behooves the professional to carefully consider the meaning of a client's gift and establish prudent guidelines governing the acceptance of gifts. Many social service agencies do not permit staff members to accept gifts because of the potential conflict of interest or appearance of impropriety, or they permit gifts of only modest value. Some agencies permit staff to accept gifts only with the understanding—which is conveyed to clients—that the gifts represent a contribution to the agency, not to the individual professional.

The human service professions agree that friendships with current clients constitute inappropriate dual relationships. There is less clarity, however, about friendships between professionals and *former* clients. Although professionals generally understand the risk involved in befriending a former client—the possibility of confused boundaries—some professionals argue that friendships with former clients are not inherently unethical and reflect a more egalitarian, nonhierarchical approach to practice. These professionals typically claim that emotionally mature practitioners and former clients are quite capable of entering into new kinds of relationships after termination of the professional-client relationship and that such new relationships often are, in fact, evidence of the former client's substantial therapeutic progress. Later I will explore this complex debate more thoroughly.

PERSONAL BENEFIT

Beyond these various manifestations of intimacy, human service professionals can become involved in dual relationships that produce other forms of personal benefit, including monetary gain, goods, services, or useful information.

Monetary gain. In some situations a practitioner stands to benefit financially as a result of a dual relationship (Bonosky 1995). In one case, a counselor's former client decided to change careers and become a therapist. After completing graduate school, the client contacted her former therapist and asked to become the former therapist's supervisee (supervision was required for a state license). The counselor was tempted to take on the supervision for a fee, in part because he enjoyed their relationship and in part because of the financial benefit. But the counselor also recognized that the shift from the counselor-client relationship to a collegial relationship would introduce a number of boundary issues.

In another case, a client named a counselor in his will. After the client's death and probate of the will, the client's family accused the counselor of undue influence (the family alleged that the counselor had encouraged the client to bequeath a portion of the estate to the counselor).

Goods and services. On occasion, human service professionals receive goods or services, rather than money, as payment for their professional services. This occurs especially in some rural communities, where barter is an accepted form of payment. In one case, a rural practitioner's client lost his mental health insurance coverage yet still needed counseling services. The client, a house painter, offered to paint the counselor's home in exchange for clinical services. The counselor decided not to enter into the barter arrangement; after consulting with colleagues, she realized that the client's interests could be undermined should some problem emerge with the paint job that would require some remedy or negotiation (for example, if the paint job proved to be inferior in some way). In another case, a social worker received several paintings from a client, an artist, as payment for services rendered. This social worker reasoned that accepting goods of this sort was not likely to undermine the clinical relationship, whereas accepting a service might.

The NASW *Code of Ethics* is an example of a prominent code that includes a specific standard on barter. The NASW Code of Ethics Revision Committee, which I chaired, struggled to decide whether to prohibit or merely discourage all forms of barter. On the one hand, bartering entails potential conflicts of interest; on the other hand, bartering is an accepted practice in some communities. Ultimately, the committee decided to strongly discourage barter because of the risks involved while recognizing that barter is not inherently unethical. Further, the code establishes strict standards for the use of barter by social workers:

> Social workers should avoid accepting goods or services from clients as payment for professional services. Bartering arrangements, particularly involving services, create the potential for conflicts of interest, exploitation, and inappropriate boundaries in social workers' relationships with clients. Social workers should explore and may participate in bartering only *in very limited circumstances* when it can be demonstrated that such arrangements are an accepted practice among professionals in the local community, considered to be essential for the provision of services, negotiated without coercion, and entered into at the client's initiative and with the client's informed consent. Social workers who accept goods or services from clients as payment for professional services assume the full burden of demonstrating that this arrangement will not be detrimental to the client or the professional relationship.
>
> (standard 1.13[b]; emphasis added)

The ethics codes of the American Counseling Association (2005; standard A.10.d) and the American Association for Marriage and Family Therapy (AAMFT) (2001; standard 7.5) include somewhat similar standards.

Useful information. A human service professional occasionally has an opportunity to benefit from a client's unique knowledge. A counselor with a complex health problem may be tempted to consult her client who is a physician and who happens to specialize in the area relevant to the counselor's chronic illness. A psychologist who is interested in adopting a child, and whose client is an obstetrics and gynecology nurse who works in a teen pregnancy clinic, may be tempted to talk to his client about adoption opportunities through the client's clinic. An agency administrator who is an active stock-market investor may be tempted to consult a client who happens to be a stockbroker. A social worker with automobile problems may be tempted to consult a client who happens to be a mechanic. These situations entail the clear potential for an inappropriate dual relationship because the professional uses a portion of the client's therapeutic session for the practitioner's own purposes, and the practitioner's judgment and services may be shaped and influenced by access to a client's specialized knowledge. The client's transference also may be adversely affected. Conversely, relatively brief, casual, and nonexploitative conversation with a client concerning a topic on which the client is an expert may empower the client, facilitate therapeutic progress, and challenge the traditionally hierarchical relationship between professional and client.

EMOTIONAL AND DEPENDENCY NEEDS

A number of boundary issues arise from practitioners' efforts to address their own emotional needs. Many of these issues are subtle, although some are more glaring and egregious. Among the more egregious are the following examples on which I have consulted:

■ The administrator of a state child welfare agency that serves abused and neglected children was having difficulty coping with his failing marriage. He was feeling isolated and depressed. The administrator was arrested based on evidence that he had developed a sexual relationship with a sixteen-year-old boy who was in the department's custody and that he used illegal drugs with the boy.

■ A psychologist in a private psychiatric hospital provided counseling to a resident who was diagnosed with paranoid schizophrenia. The psychologist, who was religiously observant, began to read biblical passages to his client in the context of counseling sessions. The client was not religiously observant and complained to other hospital staff about the psychologist's conduct.

■ A psychiatric nurse in private practice provided psychotherapy services to a forty-two-year-old woman who had been sexually abused as a child. During the course of their relationship, the nurse invited the client to her home for several candlelight dinners, went on a camping trip with the client, gave the client several expensive gifts, and wrote the client several very affectionately worded notes on personal stationery.

■ A social worker in a public child welfare agency was responsible for licensing foster homes. The social worker, who was recently divorced, became friendly with a couple who had applied to be foster parents. The social worker also became involved in the foster parents' church. The social worker, who approved the couple's application and was responsible for monitoring foster home placements in their home, moved with her son into a trailer on the foster parents' large farm.

Other boundary issues are more subtle. Examples include professionals whose clients invite them to attend important life-cycle events (such as a wedding or graduation, or a key religious ceremony), professionals who conduct home visits as a meal is being served and whose clients invite them to sit down to eat, and professionals who themselves are in recovery and encounter a client at an Alcoholics or a Narcotics Anonymous meeting. Professionals sometimes disagree about the most appropriate way to handle such boundary issues. For example, some professionals are adamantly opposed to attending a client's life-cycle event because of potential boundary problems (for example, the possibility that the client might interpret the gesture as a sign of the practitioner's interest in a social relationship or friendship); others, however, believe that attending such events can be ethically appropriate and, in fact, therapeutically helpful, so long as the clinical dynamics are handled skillfully. Further, some professionals believe that practitioners in recovery should never attend or participate in AA or NA meetings that a client might attend, because of the difficulty that clients may have reconciling the practitioner's professional role and personal life. Others, however, argue that recovering practitioners have a right to meet their own needs and can serve as compelling role models to clients in recovery.

ALTRUISM

Some boundary issues and dual relationships arise from professionals' genuine efforts to be helpful. Unlike a professional's involvement in a sexual relationship, or a dual relationship that is intentionally self-serving, altruistic gestures are benevolently motivated. Although these dual relationships are not always inherently unethical, they do require skillful handling, as in the following examples:

■ A psychiatrist in private practice was contacted by an acquaintance—not a close friend—who was in the midst of a marital crisis. The acquaintance told the psychiatrist that she and her husband "really trusted" the psychiatrist and wanted the psychiatrist's professional help. The psychiatrist agreed to see the couple professionally but later realized that being objective was difficult.

■ A social worker in a family service agency provided casework services to a client who had a substance abuse problem. The client asked the social worker if she would like to purchase wrapping paper that the client's daughter was selling as a school fund-raiser.

■ A woman who had been diagnosed with agoraphobia sent an email message to a psychologist asking whether the psychologist would be willing to provide Internet counseling for a period of time as a prelude to a possible office-based visit.

■ A counselor in a community mental health center provided psychotherapy services for many years to a young man with a history of clinical depression. The client asked the counselor to say a few words during the ceremony at the client's upcoming wedding.

■ A psychiatric nurse in a small rural community provided counseling to a ten-year-old boy who struggled with self-esteem issues. In his spare time the nurse coached the community's only youth basketball team, which played in a regional league. The nurse believed that the boy would benefit from joining the basketball team (for example, by developing social skills and new relationships) and encouraged the boy to join the team.

UNAVOIDABLE AND UNANTICIPATED CIRCUMSTANCES

The final category of boundary issues involves situations that behavioral health professionals do not anticipate and over which they have little or no initial control. The challenge for the professional in these circumstances is to manage the boundary issues in ways that minimize any harm to a client or colleague. Consider the following examples:

- A social worker in private practice attended a family holiday gathering. The social worker's sister introduced him to her new boyfriend, who is a former client of the social worker.
- The client of a psychotherapist in a rural community was a grade school teacher. Because of an unexpected administrative decision, the client became the classroom teacher of the psychotherapist's child.
- A mental health counselor discovered that she and her client had Facebook friends in common.
- A psychologist at a community mental health center joined a local fitness club. During a visit to the club the psychologist learned that an active client also was a member.

MANAGING BOUNDARIES AND DUAL RELATIONSHIPS

As I have discussed, not all dual relationships entail unethical circumstances, although some do. Some dual relationships are clearly self-serving and exploitative. Others, however, are ambiguous and contain features about which reasonable, thoughtful human service professionals may disagree.

As I will discuss more fully later, to protect clients and minimize the potential for harm—and to minimize the possibility of ethics complaints and lawsuits that allege misconduct or professional negligence—human service professionals should establish clear risk-management criteria and procedures. These criteria and procedures increase the chances that a practitioner will protect clients and would be determinative should a disgruntled client or third party allege malpractice. A sound risk-management protocol to deal with boundary issues should contain six major elements. Human service professionals should

- Be vigilant in their efforts to recognize potential or actual conflicts of interest in their relationships with clients and colleagues. Professionals should be cognizant of red flags that may signal a boundary problem. For example, clinical practitioners should be wary when they find themselves attracted to a particular client, going out of their way to extend a client's counseling sessions (facilitated by scheduling the favored client at the end of the day), acting impulsively in relation to the client, allowing the client to accumulate a large unpaid bill, and/or disclosing personal information to the client. Professionals should be sure to inform the client and appropriate colleagues when they encounter complex boundary issues, including actual or potential conflicts of interest, and explore reasonable remedies.

■ Consult colleagues and supervisors, relevant professional literature on boundary and ethical issues, relevant statutes and regulations, agency policies, and ethical standards (codes of ethics) in order to identify pertinent boundary issues and constructive options. Professionals should take special care in high-risk circumstances. For example, a professional who attempts to make a decision about whether to enter into a friendship with a former client should consider prevailing ethical standards, including those pertaining to the amount of time that has passed since the termination of the professional-client relationship; the extent to which the former client is mentally competent and emotionally stable; the issues addressed in professional-client relationship; the length of the professional-client relationship; the circumstances surrounding the termination of the professional-client relationship; and the extent to which harm to the former client or others as a result of the new relationship is foreseeable (Reamer 2006a–b).

■ Design a plan of action that addresses the boundary issues and protects clients to the greatest extent possible. In some circumstances protecting the client's interests may require termination of the professional relationship with proper referral of the client.

■ Document all discussions, consultation, supervision, and other steps taken to address boundary issues.

■ Develop a strategy for monitoring the implementation of the action plan—for example, by periodically conducting assessments with relevant parties (clients, colleagues, supervisors, lawyers) to determine whether the strategy minimized or eliminated the boundary problems.

These steps can help professionals protect clients and prevent ethics complaints and lawsuits alleging negligent conduct. In all the human service professions, state licensing or regulatory boards receive ethics complaints. These publicly sponsored bodies—which are established under the authority of state licensing statutes—are charged with reviewing, investigating, and, when warranted, adjudicating ethics complaints filed against professionals. When a licensing and regulatory board concludes that a practitioner has violated a client's boundaries or engaged in an unethical dual relationship, it may impose various sanctions and requirements for corrective action, including censure; mandated continuing education, supervision, and consultation; probation; and license suspension or revocation.

Some national professional associations also have a mechanism for reviewing and, when necessary, adjudicating ethics complaints against members. For example, the National Association of Social Workers permits individuals to file ethics complaints against its members. Based on the concept of peer review, each state chapter has an ethics committee whose function is to process ethics complaints in collaboration with the National Ethics Committee. If the complaint is accepted by the national intake committee, it decides whether to offer mediation as an option or to refer the matter for formal adjudication. As a matter of policy, cases involving allegations of sexual harassment, relationships, and physical contact are not eligible for mediation. Cases involving allegations of other boundary-related issues may be eligible for mediation.

If the case is referred for adjudication, the chapter ethics committee conducts a formal hearing during which the complainant (the person filing the complaint), the respondent (the person against whom the complaint is filed), and witnesses have the opportunity to testify. After hearing all parties and discussing the testimony, the ethics committee summarizes its findings and presents recommendations. NASW members who are found in violation of ethical standards concerning boundaries and dual relationships may be sanctioned or required to engage in some form of corrective action. These measures may include suspension or expulsion from NASW, censure, or a requirement to obtain continuing education, consultation, or supervision. In some instances, the findings may be publicized through local and national NASW publications. Other professional associations have a similar protocol, although specific procedures vary.

In addition, individuals who believe they have been harmed by an unethical dual relationship with a practitioner may file malpractice claims and negligence lawsuits (Austin, Moline, and Williams 1990; Bernstein and Hartsell 2008 Madden 1998; Reamer 2003a). Lawsuits and liability claims that allege malpractice are civil suits, in contrast to criminal proceedings. Ordinarily, civil suits are based on tort or contract law, with plaintiffs (the individuals bringing the suit) seeking some sort of compensation for injuries they claim to have incurred. These injuries may be economic (for example, lost wages or medical expenses that resulted when a client became sexually involved with her therapist and was traumatized and unable to work), physical (for instance, as a result of a sexual assault on a client by a practitioner), or emotional (for example, depression that may result from a practitioner's sexual contact with a client).

As in criminal trials, defendants in civil lawsuits are presumed to be innocent until proved otherwise. In ordinary civil suits defendants will be found liable for their actions based on the standard of preponderance of the evidence, as opposed to the stricter standard of proof beyond a reasonable doubt used in criminal trials. In some civil cases—for example, those involving contract disputes, as opposed to boundary issues—the court may expect clear and convincing evidence, a standard of proof that is greater than preponderance of the evidence but less than for beyond a reasonable doubt.

In general, malpractice occurs when evidence exists that (1) at the time of the alleged malpractice a legal duty existed between the practitioner and the client (for example, a counselor has a duty to maintain proper boundaries with clients); (2) the practitioner was derelict in that duty, either through an action that occurred or through an omission (the practitioner engaged in a sexual relationship with a client); (3) the client suffered some harm or injury (the emotional harm associated with the boundary violation); and (4) the harm or injury was directly and proximately caused by the counselor's dereliction of duty (the unethical sexual relationship was the direct and proximate cause of the emotional harm suffered by the client).

Whether a practitioner violated his or her duty is based on current standards of care in the profession. The standard of care is defined as the way an ordinary, reasonable, and prudent professional would act under the same or similar circumstances (Austin, Moline, and Williams 1990; Bernstein and Hartsell 2004; Madden 1998; Reamer 2003a). Some standards of care related to boundaries and dual relationships are clear; others are not. For example, an ordinary, reasonable, and prudent professional clearly would not engage in a sexual relationship with a clinical client or enter into a business relationship with a client. In contrast, professionals disagree about whether barter between a professional and a client should be prohibited in all instances, whether practitioners should decline all gifts and social invitations from clients, and whether friendship between a practitioner and a former client should always be prohibited. As we will see shortly, professionals face the greatest challenges when they encounter boundary and dual relationship issues for which no clear standards of care exist.

SOUND DECISION MAKING

The best strategy for protecting clients and preventing ethics complaints and lawsuits—especially when human service professionals face complex boundary issues for which no clear standards of care exist—is to engage in a systematic, deliberate, and comprehensive series of decision-making steps. Ethicists generally agree that approaching ethical decisions in this fashion is important to ensure that all aspects of an ethical dilemma are addressed. In my experience it is helpful for human service professionals to follow specific steps when attempting to make difficult decisions related to boundaries and dual relationships (Reamer 2006c, 2009a–d).

1. *Identify the boundary and dual relationship issues, including the professional duties and obligations that conflict.* Complex boundary and dual relationship issues often entail conflicts among, or ambiguities related to, professional duties and obligations. For example, practitioners who are in recovery from alcohol abuse may face difficult decisions when they unexpectedly encounter a client, who is also in recovery, at an Alcoholics Anonymous meeting. Practitioners in recovery need to handle conflicts between their duty to protect clients from harm and their right to address their own recovery issues. Whether practitioners decide to participate in or leave AA meetings when a client is present depends on their views about these conflicting duties and obligations. Carefully identifying the issues and alternative ways of handling them increases the chances that the practitioner will analyze the situation thoroughly and thereby enhance protection of clients and themselves.

2. *Identify the individuals, groups, and organizations that the ethical decision is likely to affect.* In each instance human service professionals should do their best to identify the parties that their decision may affect and the ways in which it is likely to affect them. A counselor in recovery who is trying to decide how to handle her and her client's coincidental attendance at the same AA meetings needs to think about the potential effect on the client primarily but also on the client's family and close acquaintances, the counselor herself, the counselor's employer, the counselor's malpractice and liability insurer, and the counselor's profession and professional colleagues.

Clearly, the counselor's participation in the AA meeting could affect the client and these other parties.

3. *Tentatively identify all viable courses of action and the participants involved in each, along with the potential benefits and risks for each.* Human service professionals should think through all realistic options and then engage in the conceptual equivalent of a cost-benefit analysis. In the AA example, in principle the practitioner faces several possibilities upon seeing a client at an AA meeting: attend the meeting and speak to the group about her own recovery issues; attend the meeting without speaking about her own recovery issues; and leave the meeting and explore an alternative meeting site. In addition, the practitioner would need to decide what to say to the client about their unanticipated, chance encounter and its implications for their future clinical relationship. The first option offers several potential benefits. Attending the meeting and speaking would provide the practitioner with an opportunity to address her own recovery issues. She would also serve as a role model for her client, which may enhance the client's recovery efforts. In addition, the practitioner may have greater credibility in the client's eyes because of the practitioner's personal experience with recovery issues.

However, risks are involved as well. The dual relationship may confuse the client, who may have some difficulty distinguishing between the practitioner's role as a professional counselor and as another recovering alcoholic who needs the client's support and understanding. This confusion could undermine the client's recovery efforts. In principle the practitioner's credibility may suffer if the client concludes that a counselor who is struggling with her own recovery issues is not in a position to counsel others who are in recovery. In addition, the client's presence at an AA meeting could undermine the practitioner's recovery; the practitioner may feel self-conscious and constrained by the client's presence and may be reluctant to address personal issues that she would address in the client's absence. Thus the practitioner's earnest efforts to protect her client could interfere with the practitioner's own therapeutic progress.

The second option—attending the AA meeting without speaking—also entails potential costs and benefits. The practitioner's presence could be reassuring to the client and may enhance the practitioner's credibility. Participating in the group discussion, even though she chooses not to speak at this particular meeting, may enhance the practitioner's own recovery efforts. At the same time, however, this course entails potential costs. As with the first option, the client may be confused about the practitioner's role in his life, and the practitioner may feel constrained in her efforts to address her own recovery issues. The practitioner's credibility may decline in the client's opinion if the client concludes that a counselor who is struggling with her own recovery issues is in no position to guide the client effectively.

The third option—leaving the meeting and perhaps finding an alternative twelve-step meeting—would help the practitioner and client avoid a potentially problematic dual relationship. At the same time this would remove the possibility of any benefits that could result from the practitioner's and client's simultaneous attendance at the AA meeting and efforts to address their respective recovery issues.

4. *Thoroughly examine the reasons in favor of and opposed to each course of action, considering relevant ethical theories, principles, and guidelines.*

Analysis and resolution of practical ethical dilemmas. As I noted earlier, since the mid-1970s interest in professional ethics has grown dramatically, particularly in relation to boundary and dual relationship issues. One feature of this development, especially since the 1980s, has been the deliberate exploration of the relevance of moral philosophy and ethical theory to the analysis and resolution of practical ethical dilemmas that human service professionals face; similar developments occurred in nearly all major professions, such as medicine, nursing, business, journalism, law, engineering, and the military. Currently, most professional education programs acquaint students with core ethics concepts, theories, and conceptual frameworks to enhance their management of ethical challenges.

Briefly, pertinent ethical theories and principles concern what moral philosophers call *metaethics* and *normative ethics*. Metaethics concerns the meaning of ethical terms or language and the derivation of ethical principles and guidelines. Typical metaethical questions concern the meaning of the terms *right* and *wrong* and *good* and *bad*. What criteria should we use to judge whether a social worker, counselor, or psychologist has engaged in unethical conduct by violating professional boundaries and engaging in an inappropriate dual relationship? How should we go about formulating ethical principles to guide individuals who struggle with moral choices related to boundary issues and dual relationships?

In contrast to metaethics, which is relatively abstract, normative ethics tends to be of particular interest to human service professionals because of its immediate relevance to practice. Normative ethics consists of attempts to apply ethical theories and principles to actual ethical dilemmas. Such guidance is especially useful when professionals face conflicts among duties they are ordinarily inclined to perform—what the philosopher W. D. Ross (1930) refers to as the challenge to identify one's principal duty (or *actual* duty, to use Ross's term) from among competing or conflicting prima facie duties (that is, duties that should be performed at first view).

Reconciling conflicting prima facie duties is a common challenge with respect to professional boundaries. In the case of the AA meeting, for example, the practitioner faces a choice involving conflicting prima facie duties to her client, herself, and her profession. Deciding on one's actual duty can be daunting.

Theories of normative ethics can be useful in the analysis of boundary and dual relationship issues. Philosophers generally group theories of normative ethics under two main headings. Deontological theories (from the Greek, *deontos*, 'of the obligatory') are those that claim that certain actions are inherently right or wrong, or good or bad, without regard for their consequences. Thus a deontologist—the best known is Immanuel Kant, the eighteenth-century German philosopher—might argue that engaging in a sexual relationship with a client is inherently wrong and that practitioners should never exploit clients in this way. The same might be said about investing in a client's business, socializing with a client, or accepting expensive gifts from a client. For deontologists moral rules, rights, and principles are sacred and inviolable. The ends do not justify the means, particularly if the means require violating some important moral rule, right, principle, or the law (Cahn and Markie 2008; Frankena 1973).

The second major group of theories, teleological theories (from the Greek *teleios*, 'brought to its end or purpose'), takes a different approach to ethical choices. From this point of view the rightness of any action is determined by the goodness of its consequences. For teleologists (also known among moral philosophers as consequentialists), making ethical choices without weighing potential consequences is naive. To do otherwise is to engage in what the philosopher J. J. C. Smart (1971) refers to as "rule worship." Hence from this consequentialist perspective, the responsible decision-making strategy entails an attempt to anticipate the outcomes of various courses of action and to weigh their relative benefits and costs. For example, a practitioner who is contemplating disclosing personal information to a client, accepting a client's gift or social invitation, or attending the same AA meeting that a client attends would identify the potential and likely outcomes of these choices and speculate about the potential benefits and costs for all relevant parties (the client, practitioner, practitioner's employer, and relevant third parties).

The two major teleological schools of thought are known by moral philosophers as *egoism* and *utilitarianism*. Egoism typically has no place in the human services; according to this self-serving perspective, practitioners faced with conflicting prima facie duties should act in ways that maximize their personal self-interest. Thus a practitioner contemplating a sexual relationship with a client would be concerned primarily, and perhaps exclusively, with his own potential satisfaction and contentment. Although few human service practitioners think along these egoistic lines, some do. When I have testified as an expert witness in court and licensing board cases brought against practitioners for alleged boundary violations, I have met a number of practitioners who seemed primarily concerned about their own emotional satisfaction and, narcissistically and egoistically, entered into self-serving dual relationships that harmed clients. As I will discuss more fully, many of these practitioners struggled with personal issues that led to some form of impaired judgment. These personal challenges often involve troubled marriages or primary relationships, career frustration, and a wide range of mental health issues (such as depression or addiction).

In contrast to egoism, the school of thought known as utilitarianism holds that an action is morally right if it promotes the maximum good. Historically, utilitarianism has been the most popular teleological theory among human service professionals and has, at least implicitly, served as justification for many decisions that practitioners make regarding boundaries and dual relationships. According to the classic form of utilitarianism—as generally formulated by the English philosophers Jeremy Bentham in the eighteenth century and John Stuart Mill in the nineteenth century—when faced with conflicting moral duties, one should perform the action that is likely to produce the greatest good. In principle, then, a practitioner should engage in a calculus to determine which set of consequences will produce the greatest good. (An alternative view is that practitioners should aim to minimize harm rather than maximize good. Donagan [1977] refers to this as "negative utilitarianism," and Popper [1966] refers to it as the "minimization of suffering.") Thus a counselor might argue on utilitarian grounds that the harm that may result from a sexual relationship with a former client—no matter how voluntary, satisfying, and consensual—outweighs any likely benefits. That is, the emotional harm that could result for the client—and perhaps the counselor and other relevant parties—would be more substantial than any pleasure (emotional and physical) that would result from the sexual relationship.

Some philosophers argue that it is important and helpful to distinguish between two subtypes of utilitarianism: act and rule utilitarianism (Gorovitz 1971). According to act utilitarianism, the goodness of the consequences in *that individual case* (or act) determines the rightness of an action. One does not need to look beyond the implications of this one instance. In contrast rule utilitarianism takes into account the long-run consequences when one treats the case as a precedent. Thus an act utilitarian might justify a sexual relationship with a former client if there is evidence that this would result in the greatest good for the parties involved in this particular set of circumstances. A rule utilitarian, however, might argue that the precedent established by this boundary violation would generate more harm than good if *all* human service professionals used this cost-benefit reasoning, regardless of the benefits produced in this one case. That is, a rule utilitarian might argue that the precedent would undermine clients' and the public's trust in human service professionals, particularly regarding professionals' determination to protect clients from harm and exploitation, thus limiting the human services' general effectiveness as a profession. The distinction between act and rule utilitarianism is similarly useful with regard to other boundary issues, for example, whether it is morally acceptable to disclose personal information to a client, accept a client's gift, perform favors for a client, attend an AA meeting with a client, or barter with a client for professional services. What may seem ethically justifiable in any one case (act utilitarianism) may seem unjustifiable if one treats that one case as a precedent that one then generalizes to all human service professionals who are in comparable circumstances.

Codes of ethics and legal principles. Other tools to help human service professionals examine the reasons in favor of and opposed to a course of action are professional codes of ethics and pertinent legal principles. Ethical standards have matured greatly in all the human service professions. Earlier versions were much more superficial and abstract than they are today. For example, the first code of ethics ratified by the National Association of Social Workers, in 1960, was one page long and consisted of only fourteen broadly worded proclamations concerning, for example, every social worker's duty to give precedence to professional responsibility over personal interests; to respect the privacy of clients; to give appropriate professional service in public emergencies; and to contribute knowledge, skills, and support to human welfare programs. In contrast, the current version of the NASW *Code of Ethics* contains 155 specific ethical standards (along with more abstract ethical principles, core values, and a mission statement for the profession) to guide social workers' conduct and provide a basis for adjudication of ethics complaints filed against NASW members. These guidelines are used as well by many state licensing boards that have formally adopted the NASW code standards, in whole or in part. This trend, toward more detailed and specific ethical standards, has occurred in all major human service professions, reflecting the dramatic growth of knowledge related to professional ethics.

The codes of ethics of the various human service professions (especially counseling, marriage and family therapy, psychiatry, psychology, social work) include a wide range of standards related to boundary issues and dual relationships. The number of standards devoted to boundary issues and dual relationships has increased significantly in recent code revisions. Although the content and substantive issues addressed by the various codes overlap somewhat, note that they have some significant differences, which reflect the professions' diverse norms and ideological perspectives. I will draw on these various standards throughout this discussion (see the appendix for excerpts from relevant codes of ethics pertaining to boundaries, dual relationships, and conflicts of interest).

In addition to consulting relevant codes of ethics, human service professionals facing difficult ethical decisions should carefully consider relevant legal principles, including statutes (laws enacted by state legislatures and Congress), legal regulations (regulations established by public agencies that have the force of law), and case law (legal precedents established by courts of law). Although ethical decisions should not necessarily be dictated by prevailing statutory, regulatory, and case law, practitioners should always take legal guidelines and requirements into account. In some instances the law may reinforce practitioners' ethical instincts, such as when a state law stipulates that sexual contact with a former client is a felony punishable by imprisonment and/or a monetary fine. In fact, several states have enacted such a law.

Practice theory and principles from the literature of the human service professions. Practitioners should also consider the relevance of pertinent practice theory and principles. For example, if a therapist is struggling to decide whether to have posttermination social contact with a client who has been diagnosed with borderline personality disorder, the therapist should pay close attention to practice theory related to this clinical phenomenon. In light of what we know about borderline personality disorder, the therapist may want to avoid adding boundary-related complications to this client's life. Similarly, a counselor who is considering establishing a sexual relationship with

a former client who has a history of sexual abuse should pay close attention to practice-based knowledge about posttraumatic stress disorder. And a
community mental center administrator who is considering hiring former
clients as employees should draw on available knowledge about relapse
prevention and risks before making a decision about this unique boundary
issue.

*Values (including religious, cultural, and ethnic values and political ideol-
ogy), particularly those that conflict with one's own.* Human service professionals sometimes want to share their values with clients. Further, practitioners
sometimes face conflicts between their personal values and their professional
obligations. A practitioner may have very strong religious beliefs that, in her
judgment, are relevant to a client's circumstances (for instance, when a client
is struggling with moral issues related to an unplanned pregnancy or a marital
affair); a practitioner who shares these religious beliefs with a client, or who
invites a client to attend a church-sponsored event, would produce complex
boundary issues. Boundary issues are especially complex when clients' values
conflict with the practitioner's values (for example, related to abortion or engaging in tax or insurance fraud).

A similar challenge may arise when a politically active professional is
tempted to organize clients to engage in some form of social lobbying or
protest. Supporting one's own political agenda—by recruiting clients to support one's political agenda—may conflict with the ethical prescription to
avoid inappropriate dual relationships.

5. *Consult with colleagues and appropriate experts (such as agency staff,
supervisors, agency administrators, ethics experts, and attorneys).* Ordinarily,
human service professionals should not make complex ethical decisions
alone. The quality of practitioners' judgments about the management of complicated boundary issues can be greatly enhanced by conferring with thoughtful, principled colleagues. This is not to suggest that ethical decisions are always group decisions. Sometimes they are, but in many instances individual
practitioners ultimately make the decision once they have had an opportunity
to consult with colleagues, supervisors, administrators, and other experts.

Typically, practitioners should consider consulting with colleagues who
are involved in similar work and who are likely to understand the issues. As
the NASW *Code of Ethics* (2008) states: "Social workers should seek the advice and counsel of colleagues whenever such consultation is in the best interest of clients" (standard 2.05[a]), and "social workers should keep themselves informed about colleagues' areas of expertise and competencies. Social

workers should seek consultation only from colleagues who have demonstrated knowledge, expertise, and competence related to the subject of the consultation" (standard 2.05[b]). Sometimes the consultation may be obtained informally, in the form of casual and spontaneous conversation with colleagues, and sometimes, particularly in agency settings (such as community mental health centers, family service agencies, schools, psychiatric hospitals, nursing homes, and public child welfare departments), through more formal means, as with institutional ethics committees (Amdur and Bankert 2010; Hester 2007; Post, Blustein, and Dubler 2006; Reamer 1987, 1995b).

The concept of institutional ethics committees emerged most prominently in 1976, when the New Jersey Supreme Court ruled that Karen Anne Quinlan's family and physicians should consult an ethics committee in deciding whether to remove her from life-support technology (a number of hospitals have had something resembling ethics committees since the 1920s). The court based its ruling in part on an important article that appeared in the *Baylor Law Review* in 1975, in which a pediatrician advocated the use of an ethics committee when health-care professionals face difficult ethical choices (Teel 1975).

Ethics committees, which can include representatives from various disciplines, often provide case consultation in addition to education and training (Amdur and Bankert 2010; Cranford and Doudera 1984). Many agency-based ethics committees provide nonbinding ethics consultation and can offer an opportunity for practitioners who encounter complex boundary issues to think through case-specific issues with colleagues who have ethics expertise. Although ethics committees are not always able to provide definitive options about the complex issues that are frequently brought to their attention (nor should they be expected to), they can provide a valuable forum for thorough and critical analyses of difficult ethical dilemmas related to boundaries and dual relationships.

Obtaining sound consultation is important for two reasons. The first is that experienced and thoughtful consultants may offer useful insights concerning complicated boundary issues and may raise important questions that the human service professional had not considered. The expression "two heads are better than one" may seem trite, but it is often true.

The second reason is that such consultation may help practitioners protect themselves if they are sued or have complaints filed against them because of the decisions they make. That a practitioner sought consultation demonstrates that the practitioner approached the decision carefully and prudently, and made a good faith effort to make a responsible decision and adhere to prevailing professional standards; this can help if someone alleges that the practitioner made an inappropriate decision hastily and carelessly.

6. *Make the decision and document the decision-making process.* Once the practitioner has carefully considered the various boundary issues, including the values and duties that may conflict; identified the individuals, groups, and organizations that are likely to be affected by the decision; tentatively identified all potential courses of action and the participants involved in each, along with any benefits and risks for each; thoroughly examined the reasons in favor of and opposed to each course of action (considering relevant ethical theories, principles, and guidelines; codes of ethics and legal guidelines; human service practice theories and principles; and personal values); and consulted with colleagues and appropriate experts, it is time to make a decision. In some instances the decision will seem clear. Going through the decision-making process will have clarified and illuminated the issues so that the practitioner's ethical obligation seems unambiguous.

In other instances, however, practitioners may still feel somewhat uncertain about their ethical obligations related to the proper management of boundaries. These are the hard cases and are not uncommon in ethical decision making. After all, situations that warrant full-scale ethical decision making, with all the steps that this entails, are, by definition, complicated. If they were not complex, the practitioner could have resolved the situation easily and simply at an earlier stage. Thus it should not be surprising that many ethical dilemmas related to boundaries and dual relationships remain controversial even after practitioners have taken the time to examine them thoroughly and systematically. Such is the nature of ethical dilemmas.

Once the decision is made, human service professionals should always be careful to document the steps involved in the decision-making process. Ethical decisions are just as much a part of practice as clinical, community, organizational, and policy interventions, and they should become part of the record (Luepker 2002; Kagle and Kopels 2008; Moline, Williams, and Austin 1998; Sidell 2011). This is simply sound professional practice. Both the practitioner involved in the case and other professionals who may become involved in the case (e.g., supervisors, administrators, defense counsel) may need access to these notes at some time in the future to assess the practitioner's actions and judgment. As the NASW *Code of Ethics* (2008) states, "Social workers should include sufficient and timely documentation in records to facilitate the delivery of service and to ensure continuity of services provided to clients in the future" (standard 3.04[b]). Similarly, the ethics code of the American Psychological Association (2010) states, "Psychologists create, and to the extent the records are under their control, maintain, disseminate, store, retain, and dispose of records and data relating to their professional and scientific work in order to (1) facilitate provision of services later by them or by other professionals, (2) allow for replication of research design and analyses, (3) meet institutional requirements, (4) ensure accuracy of billing and payments, and (5) ensure compliance with law" (standard 6.01).

Preparing notes on the ethical decision-making process is extremely important in the event that the case results in an ethics complaint or legal proceedings (for example, a lawsuit or licensing board complaint filed against the practitioner). Carefully written notes documenting the professional's diligence can be protection from allegations of malpractice or negligence (Reamer 2003a).

Professionals need to decide how much detail to include in their documentation. Too much detail can be problematic, particularly if the practitioner's records are subpoenaed. Sensitive details about the client's life and circumstances may be exposed against the client's wishes. At the same time practitioners can encounter problems if their documentation is too brief and skimpy, especially if the lack of detail affects the quality of care provided in the future by other professionals. In short, practitioners need to include the level of detail that facilitates the delivery of services without exposing clients unnecessarily, consistent with generally accepted standards in the profession. According to the NASW *Code of Ethics* (2008), "Social workers' documentation should protect clients' privacy to the extent that is possible and appropriate and should include only information that is directly relevant to the delivery of services" (standard 3.04[c]).

7. *Monitor, evaluate, and document the decision.* Whatever ethical decision a practitioner makes about the management of boundary issues is not the end of the process. In some respects it constitutes the beginning of a new stage. Human service professionals should always pay close attention to and evaluate the consequences of their ethical decisions related to boundaries. This is important in order to be accountable to clients, employers, funding sources, and other relevant third parties and, if necessary, to provide documentation in the event of an ethics complaint or lawsuit. This may take the form of routine case monitoring, recording, or more extensive evaluation using the variety of research tools now available to practitioners (Bloom,

Fischer, and Orme 2009; Corcoran and Fischer 2000; Nugent, Sieppert, and Hudson 2001; Vonk, Tripodi, and Epstein 2007).

As I noted in the preceding discussion, it would be a mistake to assume that systematic and ethical decision making will always produce clear and unambiguous results. To expect this would be to misunderstand the nature of ethics. The different theoretical perspectives of human service professionals, their personal and professional experiences, and their biases will inevitably combine to produce differing points of view. This is just fine, particularly if we are confident that sustained dialogue among practitioners about the merits of their respective views is likely to enhance their understanding and insight. As in all other aspects of practice, the process is often what matters most. As Jonsen notes, ethics guidelines by themselves "are not the modern substitute for the Decalogue. They are, rather, shorthand moral education. They set out the concise definitions and the relevant distinctions that prepare the already well-disposed person to make the shrewd judgment that this or that instance is a typical case of this or that sort, and, then, decide how to act" (1984:4).

THE ROLE OF PRACTITIONER IMPAIRMENT

In a significant percentage of cases involving boundary violations and inappropriate dual relationships, we find evidence of some form of practitioner impairment. In recent years the subject of impaired professionals has received increased attention (Berliner 1989; Celenza 2007; Gutheil and Brodsky 2008; Kilburg, Nathan, and Thoreson 1986; Laliotis and Grayson 1985; McCrady 1989; Reamer 2006a, 2009b; Syme 2003).

Organized efforts to address impaired employees began in the late 1930s and early 1940s after Alcoholics Anonymous was formed and in response to the need that arose during World War II to sustain a sound workforce. These early occupational alcoholism programs eventually led, in the early 1970s, to the emergence of employee assistance programs, designed to address a broad range of problems experienced by employees. Also, in 1972 the Council on Mental Health of the American Medical Association issued a statement that said that physicians have an ethical responsibility to recognize and report impairment among colleagues. In 1976 a group of attorneys recovering from alcoholism formed Lawyers Concerned for Lawyers to address chemical dependence in the profession, and in 1980 a group of recovering psychologists began a similar group, Psychologists Helping Psychologists (Kilburg, Nathan, and Thoreson 1986).

Social work's first national acknowledgment of the problem of impaired practitioners came in 1979, when NASW issued a public policy statement concerning alcoholism and alcohol-related problems (Commission on Employment 1987). By 1980 a nationwide support group for chemically dependent practitioners, Social Workers Helping Social Workers, had formed. In 1982 NASW formed the Occupational Social Work Task Force, charged with developing a strategy to deal with impaired NASW members. Two years later the NASW Delegate Assembly issued a resolution on impairment, and in 1987 NASW published the *Impaired Social Worker Program Resource Book* to help members of the profession design programs for impaired social workers. The introduction to the resource book states:

> Social workers, like other professionals, have within their ranks those who, because of substance abuse, chemical dependency, mental illness or stress, are unable to function effectively in their jobs. These are the impaired social workers. . . . The problem of impairment is compounded by the fact that the professionals who suffer from the effect of mental illness, stress or substance abuse are like anyone else; they are often the worst judges of their behavior, the last to recognize their problems and the least motivated to seek help. Not only are they able to hide or avoid confronting their behavior, they are often abetted by colleagues who find it difficult to accept that a professional could let his or her problem get out of hand.
>
> (6)

More recently, strategies for dealing with professionals who encounter boundary challenges that stem from problems such as substance abuse, mental illness, and emotional stress have become more prevalent. Professional associations and informal groups of practitioners meet periodically to discuss the problem of impaired colleagues and to organize efforts to address the problem.

Both the seriousness of impairment among human service professionals and the forms it takes, especially related to boundary violations and crossings, vary. Impairment may involve failure to provide competent care or violation of the profession's ethical standards, such as serious boundary violations involving sexual misconduct with a client (Reamer 1995b, 1997). It may also take such forms as providing flawed or inferior psychotherapy to a client or failure to carry out professional duties as a result of substance abuse or mental illness (Johnson and Stone 1986; Koeske and Koeske 1989). Lamb and colleagues provided one of the earliest, and still relevant, definitions of impairment among professionals:

> Interference in professional functioning that is reflected in one or more of the following ways: (a) an inability and/or unwillingness to acquire and integrate professional standards into one's repertoire of professional behavior; (b) an inability to acquire professional skills in order to reach an acceptable level of competency; and (c) an inability to control personal stress, psychological dysfunction, and/or excessive emotional reactions that interfere with professional functioning.
>
> (1987:598)

Although we have no precise estimates of the extent of impairment among human service professionals, speculative data are available based on pioneering research that began in the 1980s (Besharov 1985; Bissell and Haberman 1984; Bullis 1995). For example, in the foreword to the *Impaired Social Worker Resource Book*, published by the Commission on Employment and Economic Support of the National Association of Social Workers, the commission chair states, "Social workers have the same problems as most working groups. Up to 5 to 7 percent of our membership may have a problem with substance abuse. Another 10 to 15 percent may be going through personal transitions in their relationships, marriage, family, or their work life" (1987:4). The report goes on to conclude, however, that "there is little reliable information on the extent of impairment among social workers" (6).

The earliest prevalence studies among psychologists suggested a significant degree of distress within the profession. In a study of 749 psychologists, Guy, Poelstra, and Stark (1989) found that 74.3 percent reported "personal distress" during the previous three years, and 36.7 percent of this group believed that their distress decreased the quality of care they provided to clients. Pope, Tabachnick, and Keith-Spiegel report that 62.2 percent of the members of Division 29 (Psychotherapy) of the American Psychological Association admitted to "working when too distressed to be effective" (1988:993). In their survey of 167 licensed psychologists, Wood and colleagues (1985) found that nearly one-third (32.3 percent) reported experiencing depression or burnout to an extent that interfered with their work. Wood and colleagues also found that a significant portion of their sample reported being aware of colleagues

BOUNDARIES AND DUAL RELATIONSHIPS 37

whose work was seriously affected by drug or alcohol use, sexual overtures toward clients, or depression and burnout. In addition, evidence suggests that psychologists and psychiatrists commit suicide at a rate much higher than the general population (Farber 1983, cited in Millon, Millon, and Antoni 1986).

In an important interdisciplinary study, Deutsch (1985) found that more than half her sample of social workers, psychologists, and master's-level counselors reported significant problems with depression, which can be a correlate of boundary problems. Nearly four-fifths (82 percent) reported problems with relationships, 11 percent reported substance abuse problems, and 2 percent reported suicide attempts.

In a groundbreaking, comprehensive review of a series of empirical studies focused specifically on sexual contact between therapists and clients, K. S. Pope (1988) found that the aggregate average of reported sexual contact is 8.3 percent by male therapists and 1.7 percent by female therapists. Pope reports that one study (Gechtman and Bouhoutsos 1985) found that 3.8 percent of male social workers admitted to sexual contact with clients.

Impairment among professionals is the result of various causes. Stress related to employment, illness or death of family members, marital or relationship problems, financial problems, midlife crises, physical or mental illness, legal problems, and substance abuse may lead to impairment (Guy, Poelstra, and Stark 1989; Thoreson, Miller, and Krauskopf 1989). Stress induced by professional education and training can also lead to impairment, because of the close clinical supervision and scrutiny students receive, the disruption in students' personal lives caused by the demands of schoolwork and internships, and the pressures of academic programs (Lamb et al. 1987).

According to Wood and colleagues (1985), psychotherapists encounter special sources of stress that may lead to impairment because their therapeutic role often extends into nonwork areas of their lives (such as relationships with family members and friends) and because of the lack of reciprocity in relationships with clients (therapists are "always giving"), the slow and erratic nature of therapeutic progress, and personal issues that therapeutic work with clients may stir up. Psychotherapists who feel unusually stressed may cope in destructive ways that lead to boundary violations, for example, by seeking solace in an intimate relationship with an appealing client. As Kilburg, Kaslow, and VandenBos observe,

> The stresses of daily life—family responsibilities, death of family members and friends, other severe losses, illnesses, financial difficulties, crimes of all

kinds—quite naturally place mental health professionals, like other people, under pressure. However, by virtue of their training and place in society, such professionals face unique stresses. And although they have been trained extensively in how to deal with the emotional and behavioral crises of others, few are trained in how to deal with the stresses they themselves with face. . . . Mental health professionals are expected by everyone, including themselves, to be paragons. The fact that they may be unable to fill that role makes them a prime target for disillusionment, distress, and burnout. When this reaction occurs, the individual's ability to function as a professional may become impaired.

(1988:723)

Unfortunately, relatively little is known about the extent to which impaired human service professionals, especially those who violate boundaries or engage in unethical dual relationships, voluntarily seek help for their problems. Few ambitious studies have been conducted. Guy, Poelstra, and Stark (1989) found that 70 percent of the distressed clinical psychologists they surveyed sought some form of therapeutic assistance. One-fourth (26.6 percent) entered individual psychotherapy, and 10.7 percent entered family therapy. A small portion of this group participated in self-help groups (3.4 percent) or was hospitalized (2.2 percent). Some were placed on medication (4.1 percent). Exactly 10 percent of this group temporarily terminated their professional practice.

These findings contrast with those of Wood and colleagues (1985), who found that only 55 percent of clinicians who reported problems that interfered with their work (sexual overtures toward clients, substance abuse, depression, and burnout) sought help. Two-fifths (42 percent) of all clinicians surveyed, including impaired and unimpaired professionals, reported having offered help to impaired colleagues at some point or having referred them to therapists, according to Wood and colleagues. Only 7.9 percent of the sample said they had reported an impaired colleague to a local regulatory body. Two-fifths (40 percent) were aware of instances in which they believed no action was taken to help an impaired colleague.

We may draw several hypotheses concerning the reluctance of some impaired human service professionals to seek help and the reluctance of their colleagues to confront them about their problems. Until recently, professionals were hesitant to acknowledge impairment within their ranks because they feared how practitioners would react to confrontation and how such confrontation might affect future working relationships among colleagues (Bernard and Jara 1986; McCrady 1989; Prochaska and Norcross 1983; Wood et al. 1985). As VandenBos and Duthie (1986) note,

> The fact that more than half of us have not confronted distressed colleagues even when we have recognized and acknowledged (at least to ourselves) the existence of their problems is, in part, a reflection of the difficulty in achieving a balance between concerned intervention and intrusiveness. As professionals, we value our own right to practice without interference, as long as we function within the boundaries of our professional expertise, meet professional standards for the provision of services, and behave in an ethical manner. We generally consider such expectations when we consider approaching a distressed colleague. Deciding when and how our concern about the well-being of a colleague (and our ethical obligation) supersedes his or her right to personal privacy and professional autonomy is a ticklish matter.
>
> (1986:212)

Thoreson and colleagues (1983) also argue that impaired professionals sometimes find it difficult to seek help because of their mythical belief in their infinite power and invulnerability. The involvement of a large number of psychotherapists in private practice exacerbates the problem because of the reduced opportunity for colleagues to observe their unethical conduct, including boundary violations and inappropriate dual relationships (Reamer 2003b).

In Deutsch's valuable 1985 study, a diverse group of therapists who acknowledged having personal problems gave a variety of reasons for not seeking professional help, including believing that an acceptable therapist was not available, seeking help from family members or friends, fearing exposure and the disclosure of embarrassing confidential information, concern about the amount of effort required and about the cost, having a spouse who was unwilling to participate in treatment, failing to admit the seriousness of the problem, believing that they should be able to work out their problems themselves, and assuming that therapy would not help.

It is important for professionals to design ways to prevent impairment and respond to impaired colleagues, especially those whose impairment leads to serious boundary violations and inappropriate dual relationships. They must be knowledgeable about the indicators and causes of impairment, so that they can recognize problems that colleagues may be experiencing. Practitioners must also be willing to confront impaired colleagues constructively, offer assistance and consultation, and, if necessary as a last resort, refer the colleague to a supervisor or local regulatory body or professional association.

Over time various professions' codes of ethics have acknowledged and address the issue of professional impairment. In social work, for example, in 1992 the president of NASW created the Code of Ethics Review Task Force (which I chaired), which proposed adding new standards to the code on the subject of impairment. The approved additions became effective in 1994 and were then revised slightly and incorporated in the current NASW *Code of Ethics*:

> Social workers should not allow their own personal problems, psychosocial distress, legal problems, substance abuse, or mental health difficulties to interfere with their professional judgment and performance or to jeopardize the best interests of people for whom they have a professional responsibility.
>
> (standard 4.05[a])

> Social workers whose personal problems, psychosocial distress, legal problems, substance abuse, or mental health difficulties interfere with their professional judgment and performance should immediately seek consultation and take appropriate remedial action by seeking professional help, making adjustments in workload, terminating practice, or taking any other steps necessary to protect clients and others.
>
> (standard 4.05[b])

> Social workers who have direct knowledge of a social work colleague's impairment that is due to personal problems, psychosocial distress, substance abuse, or mental health difficulties and that interferes with practice effectiveness should consult with that colleague when feasible and assist the colleague in taking remedial action.
>
> (standard 2.09[a])

> Social workers who believe that a social work colleague's impairment interferes with practice effectiveness and that the colleague has not taken adequate steps to address the impairment should take action through appropriate channels established by employers, agencies, NASW, licensing and regulatory bodies, and other professional organizations.
>
> (standard 2.09[b])

Other human service professions have established similar standards. For example, the *Code of Ethics* of the AAMFT (2001) states, "Marriage and family therapists [should] seek appropriate professional assistance for their personal problems or conflicts that may impair work performance or clinical judgment" (standard 3.3). The ACA *Code of Ethics* (2005) states,

> Counselors are alert to the signs of impairment from their own physical, mental, or emotional problems and refrain from offering or providing professional services when such impairment is likely to harm a client or others. They seek assistance for problems that reach the level of professional impairment, and, if necessary, they limit, suspend, or terminate their professional responsibilities until such time it is determined that they may safely resume their work. Counselors assist colleagues or supervisors in recognizing their own professional impairment and provide consultation and assistance when warranted with colleagues or supervisors showing signs of impairment and intervene as appropriate to prevent imminent harm to clients.
>
> (standard C.2.g)

Although some cases of impairment must be dealt with through formal adjudication and disciplinary procedures, many cases can be handled primarily by arranging therapeutic, rehabilitative, and educational services for distressed and impaired practitioners.

As human service professionals increase the attention they pay to the problem of impairment and its relationship to boundary violations, they must be careful to avoid assigning all responsibility to the practitioners themselves. Professionals must also address the environmental stressors and structural factors that can cause impairment. Distress is often the result of the unique challenges in the human services, and remedial resources often are inadequate. Caring professionals who are overwhelmed by the difficulties of their clients—chronic problems of poverty, substance abuse, child abuse and neglect, hunger and homelessness, and mental illness—are prime candidates for high degrees of stress, compassion fatigue, and burnout. Insufficient funding, the stresses of managed care, unpredictable political support, and public skepticism of professionals' efforts often lead to low morale and high stress (Jayaratne and Chess 1984; Maslach 2003). Thus, in addition to responding to the individual problems of impaired colleagues, practitioners must confront the environmental and structural problems that can cause the impairment in the first place. This comprehensive effort can also help to reduce unethical behavior and professional misconduct, particularly in the form of boundary violations and inappropriate dual relationships.

There is no question that human service professionals have developed a richer, more nuanced understanding of boundary issues in the profession. To further enhance this understanding, professionals must examine dual relationships that are exploitative and those that are more ambiguous. Practitioners' firm grasp of boundary issues involving their intimate relationships with clients and colleagues, management of their own emotional and dependency issues, pursuit of personal benefit, altruistic gestures, and responses to unanticipated and unavoidable circumstances will increase their ability to protect clients, colleagues, and themselves. Most important, skillful management of boundary issues will enhance human service professionals' integrity, one of the hallmarks of a profession. Skillful management of these issues will also reduce the likelihood of ethics complaints and malpractice claims.

2

INTIMATE RELATIONSHIPS

MANY BOUNDARY ISSUES involve some form of intimate relationship. Some issues are glaring, such as those involving sexual contact between a therapist and a current client. Other issues, however, are more subtle, such as those involving seemingly innocent affectionate gestures.

I will examine a wide range of boundary issues involving intimacy. They include sexual relationships between professionals and their current or former clients; sexual relationships between professionals and clients' relatives or acquaintances; sexual relationships between professionals who are supervisors or educators and their supervisees, students, trainees, or other colleagues over whom they exercise professional authority; providing professional services to a former lover; and physical contact between professionals and clients.

SEXUAL RELATIONSHIPS WITH CLIENTS

CASE 2.1

Alfred S. was a counseling psychologist in private practice. For many years Dr. S. provided clinical services to children and families. He specialized in child behavior management problems and family therapy.

Dr. S. had been providing services to a nine-year-old child, Sam K., and his single mother, Judy K. A school counselor referred Ms. K. and her son to Dr. S.; school staffers had been concerned about Sam's acting out and aggressive behavior in school. Dr. S. met with Sam and his mother weekly for about four months. Most of the recent sessions were with Ms. K. alone, during which they discussed Ms. K.'s efforts to cope with Sam's behavior and her loneliness and sense of isolation.

> For several weeks Dr. S., who recently divorced, felt attracted to Ms. K. He found himself thinking about Ms. K. outside working hours. Dr. S. went out of his way to spend extra time with Ms. K. during their counseling sessions; often he scheduled their sessions at the end of the day so that no other client's appointment would force them to end their session after precisely fifty minutes. Toward the end of one session Dr. S. asked Ms. K. if she would like to spend a little time with him outside the office "so we can get to know each other a little better." Dr. S. went on to explain to Ms. K. that he was feeling attracted to her and that he sensed that she was feeling the same way. Dr. S. was careful to explain to Ms. K. that he would not want to do anything to harm her or her son's progress in treatment; he told Ms. K. that he would need to refer her to another therapist if they developed an intimate relationship. Within three weeks Dr. S. and Ms. K. were involved sexually.

As I noted in chapter 1, a substantial portion of intimate dual relationships entered into by human service professionals involve sexual contact (Appelbaum and Jorgenson 1991; Bohmer 2000; Celenza 2007; Gutheil and Brodsky 2008; Mittendorf and Schroeder 2004; Syme 2003). As Brodsky notes,

A sexual intimacy between patient and therapist is one example of a dual relationship. Dual relationships involve more than one purpose of relating. A therapy relationship is meant to be exclusive and unidimensional. The therapist is the expert, the patient the consumer of that expertise. Once a patient accepts an individual as a therapist, that individual cannot, without undue influence, relate to that patient in any other role. Relating to the patient as an employer, business partner, lover, spouse, relative, professor or student would contaminate the therapeutic goal. The contamination is much more intense in a psychotherapy relationship than it would be in the relationship between a client and a professional in any other field—for example, between a client and an internist, a dentist, a lawyer, or an accountant.

(1986:155)

THE NATURE OF SEXUAL MISCONDUCT

The historical record is replete with references to inappropriate sexual contact between professionals and the people they serve. The famed Hippocratic Oath makes explicit reference to this phenomenon: "Whatever houses I may visit, I will come for the benefit of the sick, remaining free of all intentional injustice, of all mischief and in particular of sexual relations with both female and male persons, be they free or slaves" (Celenza 2007:xiii). As early as 1784 the French king Louis XVI was concerned that a new medical technique, known as mesmerism (animal magnetism), might be used by unethical French physicians to sexually exploit female patients (Celenza 2007). The centuries since have been littered with troubling instances of sexual exploitation of clients by a relatively small, albeit noteworthy, percentage of practitioners.

Inappropriate sexual contact and sexualized behavior with clients can take several forms. These include touching body parts (for example, shoulder, arm, hand, leg, knee, face, hair neck), hugging, holding hands, holding a client on one's lap, engaging in sexual humor, making suggestive remarks or gestures, kissing, exposing one's genitals, touching breasts, engaging in oral sex, and engaging in sexual intercourse (Celenza 2007; Plaut 1997; Samuel and Gorton 2001; Stake and Oliver 1991). One useful typology, based on self-reports of sexual contact and behavior by a large sample of licensed psychologists, categorizes these various behaviors into three conceptual groups. The first includes overt sexual behavior, such as sexual intercourse, oral sex, fondling the genital area, touching the breasts, genital exposure, and kissing. The second group of behaviors includes touching behavior, such as touching body parts (for example, shoulders, arm, hand, leg, knee, face, hair, or neck), hugging, and holding the client on one's lap. The third group includes suggestive behavior, such as using sexual humor and making suggestive remarks or glances. State laws typically define sexual activity more narrowly as intercourse, rape, the touching of breasts and genitals, cunnilingus, fellatio, sodomy, and inappropriate or unnecessary examinations and procedures performed for sexual gratification (Simon 1999).

Beginning with the Hippocratic Oath, all major helping professions have prohibited sexual relationships with current patients and clients. The Hippocratic Oath obliges physicians to keep "far from all intentional ill-doing and all seduction, and especially from the pleasures of love with women and men" (*Dorland's Medical Dictionary* 1974:715).

A series of empirical studies demonstrates the seriousness and magnitude of boundary violations and inappropriate dual relationships involving professionals' sexual contact with clients. During a twenty-year period nearly one in five lawsuits (18.5 percent) against social workers insured through the malpractice insurance program sponsored by the National Association of Social Workers (NASW) alleged some form of sexual impropriety, and more than two-fifths of insurance payments (41.3 percent) were the result of claims concerning sexual misconduct (Reamer 2003a). Schoener and colleagues (1989) estimate that 15 to 16 percent of male and 2 to 3 percent of female therapists admit erotic contact with clients. Other national data suggest that 8 to 12 percent of male counselors or psychotherapists, and 1.7 to 3 percent of female counselors or psychotherapists, admit having had sexual relationships with a current or former client (Olarte 1997). According to Simon (1999), the reported rate of sexual contact between therapists and clients is generally in the range of 7 percent to 10 percent. Simon cautions that the actual rates are probably higher, because self-report data are known to underestimate actual incidence.

K. S. Pope (1986) reports on the frequency of successful malpractice claims filed against psychologists during a ten-year period. Although the time period covered by Pope is shorter than the period described for social workers (Reamer 2003a), the similarities are clear. As with social workers, the most frequent claims categories for psychologists during the ten-year period were sexual contact (psychologists, 18.5 percent of claims; social workers, 18.5 percent of claims) and treatment error (psychologists, 15.2 percent of claims; social workers, 18.6 percent of claims). Approximately 45 percent of dollars spent during these periods in response to claims against psychologists resulted from claims of sexual contact, and 41 percent of dollars spent in response to claims against social workers resulted from claims of sexual misconduct.

All the available data suggest that the vast majority of cases involving sexual contact between professionals and clients involve a male practitioner and female client (Brodsky 1986; Celenza 2007; K. Pope 1988; Bernsen, Tabachnick, and Pope 1994; Hedges et al. 1997). Gartrell and colleagues (1986) reported in their groundbreaking survey of psychiatrists that 6.4 percent of respondents acknowledged sexual contact with their patients; 90 percent of the offenders were male. Simon (1999) cites data that show that 80 percent of sexual contacts involving psychiatrists were between male psychiatrists and female patients, 7.6 percent between male psychiatrists and male patients, 3.5 percent between female psychiatrists and male patients, and 1.4 percent between female psychiatrists and female patients. Of the 38.4 percent who were repeaters, none was a female psychiatrist. G. G. Pope (1990:193–94) cites a study that found 93 percent of offending therapists (psychiatrists, marriage counselors, clergy, and social workers) who responded to a large-scale survey were men, and 89 percent of the victims were women.

Although suits against psychiatrists alleging sexual contact tend to be filed more frequently than such suits against psychologists, studies suggest that the prevalence rates for sexual contact with patients by psychiatrists and psychologists are similar. Studies suggest that the prevalence rate for clinical social workers is lower (Celenza 2007:7–8; Gechtman 1989).

Olarte provides a succinct profile of the offending therapist:

> The composite profile that most frequently emerges from the treatment or consultation with offenders is that the therapist is a middle-aged man who is undergoing some type of personal distress, is isolated professionally, and overvalues his healing capacities. His therapeutic methods tend to be unorthodox; he frequently particularizes the therapeutic relationship by disclosing personal information not pertinent to the treatment, which fosters confusion of the therapeutic boundaries. He is generally well trained, having completed at least an approved training program and at times formal psychoanalytic training.
>
> (1997:201)

Brodsky's overview of offending therapists who are named as defendants in lawsuits contains a number of strikingly similar attributes:

> The following characteristics constitute a prototype of the therapist being sued: The therapist is male, middle aged, involved in unsatisfactory relationships in his own life, perhaps in the process of going through a divorce. His patient caseload is primarily female. He becomes involved with more than one patient sexually, those selected being on the average 16 years younger than he is. He confides his personal life to the patient, implying to her that he needs her, and he spends therapy sessions soliciting her help with his personal problems. The therapist is a lonely man, and even if he works in a group practice, he is somewhat isolated professionally, not sharing in close consultation with his peers. He may have a good reputation in the psychological or psychiatric community, having been in practice for many years. He tends to take cases through referral only. He is not necessarily physically attractive, but there is an aura of power or charisma about him. His lovemaking often leaves much to be desired, but he is quite convincing to the patient that it is he above all others with whom she needs to be making love.
>
> (1986:157–58)

Brodsky (1986) also describes other sexually abusive therapists, including those who tend to be inexperienced and in love with one particular client, and therapists with a personality disorder (typically antisocial personality disorder) who manipulate clients into believing that the therapists should be trusted and that they have the clients' best interest at heart.

Celenza (2007:11, 29–38) studied a sample of therapists who engaged in sexual misconduct and found a number of common precursors related primarily to the therapist's personality, life circumstances, past history, and the transference/countertransference dynamics of this particular therapist-client pair. More specifically, Celenza found that clinicians who manifest certain traits are more likely to engage in sexual misconduct:

- Long-standing narcissistic vulnerability. Therapists reported a lifelong struggle with a sense of unworthiness, inadequacy, or outright feelings of failure.

- Grandiose (covert) rescue fantasies. Therapists presented a mild-mannered, self-effacing, and humble exterior that hid underlying (and unchallenged) beliefs in powers of rescue and omnipotence.

- Intolerance of negative transference. Often as a result of fragile self-esteem, some therapists have difficulty tolerating and exploring disappointments, frustrations, and criticisms that the client may have about the services she or he is receiving.

- Childhood history of emotional deprivation and sexualized over-stimulation. Some therapists reported sexualization in their relationship with a primary caregiver (usually the mother), often in the form of over-stimulation of the child in a sexualized manner rather than outright sexual abuse.

- Family history of covert and sanctioned boundary transgressions. Some therapists' families showed evidence of high moralism accompanied by hypocrisy, for example, in the form of marital infidelity or fraudulent financial activity.

- Unresolved anger toward authority figures. Some therapists appeared to engage in sexual misconduct as a way to rebel against the authority of their profession and as a result of an underlying desire to break the rules, perhaps because of anger toward an authoritarian parent.

- Restricted awareness of fantasy (especially hostile/aggressive). Many therapists, especially those who felt intense guilt and remorse, were unable to admit to or access hateful or desirous wishes except in conventional or muted ways. These therapists had difficulty perceiving aggression in themselves or others.

- Transformation of countertransference hate to countertransference love. Some therapists had difficulty tolerating their own aggression and perceiving themselves as depriving or non-nurturing with clients. They harbored the unrealistic belief that they should love and help every client.

Reaves (1986:175) cites a case that typifies the sexual abuse of a client by a therapist. According to court records, a psychiatrist had sex with a female client during a two-and-a-half year period, all the while charging her an hourly counseling fee. The plaintiff eventually divorced her husband, lost her rights under California community property law, and lost custody of her two children. The psychiatrist had also prescribed excessive medication for the plaintiff, who claimed that she had tried to commit suicide more than a dozen times using pills obtained from the psychiatrist or his office, according to court records. The psychiatrist ultimately referred the plaintiff to another practitioner, labeling her as borderline psychotic. The jury awarded damages in the amount of $4,631,666.

A small number of therapists named in ethics complaints and lawsuits try to defend their sexual contact with clients (Gutheil and Brodsky 2008; Schutz 1982). One argument they sometimes advance is that the sexual contact was an essential, constructive, and legitimate component of therapy. The therapist typically claims that he was merely trying to be helpful to the client. The defense offered by the lawyer for a Dr. Cooper, who sued the California Board of Medical Examiners, is illustrative: "Dr. Cooper is a firm believer in the fact that the body has a tremendous significance and influence on our actions; and the awareness of one's body is one of the keys to personal health; mental health; and his techniques may be considered new, revolutionary, and even bizarre perhaps to some people. But none of us knows the potential of the human body in relation to the human mind, and to explore that and make a person whole is Dr. Cooper's dedicated professional goal" (Schutz 1982:34–25).

Another defense mounted by some clinicians accused of misconduct is that the sexual relationship was independent of the therapeutic relationship. In these instances the defendant-therapist usually argues that he and the client were able to separate their sexual involvement from their professional relationship. However, as Schutz suggests in one of the earliest discussions of this phenomenon, this argument "has not been a very successful defense, since courts are reluctant to accept such a compartmentalized view of human relationships. A therapist attempting to prove the legitimacy of sexual relations between himself and a patient by establishing that two co-terminous-in-time but utterly parallel relations existed has a difficult task" (1982:35).

Sexual misconduct by therapists is now a criminal offense in a number of states (Celenza 2007). Some formerly licensed clinicians have been sentenced to prison following conviction in criminal court.

Also, state licensing boards have addressed a significant number of sexual misconduct cases in response to formal complaints. Because many licensing board websites feature disciplinary reports, anyone with Internet access can review considerable detail about clinicians' sexual misconduct and any sanctions imposed by licensing boards.

Further, many clinicians have been sued in civil court by clients or former clients who allege that they were harmed by therapists' sexual exploitation. Other clinicians have had formal complaints filed against them with national professional associations (such as the NASW) of which they are members. The list that follows is a mere sample, a diverse cross section of a distressingly large number of court cases and professional disciplinary proceedings involving allegations of sexual misconduct:

- A Michigan social worker was sentenced to two to ten years in prison after pleading guilty to eleven counts of criminal sexual conduct involving a mental health professional and one count of assault with intent of sexual penetration. The social worker sexually assaulted clients he treated during his employment in a major university health system's program for people suffering from traumatic brain injury. The incidents occurred in his office, in the patients' homes, and, in some cases, a university van he secretly used to run errands. In court the social worker admitted to fondling the breasts and buttocks of each victim for his own sexual gratification and escalating the sexual contact with one of the women under his care (Aisner 2008).

- A Pennsylvania court upheld the state licensing board's revocation of a psychologist's license to practice because of substantial evidence that he had had sexual relations with a patient before termination of the therapeutic relationship. The psychologist had neither formally terminated nor even discussed termination of the therapeutic relationship before he had sexual relations with the client. He stopped billing the client for therapy sessions around the time they started their sexual relationship, but a psychologist cannot terminate a patient relationship merely by ceasing to bill the patient ("Court Upholds Revocation" 1998:6).

▪ Two weeks after a social worker took a job at an outpatient mental health program, management observed him socializing with clients while on breaks from therapy sessions. The social worker induced a client—who had been diagnosed with bipolar disorder and alcoholism—to meet him outside the treatment program's facilities. The client testified that the social worker often had quoted from the Bible, and she thought he was a good Christian man who could help her by going for long walks and talking. After meeting the social worker off the program's premises, the client entered into a sexual relationship with him. After the second meeting the client felt tremendous remorse and guilt and had a relapse with alcohol. The jury awarded the client $123,500 in damages ("Social Worker Engages in Sexual Relationship" 1999:2).

▪ A Florida appeals court upheld the constitutionality of a state statute that was used to convict a psychotherapist for criminal sexual misconduct. In counseling a client with low self-esteem, a licensed psychologist had raised issues involving the client's sexuality, digitally penetrated her, tried to kiss her, and lowered his pants in front of her. The appeals court found ample evidence in the record that the psychologist had committed the misconduct by means of a therapeutic deception, meaning a "representation to the client that sexual contact by the psychotherapist is consistent with or part of the treatment of the client." The client met with the psychologist while wearing a wire, and the police obtained a tape-recording of the psychologist admitting that he had offered to have sex with her as an incentive for her to reach her weight goal and stating that he did not think that what had happened was hurtful but that it helped build her self-esteem. Evidence of similar misconduct with another former client was admitted into evidence ("Court Upholds Law" 1998:2).

▪ A thirty-seven-year-old woman, who complained of discontent in her life and failure to meet her family's expectations, sought help from a psychiatrist. She claimed that the psychiatrist had committed malpractice during the psychotherapy relationship when, after counseling her for six months, he told her their relationship was going to change and told her to sit on his lap. He then lifted her blouse and kissed her breast. The patient sat there and watched the psychiatrist because she was too stunned to react. He told her that he would kiss her other breast on the next visit. The psychiatrist admitted that the incident had occurred but contended that it did not constitute malpractice and the patient was not harmed by his actions. The psychiatrist also claimed that the patient had actually seduced him. The jury awarded damages of $142,371 ("Improper Sexual Contact" 1997:4).

■ A nineteen-year-old woman received treatment from a psychologist at a mental health center. The therapeutic relationship continued for about ten years. After about one year the psychologist began having sex with the woman. She had been abused as a child and did not have a father figure in her life. The client alleged that the psychologist had responded to this disclosure by viewing her as a friend, a daughter figure, and a lover. The client claimed that she has poor social skills as a result of the abuse and will never get married or be able to have a normal relationship with a man. She received $425,000 in a pretrial settlement ("Woman Blames Psychological Problems" 1997:2).

■ A woman sought mental health treatment from a counselor, who was a lesbian, to address issues related to a sexual problem she was having with her female roommate and occasional lover. The client believed that the counselor's own sexual orientation would help her deal with the clinical issues. During the course of treatment the client invited the counselor to have dinner with her and three other women. The counselor and client became sexually involved while the counselor was still providing the woman with counseling services. The California licensing board ruled that the counselor was grossly negligent and revoked her license ("Counselor Begins Sexual Relationship" 1991:1).

■ A psychiatrist hospitalized a thirty-year-old housewife and had sexual contact with her in the hospital and subsequently during office visits. The patient also accused a psychologist involved in her care of having encouraged her to have sexual relations with the psychiatrist. The psychiatrist did not deny the sexual contact but claimed that he was in love with the patient. The psychologist argued that she did not encourage their relationship. The client received $275,000 in a pretrial settlement ("Psychologist Encourages Sexual Misconduct" 1989:2).

CAUSAL FACTORS

A large percentage of clinical practitioners report having felt attracted to their clients—although most do not act on this attraction. In one of the earliest major surveys of practicing psychotherapists, 96 percent of men and 76 percent of women acknowledged attraction to one or more clients. A relatively small percentage of this particular sample—9.4 percent of the men and 2.5 percent of the women—reported having had sexual relations with their clients (Pope, Tabachnick, and Keith-Spiegel 1988). More than half of a statewide sample of clinical social workers (52.4 percent)—two-thirds of whom were women—reported having felt sexually attracted to a client (Jayaratne, Croxton, and Mattison 1997). In a survey of trainees 86 percent of men and 52 percent of women acknowledged sexual attraction to one or more clients (Gartrell et al. 1986).

The literature offers diverse theories about the causes of, and factors associated with, practitioner sexual misconduct. For example, Simon (1999), a pioneer in research on practitioner misconduct, argues that boundary violations are a function of the nature of the client's clinical issues, type of treatment, status of the therapeutic alliance (whether it is strong or weak, functional or dysfunctional), and personality of the therapist, combined with his or her training and experience.

From a psychodynamic perspective a clinician violates a client's boundaries because of the therapist's difficulty in handling countertransference phenomena—that is, the therapist's transference reaction to the client (countertransference involves unconsciously feeling toward a client the same feelings the clinician originally had toward someone else). Simon asserts that one common countertransference trap occurs when

the therapist subconsciously overidentifies with a patient who he or she then tries to rescue. The therapist is usually struggling with conflicts or has experienced traumatic life events that are also observable in the patient. The patient is treated like a favorite child, with increasing exceptions made to the maintenance of treatment boundaries. As the therapist becomes more deeply immersed in the patient's life, the patient's demands become greater on the therapist. Eventually, the therapist abrogates the role of therapist and enters into a personal, sexual relationship with the patient. Although the therapist becomes aware of increasing boundary violations, he or she feels "powerless" to restore the treatment situation. This scenario is akin to therapists who become sexually involved with patients through "masochistic surrender," one of a variety of countertransference developments in sexual misconduct cases.

(1999:38)

Myers also examines therapist sexual misconduct through a psychodynamic lens as he summarizes a number of countertransference issues that have arisen during supervision he has provided: "These include the covert encouraging of sexual acting out by the patient with various partners or the provoking of other varieties of 'Sturm und Drang' within a patient's life in order to overcome feelings of deprivation or of emptiness within the therapist's life. It is also important to be aware of the wish to protect various patients from the exigencies of life in order to rescue them, as therapists may have wished to rescue various important persons in their lives" (1994:293–94).

Gutheil (1989, cited in Simon 1999) also uses a psychodynamic perspective and focuses on the influence of love in the therapist-client relationship. Gutheil argues that many clients enter treatment with the subconscious wish that a loving, nurturing relationship with the therapist will gratify all needs and repair all hurts. According to Simon,

> The ministrations of the therapist are often perceived by patients as acts of love. For this and a myriad of other conscious and subconscious reasons, patients regularly "fall in love" with their therapists. Some therapists exploit these love feelings for therapist-patient sex. Other therapists mistake these feelings as "true love" and respond to their own needs by establishing a sexual relationship with the patient. Even well-trained therapists may rationalize their behavior by telling themselves that this relationship with the patient is very special and "truly an exception" to the prohibition against sexual involvement with patients. In fact, "love transference" can be extremely capricious, often hiding a destructive hate transference that frighteningly erupts and engulfs the therapist and patient.
>
> (1999:37)

Some authors reject this particular psychodynamic interpretation of boundary violations, preferring instead to view violations as manifestations of clinicians' "undue influence" on, and exploitation of, clients. Gutheil (1989), for example, argues that the concepts of transference and countertransference in relation to boundary violations are demeaning, disrespectful, and unrealistic because of their tendency to characterize the client as a "functional incompetent." Gutheil believes that a client often enters into a sexual relationship with her therapist in a competent manner, although she is misguided and usually unduly influenced by the therapist. Stone (1984) offers yet another perspective, proposing that the therapist breaches the client's fiduciary trust; this theory does not require reference to the client's transference and capacity to consent.

Some authors have expressed concern about a tendency among theorists to blame the victim when exploring sexual relationships between therapists and clients. Celenza, for example, traces the evolution of concern about sexual misconduct and asserts that "up through much of the last century the focus was on the male professional as either a victim of manipulation, or on mutual responsibility for what had happened" (2007:xv).

Smith and Fitzpatrick highlight the importance of the clinician's training and theoretical orientation. They argue that human service professionals must recognize significant differences among different ideological orientations and schools of thought in psychotherapy in determining whether a sexual boundary has been crossed:

> Although all competent clinicians would probably agree that setting appropriate boundaries is a clinical imperative, the wide range of theoretical orientations and techniques pose a major problem when attempting to delineate the proper boundaries of clinical practice. For example, a psychoanalytically oriented clinician may view a colleague's supportive brand of psychotherapy as indulging the patient's transference wishes and as clearly outside the acceptable limits of therapeutic practice. Consider the difference between the clinician who believes that effective psychotherapy can only occur within the four walls of the consulting room versus the therapist who accompanies patients (e.g., those with anxiety disorders) to various locales for in vivo exposure sessions.
>
> (1995:500)

Goisman and Gutheil highlighted the practical consequences of such differences in treatment ideology and theoretical orientation:

> We are aware of a case currently in litigation where a number of the charges against an experienced behavior therapist flowed from the testimony of a psychoanalytically trained expert witness, who faulted the behavior therapist for assigning homework tasks to patients, hiring present and former patients for jobs in psychoeducational programs and other benign interventions, and performing a sexological examination and sensate focus instruction in a case of sexual dysfunction. From a psychoanalytic viewpoint all of

these would likely constitute boundary violations of a potentially harmful sort, but from a behavioral viewpoint this is not at all the case.

(1992:538)

The variation in practitioners' attitudes concerning intimate relationships with clients is noteworthy. Although some studies require updating, they provide compelling insight into clinicians' opinions. In their groundbreaking survey of forty-eight hundred psychiatrists, psychologists, and social workers, Borys and Pope (1989) found that while virtually no respondents approved of sexual activity with a current client, only 68 percent of respondents would absolutely prohibit sexual activity with a client after termination. Pope, Tabachnick, and Keith-Spiegel (1995) found that about 7 percent of a group of psychologists (psychotherapists) believed that becoming sexually involved with a former client is ethical under many circumstances or unquestionably ethical, and about 10 percent stated that kissing a client is ethical under many circumstances or unquestionably ethical. In their survey of more than eight hundred Michigan social workers, Jayaratne, Croxton, and Mattison (1997) found that about 5 percent of respondents said that having sex with a former client is appropriate, 6.4 percent said that going on a date with a former client is appropriate, and 2.6 percent said that kissing a client is appropriate. Another report provides evidence that fewer female therapists than male therapists believe that sexual contact may be beneficial to the treatment process or that it may be appropriate with former clients (Stake and Oliver 1991).

Kardener, Fuller, and Mensh (1976, cited in G. G. Pope 1990) found differences among therapists with different ideological orientations. For example, 86 percent of psychodynamically oriented therapists felt that erotic contact was never of benefit to the client, whereas 71 percent of the humanistic and 61 percent of the behavioral therapists embraced that view. Based on his comprehensive review of the data available by 1990, G. G. Pope concluded that psychoanalysts are more conservative in matters regarding sexuality than the nonpsychoanalytically oriented.

Several authors believe that practitioners who engage in sexual misconduct can be categorized conceptually. Twemlow and Gabbard (1989) characterize therapists who fall in love with clients—a particular subgroup of clinicians who become sexually involved with clients—as lovesick therapists. Lovesickness includes several key elements: emotional dependence; intrusive thinking, whereby the therapist thinks about the client almost constantly;

physical sensations like buoyancy or pounding pulse; a sense of incompleteness, of feeling less than whole when away from the client; an awareness of the social proscription of such love, which seems to intensify the couple's longing for each other; and an altered state of consciousness that fosters impaired judgment on the part of the therapist when in the presence of the loved one.

According to Schoener (1989, 1995), he and his colleagues base their widely cited classification scheme—which includes a broader range of offending therapists—on empirical evidence gathered from psychological and psychiatric examinations of sexually exploitative therapists. These clinical clusters (the italicized terminology is Schoener's) include:

1. *Psychotic and severe borderline disorders.* While relatively few in number, these professionals have difficulties with boundaries because of problems with both impulse control and thinking. They are often aware of current ethical standards but have difficulty adhering to them because of their poor reality testing and judgment.

Manic disorders. Most typically these are practitioners who have been diagnosed with mania, go off medication, and become quite impulsive.

2. *Sociopaths and severe narcissistic personality disorders.* These are self-centered exploiters who cross various boundaries when it suits them. They tend to be calculating and deliberate in their abuse of their clients (Olarte 1997). They often manipulate the treatment by "blurring the professional boundaries with inappropriate personal disclosure that enhances and idealizes transference, and by manipulating the length or the time of the sessions to facilitate the development of a sexual relationship with the client. . . . If caught, they might express remorse and agree to rehabilitation to protect themselves or their professional standing, but they will show minimal or no character change through treatment" (Olarte 1997:205).

3. *Impulse control disorders.* This group includes practitioners with a wide range of paraphilias (sexual disorders in which unusual fantasies or bizarre acts are necessary for sexual arousal) and other impulse control disorders. These professionals often have impulse control problems in other areas of their lives. They are typically aware of current ethical standards, but these do not serve as a deterrent. These practitioners often fail to acknowledge the harm that their behavior does to their victims and show little remorse.

4. *Chronic neurotic and isolated.* These practitioners are emotionally needy on a chronic basis and meet many needs through their relationships

with clients. They may suffer from long-standing problems with depression, low self-esteem, social isolation, and lack of confidence. At times these practitioners disclose personal information to clients inappropriately. Typically, they deny engaging in misconduct or justify the unethical behavior as their therapeutic technique designed to enhance their suffering client's self-esteem. They may also blame the client's claims on the client's pathology. Such practitioners are often repeat offenders.

5. *Situational offenders.* These therapists are generally healthy with a good practice history and free of boundary problems, but a situational breakdown in judgment or control has occurred in response to some life crisis or loss. These practitioners are generally aware of current ethical standards. According to Olarte, "Their sexual contact with a client is usually an isolated or limited incident. Frequently at the time of the boundary violation, these therapists are suffering from personal or situational stresses that foster a slow erosion of their professional boundaries. They most often show remorse for their unethical behavior, frequently stop such violations on their own, or seek consultation with peers" (1997:204).

6. *Naïve.* These therapists have difficulty understanding and operating within professional boundaries because they suffer from deficits in social judgment, not pathology. Their difficulties stem in part from their lack of knowledge of current ethical standards and their confusion about the need to separate personal and professional relationships.

In contrast to this framework, Simon (1999) offers a typology that includes somewhat different clinical dimensions. Simon places vulnerable therapists in five categories (the italicized terminology is Simon's):

- *Character disordered.* Therapists diagnosed with symptoms of borderline, narcissistic, or antisocial personality disorder.
- *Sexually disordered.* Therapists diagnosed with frotteurism (recurrent intense sexual urges and sexually arousing fantasies in regard to a nonconsenting person), pedophilia, or sexual sadism.
- *Incompetent.* Therapists who are poorly trained or have persistent boundary blind spots.
- *Impaired.* Therapists who have serious problems with alcohol, drugs, or mental illness.
- *Situational reactors.* Therapists who are experiencing marital discord, loss of important relationships, or a professional crisis.

Drawing on the concept of transference, Simon (1999) highlights several themes in therapist-client sexual relationships—for example, clients who idealize their therapist or regard the therapist as a savior or as omniscient. Simon classifies these themes, reflecting clients' perceptions of their therapists, as follows (the italicized terminology is Simon's):

Dr. Perfect. The client idealizes the therapist's attributes.

Dr. Prince. The client idolizes the therapist romantically, hoping the therapist will rescue him or her.

Dr. Good Parent. The client experiences the therapist as a nurturing parent and may use therapy for reparenting purposes.

Dr. Magical Healer. The client regards the therapist as his or her savior.

Dr. Beneficent. The client regards the therapist as the devoted caretaker, akin to a nanny or first doctor.

Dr. Indispensable. The client believes that only this therapist is able to cure.

Dr. Omniscient. The client believes that the therapist knows and understands all.

Based on his extensive experience with vulnerable and offending therapists, Simon (1999) argues that boundary violations are often progressive and follow a sequence, or "natural history," that leads ultimately to a therapist-client sexual relationship. Here is a common sequence in an office-based one-on-one clinical relationship:

1. The therapist's neutrality gradually erodes. The therapist begins to take special interest in the client's issues and life circumstances.
2. Boundary violations begin between the chair and the door. As the client is leaving the office, and both client and worker are standing, the therapist and client may discuss personal issues that are not part of the more formal therapeutic conversation.
3. Therapy becomes socialized. More time is spent discussing nontherapy issues.
4. The therapist discloses confidential information about other clients. The therapist begins to confide in the client, communicating to the client that she is special.
5. Therapist self-disclosure begins. The therapist shares information about his own life, perhaps concerning marital or relationship problems.
6. Physical contact begins (for example, touching, hugs, kisses). Casual

physical gestures convey to the client that the therapist has warm and affectionate feelings toward her.

7. Therapist gains control over client. The client begins to feel more and more dependent on the therapist, and the therapist exerts more and more influence in the client's life.

8. Extratherapeutic contacts occur. The therapist and client may meet for lunch or for a drink.

9. Therapy sessions are longer. The customary fifty-minute session is extended because of the special relationship.

10. Therapy sessions are rescheduled for the end of day. To avoid conflict with other clients' appointments, the therapist arranges to see the client as the day's final appointment.

11. Therapist stops billing client. The emerging intimacy makes it difficult for the therapist to charge the client for the time they spend together.

12. Dating begins. The therapist and client begin to schedule times when they can be together socially.

13. Therapist-client sex occurs.

Simon presents the following clinical vignette to illustrate this progression or natural history:

Ms. G, a 34-year-old single woman with previously diagnosed Borderline Personality Disorder and drug abuse, seeks treatment for severe depression following a spontaneous abortion. The psychiatrist is 49 years old and recently divorced. His ex-wife was a very attractive, talented artist who ran off with a concert pianist. The psychiatrist increasingly relies on alcohol to tranquilize his grief.

Ms. G is very bright and attractive. She comes to treatment to find relief from feelings of depression, isolation, and emptiness. Clear vegetative signs of depression are present. Ms. G had hoped for a child as a cure for her loneliness and despondency.

The psychiatrist is vaguely aware of Ms. G's resemblance to his ex-wife. He quickly becomes enamored of Ms. G, overlooking and minimizing her major depression. His clinical judgment is further distorted by the appearance of improvement in Ms. G's depression as the psychiatrist shows a personal interest in her. The psychiatrist looks forward to seeing Ms. G for twice-a-week appointments, finding solace and relief from his own loss. For the first 2 months, the treatment boundary remains reasonably intact. But then, gradually, the sessions take on a conversational, social tone.

The psychiatrist and Ms. G begin to address each other by their first names. The psychiatrist discloses the facts surrounding his divorce, talking at length about his wife's infidelity and his feelings of betrayal. He also confides in Ms. G intimate details about his other patients, thus treating her as a confidant. Ms. G is distressed at hearing the psychiatrist's unhappiness and feels guilty that she cannot be of more assistance.

In the beginning, the psychiatrist sits a comfortable distance from Ms. G, but gradually moves his chair closer. Eventually, the psychiatrist and Ms. G sit together on the sofa. Occasionally, the psychiatrist puts his arm around Ms. G when she tearfully describes her childhood physical and sexual abuse. Treatment sessions become extended in time, some lasting as long as 3 hours. Ms. G feels grateful that she is receiving so much special treatment.

Because the extended sessions disrupt the psychiatrist's schedule, Ms. G is seen at the end of the day. Occasionally, the psychiatrist and Ms. G also meet at a nearby park or at a bar for a drink. Because Ms. G complains of sleeping problems, the psychiatrist prescribes barbiturates. He has not kept up with the developments in psychopharmacology, having used medications very sparingly in his practice over the years. The psychiatrist is unaware of Ms. G's previous addiction to narcotics. He does not explain to her the risk of taking barbiturate medications. Over time, Ms. G requires increasingly higher doses of barbiturates that eventually interfere with her ability to function independently. The psychiatrist begins to make day-to-day decisions for Ms. G, including balancing her checkbook.

During sessions, the psychiatrist and Ms. G begin to embrace and kiss. The psychiatrist finds Ms. G more compliant to his advances when she has had a few drinks. During one session when Ms. G becomes intoxicated, sexual intercourse takes place. The psychiatrist stops billing Ms. G as their sexual relationship continues.

A few months later, the psychiatrist takes an extended vacation. While he is away, Ms. G learns from another patient that the psychiatrist revealed details of her childhood sexual abuse. Ms. G becomes extremely depressed and takes a near-lethal overdose of barbiturates. While hospitalized, she is weaned from barbiturates. She discloses the fact of her sexual involvement with her outpatient psychiatrist. Ms. G is successfully treated for major depression with antidepressants and supportive therapy. The diagnosis of Borderline Personality Disorder is also made by her treating psychiatrist. This disorder is severely aggravated due to the sexual exploitation by her therapist. The exploiting psychiatrist attempts to contact Ms. G on his return. She refuses. One year later, Ms. G brings a $1 million malpractice suit against the psychiatrist for sexual misconduct and psychological damages.

(1995:90–91)

Gutheil and Gabbard agree with Simon that sexual misconduct usually begins with relatively minor boundary violations "which often show a crescendo pattern of increasing intrusion into the patient's space that culminates in sexual contact" (1993:188). They caution, however, that not all boundary crossings, or even boundary violations, lead to or represent evidence of sexual misconduct:

> A clear boundary violation from one ideological perspective may be standard professional practice from another. For example, the so-called "Christian psychiatry movement" might condone the therapist's attendance at a church service with one or more patients, and various group therapeutic approaches or therapeutic communities may involve inherent boundary violations, as when some behaviorist schools permit hiring patients in therapy to do work in the treatment setting. Bad training, sloppy practice, lapses of judgment, idiosyncratic treatment philosophies, regional variations, and social and cultural conditioning may all be reflected in behavior that violates boundaries but that may not necessarily lead to sexual misconduct, be harmful, or deviate from the relevant standard of care.
>
> (Gutheil and Gabbard 1993:188–89)

One common theme in the literature on sexual misconduct is the inadequacy of professional education and training. Comprehensive surveys of practicing clinicians and trainees (Gartrell et al. 1987; Olarte 1997; Pope, Keith-Spiegel, and Tabachnick 1986) have found that most cite training that is inadequate for helping them deal constructively with their sexual attraction to their clients. According to Olarte, "The majority reported insufficient training on the recognition and resolution of erotic transference phenomena and minimal discussion during supervision of countertransference feelings pertaining to the development of clients' erotic transference onto therapists" (1997:197). And, unfortunately, at-risk clinicians may be the least likely to get consultation about the boundary-related challenges they encounter. According to Celenza, "When therapists are at risk for engaging in sexual intimacies, they are least likely to get consultation. This is presumably related to their fear of exposing inappropriate feelings and their shame at losing the capacity to maintain the boundaries of the therapeutic frame. In some cases, the resistance to obtaining consultation may also be related to an anticipation of being told to end the relationship" (2007:41).

CLINICAL AND PROFESSIONAL CONSEQUENCES

Sexual misconduct typically has devastating consequences. For victimized clients common consequences include destroyed self-esteem, destructive dependency, mistrust of the opposite sex, distrust of therapists, difficulty in subsequent intimate relationships, impaired sexual relationships, guilt, self-blame, suicidal ideation, substance abuse, loss of confidence, cognitive dysfunction, increased anxiety, identity disturbance, sexual confusion, mood lability, suppressed rage, depression, psychosomatic disorders, and feelings of anger, rejection, isolation, and abandonment (Celenza 2007; Elliot, Wolber, and Ferriss 1997; Gutheil and Brodsky 2008; Luepker 1999; Olarte 1997; Smith and Fitzpatrick 1995; Stake and Oliver 1991). Bouhoutsos and colleagues (1983) had psychologists describe the effects of therapist-client sex on clients (current and former) who had reported sexual involvement with therapists. Nearly all the respondents (90 percent) reported adverse effects, ranging from negative feelings about the experience to suicide. According to G. G. Pope,

> The effects of sexual exploitation on patients may vary, depending on individual personality and situational factors. Questionnaires in previously mentioned studies dealt also with the issue of patients' reactions. From 80 to 98% of the therapist responders felt that such contact was "usually or always harmful" to the patient. Others considered it "as a serious public health problem" and many courts labeled it as deceit, assault, coercion and abuse of trust, perpetrated upon the patient. The victim's emotional-psychological reactions may be akin to psychopathology occurring in rape and/or incest. . . . Common reactions may include guilt and shame, grief, anger/rage, loss of self-esteem and depression, ambivalence and confusion, fear and generalized distrust.
>
> Some authors describe the damage done to the patient as multifaceted: (1) delay of competent therapy; (2) psychopathology exacerbated when the "love affair" is terminated; (3) mistrust and ambivalence may grossly interfere with a new therapeutic relationship; (4) if a therapeutic relationship is

established, the patient's expectations may be exaggerated and inappropriate; (5) the patient's ability to relate to spouse, etc., may be severely damaged.

(1990:195)

Although human service professionals must be concerned primarily with the detrimental consequences of sexual misconduct for victimized clients, they should not ignore the effect on the therapists who are involved in these relationships. Both practicing therapists and trainees report that being attracted to their clients evoked guilt, confusion, and anxiety (Gartrell et al. 1987; Olarte 1997; Pope, Keith-Spiegel, and Tabachnick 1986; Syme 2003). In addition, in a growing number of states, practitioners who sexually exploit clients may face criminal charges; in 1983 Wisconsin became the first state to enact a statute making psychotherapist-client sexual exploitation a criminal offense (Celenza 2007). According to Strasburger, Jorgenson, and Randles,

> Deterrence is the primary argument in favor of criminalization of psycho-therapist-patient sexual activity. A criminal law articulates to everyone the wrongfulness of such behavior. Proponents believe that sexual contact would be restrained by an unmistakable legal message that such behavior is severely damaging and totally unconscionable backed by the threat of a felony conviction and a prison sentence. Controversy exists over the probable effectiveness of this deterrence, but among the categories of exploitative therapists, those who are naïve, uninformed, or undergoing the effects of midlife crisis may well respond to the prospect of punishment.

(1995:299)

Some victims report feeling intimidated by and fearing the offending therapist even after the misconduct has been exposed. According to Celenza,

> Victims often report continuing to fear the transgressing therapist, even after the case has been adjudicated. This is especially true for those exploited by a psychopathic predator who may have threatened the patient or otherwise intimidated her during the relationship and perhaps throughout the adjudicative process as well. One patient received a bill for the last month of treatment even though the abuse had begun months before. This patient became extremely anxious about *not* paying the bill, despite knowing that the treatment was a sham. She was afraid the abuser would sue her or take her to court and ruin her credit standing. She was fearful of having any kind

of contact with him, so she immediately paid the bill, feeling this was the best alternative and a way for her to obtain some peace of mind, at least in the short run.

(2007:133)

RISK-MANAGEMENT STRATEGY

Practitioners can take various steps to protect clients and to minimize the likelihood of ethics complaints and lawsuits associated with sexual misconduct. Simon highlights several useful basic principles underlying constructive maintenance of boundaries:

1. Rule of abstinence: Practitioners should strive, above all else, to avoid sexual involvement with clients and to resist acting on sexual attraction toward clients.

2. Duty of neutrality: Practitioners should seek to relate to clients as neutrally as possible. Neutrality entails the absence of favoritism, preferential consideration, and special treatment.

3. Patient autonomy and self-determination: Practitioners should respect clients' right to self-determination, which means avoiding any manipulative behavior or behaviors that might promote clients' dependence or constitute "undue influence."

4. Fiduciary relationship: Fiduciary relationships are based on trust. Clients must be able to trust their therapists and to assume that their therapists would not engage in manipulative, exploitative, or seductive behaviors for self-interested purposes.

5. Respect for human dignity: Practitioners must maintain deep-seated respect for their clients, act only in a caring and compassionate manner, and avoid engaging in destructive behaviors.

(1999:32)

More concretely, practitioners should adhere to a number of guidelines to protect clients and minimize risks associated with sexual attraction (Calfee 1997; Simon 1999):

- Maintain relative therapist neutrality (the absence of favoritism).
- Foster psychological separateness of the client.

- Protect client confidentiality.
- Obtain informed consent for treatment and procedures.
- Interact with clients verbally.
- Ensure no previous, current, or future personal relationship with the client.
- Minimize physical contact.
- Preserve relative anonymity of the therapist.
- Establish a stable fee policy.
- Provide a consistent, private, and professional setting for treatment.
- Define the time and length of the treatment session.

Beyond these broad guidelines, therapists should pay special attention to clients' unique clinical issues that may complicate boundary phenomena (Gutheil and Simon 1995). For example, if a therapist senses that a client is feeling attracted to him or her, the therapist might avoid scheduling the client at times when no one else is in the office suite. As Gutheil and Gabbard observe, "From a risk-management standpoint, a patient in the midst of an intense erotic transference to the therapist might best be seen, when possible, during high-traffic times when other people (e.g., secretaries, receptionists, and even other patients) are around" (1993:191). Therapists in solo private practice must be especially careful because of professional isolation and the absence of institutional or collegial oversight and restraints (Simon 1995).

Working in a small or rural community poses unique challenges for practitioners because of geographic proximity. In these settings the personal and professional lives of practitioners and clients are more likely to intersect, thus increasing the possibility of boundary crossings and violations (Daley and Doughty 2006).

Therapists who sense potential boundary issues involving sexual attraction should avoid out-of-the-office contact with clients. A common example includes counseling sessions conducted during lunch in a restaurant: "This event appears to be a common way station along the path of increasing boundary crossings culminating in sexual misconduct. Although clinicians often advance the claim that therapy is going on, so, inevitably, is much purely social behavior; it does not *look* like therapy, at least to a jury. Lunch sessions are not uncommonly followed by sessions during dinner, then just dinners, then other dating behavior, eventually including intercourse" (Gutheil and Gabbard 1993:192).

Boundary violations can also arise from seemingly innocent gestures, such as offering a stranded client a ride home after a counseling session. Clinically relevant discussion may continue during the ride and while the therapist and client are parked in front of the client's home. Conducting sensitive discussion in the context of the therapist's personal space can lead to boundary ambiguity, confusion, and, ultimately, violation: "From a fact finder's viewpoint, many exciting things happen in cars, but therapy is usually not one of them" (Gutheil and Gabbard 1993:192).

As always, one must consider these guidelines in relation to different treatment approaches and ideologies. Some treatment techniques assume that therapists will spend time with clients outside the office. As Gutheil and Gabbard note,

> It would not be a boundary violation for a behaviorist, under certain circumstances, to accompany a patient in a car, to an elevator, to an airplane, or even to a public restroom (in the treatment of paruresis, the fear of urinating in a public restroom) as part of the treatment plan for a particular phobia. The existence of a body of professional literature, a clinical rationale, and risk-benefit documentation will be useful in protecting the clinician in such a situation from misconstruction of the therapeutic efforts.
>
> (1993:192)

Simon (1995) urges practitioners to conduct an "instant spot check" to identify whether the therapist has committed or is at risk of committing a boundary violation. Using this approach, the first question to ask is whether the treatment is for the benefit of the therapist or for the sake of the client's therapy. Second, is the treatment part of a series of progressive steps in the direction of boundary violations (for example, inviting the client to have lunch after a counseling session in order to continue discussion of "compelling clinical issues")? Simon argues that an affirmative answer to either question should put the therapist on notice to desist immediately and take corrective action.

As I noted earlier, Simon cautions that early boundary violations in psychotherapy usually appear in the transition zone between the chair and the door: "Attention to emerging boundary issues in this therapy space can help identify and prevent progressive boundary violations" (1995:93). In this vein Epstein and Simon (1990) have devised the Exploitation Index, which provides therapists with early warnings of treatment boundary violations.

The instrument asks practitioners to assess themselves with regard to seven categories:

- Generalized boundary violations: role conflicts that blur the line between a therapeutic relationship and a personal, social, or business relationship
- Eroticism: indulging in self-gratifying romantic feelings about a client
- Exhibitionism: boasting or in some other way obtaining personal gratification from a client's accomplishments or fame
- Dependency: feeling a need for a client to continue in therapy or to give the therapist personal emotional support
- Power seeking: a need for mastery and control over the client, in or out of therapy
- Greediness: seeking financial benefits from a client beyond the contracted fee for therapy
- Enabling: allowing rescue fantasies and a need to cure to lead the therapist to make exceptions for a client the therapist feels is special

More specifically, the Exploitation Index addresses the extent to which therapists engage in risky behaviors. Items address the extent to which a clinician

1. Prescribes medications, makes diagnoses, or offers psychodynamic explanations for the behavior of family members of social acquaintances
2. Is gratified by a sense of power when the therapist is able to control a client's activity through advice, medication, or behavioral restraint (e.g., hospitalization, seclusion)
3. Finds the chronic silence or tardiness of a client a satisfying way of getting paid for doing nothing
4. Accepts gifts or bequests from clients
5. Engages in a personal relationship with clients after termination of treatment
6. Touches clients (excluding handshakes)
7. Uses information learned from clients, such as business tips or political information, for personal financial or career gain
8. Feels it is possible to obtain personal gratification by helping to develop clients' potential for fame or unusual achievement
9. Feels a sense of excitement or longing when thinking of a client or anticipating the client's visit

10. Makes exceptions for clients, such as providing special scheduling or reducing fees, because the client is attractive, appealing, or impressive to the clinician

11. Asks clients for personal favors (e.g., get lunch, mail a letter)

12. Uses the client's first name and asks the client to reciprocate

13. Undertakes business deals with clients

14. Takes great pride that such an attractive, wealthy, powerful, or important client is seeking the therapist's help

15. Accepts for treatment a person with whom the clinician has had social involvement or knows to be in the therapist's social or family sphere

16. Experiences a client's seductive behavior as a gratifying sign of the clinician's sex appeal

17. Discloses sensational aspects of clients' lives to others (even when protecting a client's identity)

18. Accepts a medium of exchange other than money for clinical services (e.g., trading of professional services)

19. Compares the gratifying qualities observed in a client with the less gratifying qualities in the therapist's spouse or significant other (e.g., thinking, "Where have you been all my life?").

20. Feels that the client's problems would be immeasurably helped if only the client had a positive romantic involvement with the clinician

21. Makes exceptions in the conduct of treatment because the therapist feels sorry for the client, or because the therapist believes that the client is in such distress or so disturbed that the therapist has no other choice

22. Recommends treatment procedures or referrals that the therapist does not believe to be necessarily in the client's best interest but that may instead be to the clinician's direct or indirect financial benefit

23. Accepts for treatment individuals known to have been referred by a current or former patient

24. Makes exceptions for a client because the therapist is afraid the client will otherwise become extremely angry or self-destructive

25. Takes pleasure in romantic daydreams about a client

26. Fails to deal with the following client behavior(s): paying the fee late, missing appointments on short notice and refusing to pay for the time (as previously agreed), seeking to extend the length of sessions

27. Is personally revealing to clients in order to impress them

28. Tries to influence clients to support political causes or positions in which the therapist has a personal interest

29. Seeks social contact with clients outside clinically scheduled visits
30. Finds it painfully difficult to agree to a client's desire to cut down on the frequency of therapy, or to work on termination
31. Talks about the clinician's personal problems with a client and expects the client to be sympathetic
32. Joins in any activity with a client that may deceive a third party (e.g., insurance company)

A survey of 532 psychiatrists who were administered the Exploitation Index showed that 43 percent found that one or more questions alerted them to boundary violations. Another 29 percent said that the questionnaire stimulated them to make specific changes in their treatment approaches and techniques (Simon 1995). Evidence suggests that some offending therapists were vulnerable at the very start of their careers because of the motivations that brought them into the profession. Sussman (1995, cited in Gutheil and Brodsky 2008: 221) lists some unconscious motives that can lead a person to the practice of psychotherapy; among them are the wish or hope of

Gaining magical powers
Being admired and idolized
Making up for the damage the therapist believes he inflicted on his family as a child
Transcending her own aggression and destructiveness
Escaping his own problems by focusing on those of other people
Holding on to or becoming like her own therapist
Achieving a deep level of intimacy within a safe context
Meeting his own dependency needs vicariously by attending to those of his clients
Transcending ordinary limitations and frustrations by achieving breakthroughs in understanding and interpersonal connection

Practitioners should also be alert to certain gender-specific issues. That most cases of sexual misconduct involve male clinicians and female clients is compelling. This pattern reflects long-standing, enduring cultural patterns involving male dominance in heterosexual relationships. As several authors (Celenza 2007; Gabbard 1990; Gutheil and Brodsky 2008; Olarte 1997) observe, therapists of both genders need to be aware of the effect of their deep-seated sex-related interaction styles and patterns. For instance, a male clinician who has little insight into his tendency to act in a somewhat controlling, authoritative, and seductive manner may encourage his female clients' dependency, passivity, and compliance, which may serve as precursors to boundary violations involving sexual misconduct.

Moreover, sexual misconduct ultimately entails the exploitation of clients—that is, the inappropriate use of the power that therapists can exercise in their authoritative role. This too raises gender issues. As Blackshaw and Miller note,

> Boundaries are necessary to prevent exploitation when a power differential is present. Power differentials exist between therapists and patients and also between men and women. The situation of male therapist and female patient presents a large power difference; this may be one reason why male therapists are more likely than female therapists to cross boundaries and to sexually exploit patients. One approach to safeguarding patients is to strengthen boundaries. Another parallel approach is to reduce the power differential. Some inequality of power will always remain since the patient comes to the therapist for help. However, in addition to maintaining appropriate boundaries, and with a clear focus on the patient's needs and problems, more mutual relationships in therapy are possible. . . . This results in a "power-with" rather than a "power-over" dynamic.
>
> (1994:293)

The overarching concept to keep in mind is prevention. Practitioners must anticipate the possibility of boundary complications and take assertive steps to prevent problems. As Simon concludes,

> The identification of inchoate treatment boundary violations can be a powerful prevention tool in the hands of competent therapists. Although it may sound like one is preaching to the choir, the significant number of cases of otherwise competent therapists who gradually cross treatment boundaries to become sexually involved with their patients is very sobering. Marginally competent or poorly trained therapists also may benefit from identification of early boundary violations. Many of these therapists naively attempt to re-parent their patients, crossing treatment boundaries

as they become overly involved in their patients' lives. Other therapists masochistically surrender to the demands of certain patients. They
become unable to extricate themselves over the course of progressive boundary violations.

(1995:91)

REHABILITATION EFFORTS

Relatively little research has been conducted on the effectiveness of efforts
to rehabilitate impaired professionals who engage in ethical misconduct
(Celenza 2007; Gutheil and Brodsky 2008; Jorgenson 1995; Sonnenstuhl
1989; Trice and Beyer 1984). Many investigations have serious methodologi-
cal limitations; few studies control adequately for extraneous factors that
may account for changes over time in practitioners' attitudes and behavior.

In recent years several organized efforts have tried to identify and address
the problems of impaired professionals and ethical misconduct. The consensus is growing that a model strategy for addressing impairment among
professionals should have several components (Celenza 2007; Gabriel
2005; Reamer 1994; Schoener and Gonsiorek 1989; Sonnenstuhl 1989;
VandenBos and Duthie 1986). First, human service professionals need adequate means for identifying impaired colleagues. Professionals must be
willing to assume responsibility for acknowledging impairment among colleagues. And as Lamb and colleagues (1987) note, it certainly would help to
develop reasonably objective measures of what constitutes failure to live up
to professional standards, incompetent skills, and impaired professional
functioning.

Second, a professional who spots a colleague who may be impaired
should first speculate about the causes and then proceed with what Sonnenstuhl (1989) describes as "constructive confrontation." Third, the practitioner must decide whether to help the impaired colleague identify ways
to seek help voluntarily or to refer the colleague to a supervisor or local
regulatory body (such as a licensing board or professional association's ethics committee).

Assuming a rehabilitation plan is appropriate to the situation, the impaired
practitioner's colleagues, supervisor, or local regulatory body should make
specific recommendations. The possibilities include close supervision, personal psychotherapy, or other appropriate treatment (for example, substance

abuse treatment). In some cases a licensing board or professional association may need to impose some type of sanction such as censure, probation, limitations on the clinician's practice (for example, concerning type of clientele served or practice setting), suspension, license revocation, or termination of employment.

With specific regard to treatment that follows the filing and processing of a formal complaint, Schoener (1995) argues that, ideally, a comprehensive assessment of the practitioner would be conducted by a licensing or regulatory body and would involve several steps, including

- Gathering data about the practitioner's professional training, professional work history, and personal history (including noteworthy ups and downs), and the nature of the practice-related complaint (boundary violation)
- Generating hypotheses about causal factors that may be involved in the boundary violation
- Formulating a rehabilitation plan, when feasible
- Coordinating the rehabilitation plan with the licensing board, professional association, and practitioner's employer
- Implementing the corrective action (for example, psychotherapy, supervision, consultation, continuing education) and, when necessary, appropriate sanctions (for example, license suspension or revocation, expulsion from professional association)
- Evaluating the practitioner's progress with regard to the possibility of permitting reentry to practice and the profession

Gabriel (2005) argues that a comprehensive rehabilitation process may take three to five years, with yearly evaluations. Often, interviewing the original victim or complainant is essential. According to Schoener, "This often proves invaluable. Beyond helping us avoid being taken in by intentional distortions on the part of the practitioner being evaluated, it provides a much more complete picture of the events in question. Even a completely honest, nondefensive professional who is being cooperative does not know all that happened. Each party experienced the events differently" (1995:98).

Schoener (1995) believes that a formal assessment of an exploitative practitioner should not be conducted, or a rehabilitation plan developed, unless (1) the practitioner admits wrongdoing and understands that the client suffered harm; (2) the practitioner believes that he or she has a problem that requires rehabilitation; (3) the practitioner is willing to agree to the assessment and realizes that its outcome may not be favorable; and (4) the essential facts of the case are not in dispute. Once the practitioner has completed the rehabilitation plan, those responsible for overseeing it must be able to answer yes to two questions: "To a reasonable degree of psychiatric or psychological certainty, have the problems you were treating been fixed or resolved?" and "Would you have any qualms whatsoever if your spouse or child went to see this person for individual therapy?"

Studies have shown that ambitious, skilled treatment of offending practitioners can be effective (Gutheil and Brodsky 2008; Simon 1999). However, prospects are not encouraging for practitioners who have been diagnosed with serious personality disorders or paraphilias, or who are deemed incompetent (Schoener 1995; Simon 1999).

SEXUAL RELATIONSHIPS WITH FORMER CLIENTS

CASE 2.2

George M. was a licensed counselor at a community mental health center. He provided individual counseling to a thirty-eight-year-old woman, Carolyn L., a single parent who was having difficulty coping with the death of her twelve-year-old child. Ms. L.'s daughter had died after a long struggle with bone cancer. Mr. M. and Ms. L. met for counseling for six sessions. The two agreed to terminate the therapy after Ms. L. reported that she felt much better able to move on with her life and handle her loss.

A little more than five years after they terminated their professional-client relationship, Mr. M. and Ms. L. encountered each other unexpectedly at a mutual acquaintance's Fourth of July party. The host, a distant cousin, invited Mr. M. to the party. Ms. L. was the host's neighbor and acquaintance.

Mr. M. and Ms. L. recognized each other at the party and chatted briefly. Mr. M. asked Ms. L. how she was doing, and Ms. L. brought him up to date. During their encounter Mr. M., who was divorced, found himself feeling attracted to Ms. L. He began thinking about asking Ms. L. out for a dinner date. Mr. M. knew that some colleagues might not approve of his dating a former client, but he felt in his heart that enough time had passed since the termination of the professional-client relationship; he believed that Ms. L. was quite mature emotionally and would be able to handle a personal relationship with him. Being rather cautious, however, Mr. M. decided to bring up the issue at the next meeting of his peer consultation group.

CASE 2.3

Alicia D. was a psychologist who provided counseling to a lesbian couple, Melinda F. and Tanya P., who struggled with a number of relationship issues. About eight months after the counseling began, the couple decided to end their relationship. During their last counseling session Tanya told Dr. D. that she would like to continue seeing her for individual counseling. Melinda told Dr. D., "It's fine with me" if Tanya meets with Dr. D. for individual counseling.

Dr. D. and Tanya met for individual counseling for approximately six months. Four months after they terminated their counseling relationship, the two bumped into each other at a local coffee shop; Dr. D. and Tanya shared a table briefly, and Tanya gave Dr. D. a quick update. About a week later Tanya sent Dr. D. a short email message letting her know how much she enjoyed their casual encounter. Tanya also asked Dr. D. a simple question about a local wellness program that she was considering attending. Several weeks later Dr. D. and Tanya bumped into each other again at a local sandwich shop and had lunch together. During their conversation both acknowledged that they had been thinking about how nice it would be to spend time together as friends. They arranged a dinner date for the following weekend. Within a month Dr. D. and Tanya began living together. Two months later Melinda heard about their relationship and cohabitation. In short order Melinda filed a licensing board complaint against Dr. D. alleging that she engaged in an unethical dual relationship with a former client. The complaint included many details about the ways in which Melinda believed she was harmed by Dr. D.'s conduct.

Although the human service professions agree that sexual relationships with current clients are inappropriate, they are not unanimous regarding sexual relationships of practitioners with *former* clients (Gutheil and Brodsky 2008). The NASW *Code of Ethics*, for example, generally prohibits sexual relationships with former clients. However, the NASW code also states that exceptions may be warranted under "extraordinary circumstances," such as when the social worker was involved in a nonclinical relationship with the client (for example, a social worker employed as a community organizer who became involved with a neighborhood resident): "If social workers engage in conduct contrary to this prohibition or claim that an exception to this prohibition is warranted because of extraordinary circumstances, it is social workers— not their clients—who assume the full burden of demonstrating that the former client has not been exploited, coerced, or manipulated, intentionally or unintentionally" (standard 1.09[c]). In contrast, ethical standards promulgated by the American Psychological Association and the American Association for Marriage and Family Therapy prohibit sexual relationships with former clients for only the two-year period immediately following termination of treatment; the ethical standards promulgated by the American Counseling Association (2005) prohibit sexual relationships with former clients for a five-year period immediately following termination of treatment. Although the APA, AAMFT, and ACA codes discourage sexual relationships with former clients, they offer practitioners more latitude once the two-year period (APA and AAMFT) and five-year period (ACA) are reached.

Survey results demonstrate impressive diversity of opinion among professionals concerning the ethics of sexual relationships with former clients. Akamatsu (1988) found that about 45 percent of a sample of 395 members of American Psychological Association Division 29 (Psychotherapy) said that intimate relationships with former clients were highly unethical. Fewer than a third of this group (about 31 percent) felt that such relationships were neither ethical nor unethical, or even felt them to be ethical to some degree; 23.9 percent felt that such relationships were only somewhat unethical. About 14 percent of the men in this sample and about 5 percent of the women admitted to intimate relationships with former clients. The average interval between termination and the commencement of the relationships was 15.6 months. In another study Jayaratne, Croxton, and Mattison (1997) found that about 5 percent of their sample of clinical social workers believed that having sex with a former client is appropriate, and about 6 percent believed that going on a date with a former client is appropriate. About 1 percent of this sample reported having dated a former client, and about the same percentage reported having had sex with a former client.

One major practical consideration for practitioners to keep in mind is that, as I noted earlier, some state legislatures have enacted laws making sexual contact with a client or former client a criminal offense, punishable by imprisonment and/or a fine (Calfee 1997; Koocher and Keith-Spiegel 2008; Strasburger, Jorgenson, and Randles 1995). Beyond this practical consideration, however, it is most important that practitioners consider the potentially devastating emotional effect that a sexual relationship may have on the former client (Celenza 2007; Gutheil and Brodsky 2008). For example, former clients often face challenging issues in their lives after the formal termination of the professional-client relationship. New emotional issues, relationship problems, or developmental crises, for instance, may emerge, and former clients may wish to contact the practitioner for assistance. The practitioner's familiarity with the client's circumstances and the established relationship between the parties may be especially helpful in such cases; starting over with a new provider may be inefficient, emotionally taxing, and intimidating. Clearly, however, a practitioner and a former client who have entered into a sexual relationship could have difficulty resuming an effective professional-client relationship. Practitioners and former clients who enter into sexual relationships after termination of their professional-client relationship essentially forfeit any resumption of that relationship, and this may not be in the client's best interest.

In addition, former clients may encounter less challenging yet important new issues or problems in their lives and still may find it helpful to speculate about what their former therapist would have advised or said about the matter. The former client may not feel the need to resume a formal relationship with the practitioner; however, the client might find it helpful merely to reflect on the therapist's perspective. A sexual relationship between the practitioner and the former client presumably would interfere with the former client's ability to draw on what he or she has learned from the practitioner's professional expertise, given the shift from a professional to an intimate relationship. Thus practitioners generally should consider their clients as "clients in perpetuity": once a client, always a client. Epstein espouses this point of view:

> In my opinion, legalistic arguments about permissible waiting periods ignore the fundamental purpose of the therapeutic frame. I do not believe it possible for a therapist to conduct coherent psychotherapy unless he or she can *permanently* relinquish the prospect of *ever* obtaining gratification from the patient for *anything* besides the contracted compensation. The treatment frame is a reflection of the therapist's ego boundaries. If a therapist *seriously* entertains an actual plan for sex with a patient after termination, it suggests that he or she suffers from impaired ego boundaries.
>
> (1994:219)

Practitioners must also realize that courts of law may regard sexual contact with former clients as evidence of professional negligence. In one case ("Woman Claims Improper Sexual Conduct" 1996), for example, a married couple claimed that the psychologist who had treated their two sons during a fifteen-month period for emotional problems was negligent when he had sexual relations with the wife after the treatment ended. The wife presented evidence of her resulting depression, panic disorder, anxiety, and adjustment disorder. A jury found that the psychologist was negligent and that the wife was partially negligent (negligence was apportioned 40 percent to the wife and 60 percent to the psychologist). The jury found that the wife was entitled to punitive damages in the amount of $75,000.

Practitioners who believe that any nonprofessional relationship with a former client is justifiable should recognize that they are entering high-risk territory. At the very least these practitioners should ask themselves several key questions:

■ How much time has passed since termination of the professional-client relationship? Clearly, a sexual relationship that begins shortly after termination is more suspect than one that begins long after the practitioner's services to the client have ended. This question is difficult to address in part because there is no magical length of time that must elapse so that a relationship can be deemed appropriate.

■ To what extent is the client mentally competent and emotionally stable? A sexual relationship with a former client who has a lengthy history of emotional instability and vulnerability is a greater cause for concern than a relationship with a former client who is clearly competent and emotionally stable.

■ What issues were addressed in the professional-client relationship? A sexual relationship after a professional-client relationship that involved discussion or examination of emotionally sensitive and intimate issues—for example, related to the client's history of childhood sexual abuse—is more problematic than a relationship limited to anxiety or stress management.

■ How long did the professional-client relationship last? Should an intimate relationship develop, a professional-client relationship that lasted for many months is a greater cause for concern than a relationship that lasted for two brief meetings several years earlier.

■ What circumstances surrounded the termination of the professional-client relationship? Was it terminated so that the practitioner and client could begin an intimate relationship, or did it come to a natural conclusion because the compelling therapeutic work was done? The practitioner must carefully examine the motives and circumstances surrounding the termination of the professional-client relationship.

■ To what extent is there foreseeable harm to the client or others as a result of the intimate relationship? How likely is it that an intimate relationship, especially if that relationship ends traumatically, could harm the client?

Could those who are close to the client—such as a spouse or partner—be harmed by the practitioner's relationship with the former client? To what extent could the client's ability to trust therapists be harmed by the relationship? Could rumors about the relationship undermine practitioners' integrity in general?

COUNSELING FORMER SEXUAL PARTNERS

Practitioners have personal lives that may involve sexual relationships. Ideally, such relationships involve mutually intimate sharing of information and feelings. In its purest form an intimate relationship between two people is not hierarchical in nature, with one person assuming more authority, power, or control than the other.

Moving from an intimate sexual relationship to a professional-client relationship can be detrimental to the client. Former lovers who become clients—no matter how much time has elapsed—may find it difficult to shift from the role of an egalitarian partner in a relationship to a party who, to some degree, is in a dependent or subordinate position.

CASE 2.4

Dennis G. was a psychiatrist in private practice. His practice focused primarily on adults with mood and anxiety disorders. Dr. G. has been in practice for twelve years.

Toward the end of his psychiatric residency, Dr. G. began dating Dr. B., who was a resident in internal medicine at the same hospital where Dr. G. trained. Dr. G. and Dr. B. lived together for about ten months before deciding, quite amicably, to end their intimate relationship. The two remained friendly for about two years and then lost touch when Dr. B. moved to another city to pursue a fellowship.

Dr. B. recently moved back to the city where Dr. G. lived, having accepted a position at a local health center. After about six months in her new job, Dr. B. found herself struggling with symptoms of depression, which had affected her off and on since her college years. Dr. B. had not been in touch with Dr. G. for some time but decided to call him for a consultation about her depression. Dr. G. and Dr. B. met for lunch, got reacquainted, and talked about Dr. B.'s symptoms. Dr. B. felt very comfortable with Dr. G. and trusted his advice and the treatment approach he suggested. Dr. B. asked Dr. G. whether he would be willing to oversee her treatment, which would include a combination of psychotherapy and psychotropic medication.

No matter how much a therapist believes in empowering clients and engaging clients as equal partners in the helping relationship, clients are, by definition, in the position of asking for or being required to receive assistance (a form of dependency), and the practitioner is in the position of authority charged with providing assistance. This inescapable dynamic places clients in a vulnerable position that reflects the power imbalance in the relationship. This perspective is reflected in the views of a sample of clinical social workers who were surveyed about boundary issues: fewer than 2 percent stated that accepting a former romantic partner as a client is appropriate (Jayaratne, Croxton, and Mattison 1997).

Confusion about the nature of the relationship could cause a client who was sexually involved with a therapist before the onset of the professional-client relationship to be unable to benefit fully from the therapist's expertise. The client may have difficulty distinguishing between the therapist's professional and personal roles in her or his life. The couple's interpersonal history and dynamics may interfere with the client's ability to receive help and the therapist's ability to provide help. The therapist's influence and credibility might be undermined because of the client's intimate familiarity with the therapist's personal life and issues.

In psychodynamic terms the transference and countertransference involved in such a relationship are likely to limit the therapist's effectiveness and the ability of both client and practitioner to maintain appropriate professional boundaries. Transference is a frequent challenge in psychotherapy. Former experiences, relationships, or developmental conflicts in the client's life may stimulate or trigger the client's emotional reactions in the current relationship with the therapist. Given the possibility of transference, emotional experiences in the sexual relationship with the therapist that preceded the professional-client relationship may complicate the client's feelings about and reactions to the therapist. In countertransference a therapist's emotional reactions to a client may have originated in the therapist's own previous experiences, relationships, or developmental conflicts (Barker 1999). In this context the once-intimate relationship with the client that predates the professional-client relationship may affect the practitioner's feelings about and reactions to the client.

SEXUAL RELATIONSHIPS WITH CLIENTS' RELATIVES OR ACQUAINTANCES

Current ethical standards also prohibit human service professionals from engaging in sexual activities or sexual contact with a client's relative, or another individual with whom the client maintains a close personal relationship, when the relationship carries a risk of exploitation or potential harm to the client. For example, the NASW *Code of Ethics* (2008) asserts:

> Sexual activity or sexual contact with clients' relatives or other individuals with whom clients maintain a personal relationship has the potential to be harmful to the client and may make it difficult for the social worker and client to maintain appropriate professional boundaries. Social workers— not their clients, their clients' relatives, or other individuals with whom the client maintains a personal relationship—assume the full burden for setting clear, appropriate, and culturally sensitive boundaries.
>
> (standard 1.09[b])

A practitioner's sexual relationship with a client's relative or another person to whom the client is close may cause the client to feel betrayed and can undermine confidence in the practitioner and the practitioner's profession. Human service professionals are obligated to protect clients' interests and must avoid conflicts of interest that may be harmful to clients.

In some cases a practitioner's relationship with a client's relative or another individual with whom the client has a close personal relationship is clearly inappropriate, as in the examples that follow.

CASE 2.5

A counselor at a child guidance clinic provided counseling to a nine-year-old child who was referred by the principal of the child's grade school. The student, who was in foster care, was having difficulty managing his behavior in the classroom and was engaging in some physically risky activities (for example, jumping from high places and taking risks crossing busy highways).

The counselor met with the child and with the child's foster mother for an initial assessment and intake interview. The counselor then met with the child individually and, sporadically, with the child's foster mother. During the course of the counselor's professional relationship with the child, the counselor began to date the child's foster mother. On several occasions the counselor spent time socially with the child and his foster mother at their home.

CASE 2.6

A social worker at a major teaching hospital provided counseling services to an elderly patient, a seventy-two-year-old man who had fallen and fractured his hip. During the patient's hospital stay, the social worker became acquainted with the patient's son, who visited his father regularly. The patient's son was attracted to the social worker—with whom he had spent considerable time planning his father's transfer to a rehabilitation facility—and asked her out on a date. The social worker accepted the invitation, and the two began an intimate relationship.

Serious medical complications that required the patient to stay in the hospital delayed his transfer to a nursing home. The patient had developed a life-threatening infection and eventually had to be placed on a ventilator. When the patient's prognosis became grim, the social worker and the patient's son discussed the decision the son might need to make about terminating the ventilator. The social worker found that her intimate relationship with the patient's son complicated her role as a professional who was attempting to help a patient's adult child make a difficult decision about termination of life support.

CASE 2.7

A clinical psychologist at a center that provides services to people with physical disabilities facilitated a support group for caregivers. The group's primary purpose was to provide emotional support and mutual aid to relatives and acquaintances of the center's primary clients.

One group member was the sister of a center resident, a forty-two-year-old woman who was paralyzed as a result of a skiing accident. The client was living with the sister, who was having difficulty juggling the various demands in her life.

After one support group meeting the client's sister stayed to chat with the psychologist. The sister said she wanted some advice about how to handle a difficult family issue involving the client's care.

Following their brief discussion, the client's sister told the psychologist that she had something else she wanted to discuss. She told the psychologist she felt a bit foolish, but she wondered whether he would be interested in accompanying her to her employer's annual golf outing, especially since the two had spent considerable time talking informally about their mutual passion for golf. The psychologist found the client's sister appealing and accepted the invitation. Within weeks the two began to date and quickly developed an intimate relationship.

In each of these examples it is easy to imagine how the client might feel betrayed by the practitioner's intimate relationship with the relative or acquaintance and how this relationship could interfere with the practitioner's professional effectiveness. In other cases, however, practitioners may disagree about whether a sexual relationship with a client's relative or another individual to whom a client is close is inappropriate. Here are examples that may generate disagreement among practitioners:

CASE 2.8

A counselor employed in the forensic unit of a state psychiatric hospital provided counseling to a patient who had been charged with the crime of arson and in criminal court had been found not guilty by reason of insanity. The counselor happened to meet the distant cousin of the patient at a friend's dinner party, and the two started dating. At the time neither knew of the other's connection to the patient.

About two months after their intimate relationship began, the counselor learned of his sexual partner's relationship to the counselor's current patient. The counselor was unsure whether professional duty required him to terminate the professional relationship and transfer clinical responsibilities to a colleague.

CASE 2.9

A social worker in a residential program for children with serious emotional and behavioral problems provided counseling to a fifteen-year-old resident. The social worker also met occasionally with the client's parents. At a neighborhood block party the social worker met a man who was a good friend of the client's father. The social worker and the man began to date.

In such cases, where practitioners may disagree about the appropriateness of a sexual relationship with a client's relative or acquaintance, the practitioner should seek consultation with colleagues and carefully examine the potential risks to the client. In the end practitioners must assume the full burden and the associated risks if they decide to enter into an intimate relationship.

SEXUAL RELATIONSHIPS WITH SUPERVISEES, TRAINEES, STUDENTS, AND COLLEAGUES

Human service practitioners also must avoid sexual relationships with staff members whom they supervise and students, trainees, and other colleagues over whom they exercise some form of authority. Supervisees, for example, are typically dependent on their supervisors and could feel pressured to accede to a supervisor's initiation of a sexual relationship out of fear of jeopardizing the supervisory relationship (Congress 1996; Syme 2003). Such a relationship is likely to be exploitative and probably illegal, as it would constitute sexual harassment.

CASE 2.10

A psychiatric resident was receiving clinical supervision from an experienced psychiatrist at a private inpatient mental health facility. The supervision was a requirement of the resident's training. For several months the supervising psychiatrist and the resident met weekly in the supervisor's office to discuss clinical issues that arose in cases that the resident was handling. The supervisor, who was newly divorced, found that he was becoming attracted to the resident. At the end of one supervision session, he suggested that they have dinner together at a nearby restaurant. Before long the two began a sexual relationship.

The resident felt overwhelmed by her complicated relationship with her supervisor. She was afraid to terminate the sexual relationship, in part because she found him attractive and in part because she did not want to jeopardize her professional future, which could be affected by the supervisor's evaluations and recommendations.

In case 2.10 the supervisor was unethical because he took advantage of his position of authority to enter into a sexual relationship with his supervisee. The supervisee was emotionally troubled by the situation and worried that her sexual involvement with her supervisor eventually could injure her reputation and harm her career.

Students and other trainees are similarly vulnerable to exploitation (Penfold 1998). Practitioners who function as practicum or field supervisors for students, for example, maintain control over their students' lives and careers in much the same way work-setting supervisors have control over their supervisees' lives and careers. Students sometimes share personal information with faculty members in a way that leads to an intimate connection; it is important for faculty members to avoid blending or conflating their instructional and clinical roles, which can sometimes lead to blurred boundaries and inappropriate relationships.

Academic supervisors have considerable influence on the grades that students receive for internships, and students may feel that their educational and professional careers would be jeopardized if they were to resist supervisors' attempts to become involved with them sexually. Trainees may feel similarly vulnerable when practitioners have authority over them in the context of continuing education or professional development programs. Instructors who engage in sexual relationships with students or trainees expose themselves to the risk of formal ethics complaints and sexual harassment allegations. Celenza broaches several key questions regarding these phenomena:

> What are the circumstances under which two adults may be considered consenting, relatively free of transference-based pressures and structured power imbalances? How are these aspects of the supervisory relationship reconciled with the fact that a teacher and student are devoted to the same profession, thereby reflecting inherent similarities of interest and inclinations? Don't these similarities make sexual and/or romantic appeal more likely? The academic and supervisory contexts do not exactly replicate the many potentially exploitative aspects associated with the therapeutic relationship. However, there is a hierarchy and potential for exploitation embedded in the structure of academic and supervisory relationships that must be taken into account. As long as these structural features are in place, the student/supervisee cannot be considered free to consent and the relationship must be viewed within a context that is bound by professional ethics.
>
> (2007:65)

Pope (1989, cited in Celenza 2007:73) offers several recommendations for educators and supervisors in an effort to prevent boundary violations: (1) maintain the student's interests as primary; (2) remain aware of the deleterious effects of boundary transgressions on a student's training needs; (3) appreciate the effects of educator-student intimacies on the safety and openness of the learning environment; (4) appreciate the potential compromise of the evaluative function; (5) appreciate the potential exploitation of the power differential, especially with regard to future job placement, recommendations, fellowship placements, and so forth; and (6) appreciate the vulnerability of the training program to class-action lawsuits or misconduct complaints.

Practitioners are obligated to avoid engaging in sexual relationships not only with colleagues over whom they exercise professional authority but also with any colleague with whom a potential conflict of interest exists. The next case illustrates how this can be done.

CASE 2.11

A social worker employed by a state human services agency was responsible for overseeing a contract between the department and a large community mental health center that was providing clinical services to teenage parents. As part of her duties the social worker met periodically with the agency's director to discuss the program's services, goal attainment, and budget. Over time the two individuals became attracted to each other and began dating. When it appeared that the two were embarking on a sexual relationship, the social worker notified her supervisor, informed her of the evolving relationship, and suggested that the supervisor assign another staff person in the office to assume responsibility for oversight of this contract.

PHYSICAL CONTACT

Not all physical contact is explicitly sexual, although sometimes it carries sexual overtones. Practitioners must be careful to distinguish between appropriate and inappropriate physical contact with clients. Most professions' codes of ethics do not comment on this phenomenon explicitly. An exception is the NASW *Code of Ethics* (2008): "Social workers should not engage in physical contact with clients when there is a possibility of psychological harm to the client as a result of the contact (such as cradling or caressing clients).

Social workers who engage in appropriate physical contact with clients are responsible for setting clear, appropriate, and culturally sensitive boundaries that govern such physical contact" (standard 1.10).

Nonsexual physical touch has been used in therapeutic contexts in a variety of ways and, according to proponents, can enhance therapeutic relationships and progress (Downey 2001; Durana 1998; Hunter and Struve 1998; Zur 2007). Zur (2007) reviewed relevant literature and concludes that touch in a therapeutic context may be viewed as

- *Ritualistic or socially accepted gestures for greeting and good-bye on arrival and departure.* These gestures figure significantly among most cultures and include handshakes, a greeting or farewell embrace, and other culturally accepted gestures.
- *Conversational marker.* This form of light touch on the arm, hand, back, or shoulder is intended to make or highlight a point and can also take place at times of stillness, with the purpose of accentuating the therapist's presence and conveying attention.
- *Consoling touch.* This important form of touch, holding the hands or shoulders of a client or providing a comforting hug, is most likely to enhance the therapeutic alliance.
- *Reassuring touch.* This form of touch is geared to encouraging and reassuring clients and usually involves a pat on the back or shoulder.
- *Playful touch.* This form of touch, mostly of hand, shoulders, or head, may take place while playing a game with a child or adolescent client.
- *Grounding or reorienting touch.* This form of touch is intended to help clients reduce anxiety or dissociation by using touch to the hand or arm or by leading them to touch their own hands or arms.
- *Task-oriented touch.* This involves touch that is merely ancillary to the task at hand, such as offering a hand to help someone stand up or bracing an arm around a client's shoulders to keep the client from falling.
- *Corrective experience.* This form of touch may involve the holding of an adult or rocking of a child by a therapist who practices forms of therapy that emphasize the importance of corrective experiences.
- *Instructional or modeling touch.* Therapists may model how to touch or respond to touch by demonstrating a firm handshake, holding an agitated child, or responding to unwanted touch.
- *Celebratory or congratulatory touch.* The therapist may give a pat on the back or a congratulatory hug to a client who has achieved a goal.

- *Experiential touch.* This form of touch usually takes place when the therapist conducts an experiential exercise, such as teaching gestures during assertiveness training, or asking family members participating in family sculpturing to assume certain positions in relationship to each other.

- *Referential touch.* This is often done in group or family therapy when the therapist lightly taps the arm or shoulder of a client, indicating that he or she can take a turn or be silent.

- *Inadvertent touch.* This is touch that is unintentional, involuntary, and unpremeditated, such as an inadvertent brush against a client by the therapist.

- *Touch intended to prevent a client from hurting him- or herself.* This type of touch is intended to stop self-harming behavior such as head banging, self-hitting, or self-cutting.

- *Touch intended to prevent someone from hurting another.* This form of touch is intended to stop or restrain someone from hurting another person, as sometimes happens in family, couple, or group therapy or when working with extremely volatile clients.

- *Touch in therapist's self-defense.* This form of touch is used by a therapist to physically defend against the assault of a violent client by using self-defense techniques that restrain clients with minimum force.

- *Therapeutic touch in body psychotherapies.* This is different from the use of touch as an adjunct to verbal psychotherapy. Somatic and body psychotherapists regularly use touch as part of their theoretically prescribed clinical intervention. Massage, Rolfing, or other hands-on techniques, incorporated or implemented along with psychotherapy, also fit into this category.

As Zur notes, clinicians' use of physical touch raises a number of complex issues regarding boundary maintenance:

The relationship among boundaries, touch, and psychotherapy presents a unique situation that involves three main types of boundaries. The first is the distinct boundary of the physical body, the second is concerned with psychotherapeutic boundaries, and the third relates to the boundary between sexual and nonsexual touch. The boundary of the body is clear and well defined by the skin. Although the skin is physically, distinctly defined and separates individuals from their environment, it is also a gateway for numerous complex and often mysterious physiological and emotional regulatory systems that are affected when the skin is touched.

(2007:168)

The essential feature of appropriate physical touch is that it is not likely to cause the client psychological harm, as in the examples that follow.

CASE 2.12

A psychologist worked in a residential program for children who had been adjudicated delinquent. The psychologist learned from his supervisor that the court had just terminated the parental rights of the single mother of a resident, following the mother's third conviction for narcotic drug use and possession; eventually, the child, who was twelve, would be placed with a foster family and, ideally, would be adopted.

Upon learning this news, the child started to sob hysterically and cried out for his mother, whom he loved deeply. The psychologist put his arms around the boy and held him briefly in an effort to comfort him.

CASE 2.13

A couple sought counseling from a social worker following the sudden death of their infant. The social worker met with the couple weekly during a five-month period. During that time the social worker helped the couple explore their grief and cope with their tragic loss.

At the end of their last session together, the couple hugged the social worker warmly and thanked him for his invaluable help.

CASE 2.14

A hospital-based counselor worked in the facility's hospice unit. Patients in the unit had been diagnosed with a terminal illness and were in the final stages of dying.

One of the counselor's patients was a sixty-one-year-old woman who had been diagnosed with ovarian cancer. As she spoke with the counselor, the patient reminisced about important moments in her life, mainly related to her marriage and children. The patient cried as she spoke; the counselor reached over and held the patient's hand during their conversation.

In these situations the practitioner had brief and limited physical contact that is generally considered acceptable. None of these clients would likely be psychologically harmed by the contact. To the contrary, they probably would find the physical contact emotionally comforting, as a form of consolation or "therapeutic touch." To fully protect clients and ensure their comfort, as a matter of course, and when circumstances permit, clinicians should ask clients for permission before engaging in physical contact. Some clients may feel uncomfortable with physical contact, particularly if they have a history of physical trauma.

A Georgia court ruled that physical touch is not necessarily evidence of negligence ("Patient's Claims" 1998). The state appeals court affirmed the dismissal of claims brought by a patient who had been treated by a psychiatrist for nine years. The patient, who was diagnosed with anorexia nervosa and borderline personality disorder, had met with the psychiatrist for therapy once per week. On approximately six occasions the psychiatrist permitted the patient to hold his hand during therapy, and they would hug at the end of the session. The patient acknowledged that none of the contact was of a sexual nature. The court ruled that the contact between the patient and the psychiatrist did not constitute a battery and that the patient had consented to the limited physical contact as part of her treatment.

Clearly, many professionals believe that limited forms of physical contact can be appropriate. More than four-fifths of a sample of clinical social workers (83.1 percent) stated that hugging or embracing a client can be appropriate, and two-fifths (39.9 percent) stated that touching a client as a regular part of the therapy process can be appropriate. In contrast relatively few (13.7 percent) stated that it is appropriate to use massage with a client or kiss a client (2.6 percent); only about 2 percent of this sample reported having engaged in either of these activities (Jayaratne, Croxton, and Mattison 1997). Similarly, nearly all respondents in a survey of a national sample of psychologists (psychotherapists) stated that under some circumstances hugging a client is ethical, and the vast majority (nearly 87 percent) reported having hugged a client (Pope, Tabachnick, and Keith-Spiegel 1995).

In general inappropriate physical touch occurs when the nature of the touch might exacerbate the client's transference in harmful ways, thus confusing or troubling the client. In other instances the touch is inappropriate because it might suggest that the relationship between the practitioner and client extends beyond the formal professional-client relationship, as in the examples that follow.

CASE 2.15

A counselor in private practice specialized in providing group therapy to women who had been physically and sexually abused. As a routine part of therapy the counselor asked group members to sit in a circle on the floor ("to get down low, on the same level, and as a way to get in touch with the small child within themselves," the counselor said), and then she lowered the office lights and played soothing music. In the course of this part of the therapy, each client had an opportunity to experience being nurtured by the counselor: the counselor sat on the floor with her legs spread open, and the client sat with her back against the counselor's chest and the counselor's arms wrapped around her. The counselor rocked the client and spoke softly to the clients "inner hurt child." At times the counselor would wipe away the client's tears and gently stroke her hair. The counselor said this provided clients with a "corrective emotional experience" and "constructive reparenting."

CASE 2.16

A psychologist had a long-standing interest in the therapeutic value of massage. She had not received formal training as a massage therapist but had learned a number of massage techniques from a close friend who is a licensed massage therapist. The psychologist was providing counseling to a thirty-two-year-old woman who was dealing with her recent realization that she had been sexually abused as a child by her mother's boyfriend. During one session the client commented that for weeks she had felt as if her body were tied up in knots and that she was "filled with painful tension." The psychologist suggested that some massage might be helpful and offered to rub the client's shoulders, neck, head, face, arms, and back during their therapy session.

CASE 2.17

A marriage and family therapist provided counseling to a young couple who were having marital difficulties. The couple disagreed about whether to have children, and this disagreement was the source of considerable tension in their relationship. On several occasions the therapist met alone with the wife. Toward the end of one such session, the wife began to cry intensely; the therapist got up from his chair and sat next to the client on the sofa to comfort her; he put his arms around the client, and she leaned against the therapist as she cried. The therapist stroked her head softly while the client continued to talk about her distress.

These situations can be problematic because the therapists' conduct has the potential to confuse clients about the nature of the professional-client relationship and introduce complex boundary issues into the relationship. Some forms of touch—especially cradling and caressing, which typically have a sexual connotation—are likely to distract both practitioner and client from their therapeutic agenda and thus jeopardize the client's well-being. Other than brief contact for exclusively therapeutic purposes—such as a quick hug to say good-bye or to console a terribly distraught client—physical touch has the potential to cause psychological harm and interfere with the professional-client relationship. Gutheil and Gabbard offer the following wise advice:

> From the viewpoint of current risk-management principles, a handshake is about the limit of social physical contact at this time. Of course, a patient who attempts a hug in the last session after 7 years of intense, intensive, and successful therapy should probably not be hurled across the room. However, most hugs from patients should be discouraged in tactful, gentle ways by words, body language, positioning, and so forth. Patients who deliberately or provocatively throw their arms around the therapist despite repeated efforts at discouragement should be stopped. An appropriate response is to step back, catch both wrists in your hands, cross the patient's wrists in front of you, so that the crossed arms form a barrier between bodies, and say firmly, "Therapy is a talking relationship; please sit down so we can discuss your not doing this anymore." If the work degenerates into grabbing, consider seriously termination and referral, perhaps to a therapist of a different gender.
>
> (1993:195)

I would add to Gutheil and Gabbard's sound suggestions the need to carefully document this interaction, the clinician's response, and plans to address the issue going forward.

There is legitimate debate about whether some forms of therapy should be allowed to incorporate physical touch as a component of the therapeutic approach. According to Syme:

> The decision of whether to offer touch or not will depend on both theoretical and ethical considerations. Orthodox psychoanalysts do not touch their clients for theoretical reasons, though there is little research to support this. The relational theory of some psychotherapists supports the use of touch in

certain instances, as do most regressive and some humanistic theories. Here again there is little research but some of the research and some subjective accounts of clients do suggest that there are positive effects of touch. It is also clear that non-erotic touch can have negative effects. The ethical considerations are firstly whether the therapist has adequate training both theoretically and technically in the use of touch. Secondly therapists must not use touch if it is any way alien to themselves. Thirdly touch should be offered only if it is really in the service of the client's needs.

(2003:67)

The debate about clinicians' use of physical touch is not easily settled. However, practitioners who incorporate physical touch should consider one therapist's experience:

A therapist—who claimed that her school of practice involved hugging her female patient at the beginning and end of every session, without apparent harm—eventually had to terminate therapy with the patient for noncompliance with the therapeutic plan. The enraged patient filed a sexual misconduct claim against therapist. Despite the evidence showing that this claim was probably false (a specious suit triggered by rage at the therapist), the insurer settled because of the likelihood that a jury would not accept the principle of "hug at the start and hug at the end but no hugs in between." If the claim was indeed false, this is a settlement based on boundary violations alone.

(Gutheil and Gabbard 1993:195)

Practitioners should also be sensitive to cultural, ethnic, and religious norms pertaining to physical touch. For example, it would be inappropriate for a male practitioner to shake the hand of a client who is a strictly observant Orthodox Jewish woman because Orthodox rules (known as *negiah*) proscribe physical contact between unmarried members of the opposite sex. Similarly, a practitioner should not touch the head of a Cambodian (Khmer) client, because some believe that the soul resides in the head and should not be disturbed. Such gestures would violate sacred religious and ethnic norms. As Smith and Fitzpatrick note,

Like the issue of dual relationships, the issue of physical contact (exclusive of overtly sexual contact) with clients in therapy is not easily resolved. On one side, a gentle, reassuring touch or hug can be the most appropriate response at certain times or with certain clients. . . . On the other hand, clinicians practicing such behavior can run the risk of having it interpreted as a sexual advance, leading to undesired consequences for both the clinician and the client. . . . There are also cultural factors to be considered. For example, in Montreal where the dominant culture is French-Canadian, kissing on both cheeks is a widely practiced greeting among friends and even casual acquaintances. When it occurs between a therapist and client (as it sometimes does on special occasions), it does not carry the erotically charged meaning it might elsewhere in North America.

(1995:502–3)

Physical touch can also be an issue in nonpsychotherapeutic contexts. For example, in many circumstances human service professionals instinctively initiate or respond to a handshake upon meeting someone in a professional setting, such as a meeting of community residents or an administrators' meeting. However, a child-abuse-and-neglect investigator may decide not to shake the hand of a parent whom the professional is in the process of charging with child abuse. The investigator may believe that the handshake conveys a sense of familiarity, alliance, and comfort that is inconsistent with the adversarial nature of the encounter—an encounter that could lead to criminal charges and involuntary termination of parental rights. Whether to shake another party's hand in this kind of situation depends on the practitioner's judgment about the connotations of a handshake and the potential for boundary confusion and emotional harm.

Based on their review of pertinent literature, Gutheil and Brodsky (2008) encourage practitioners to take a number of precautions when contemplating any form of physical contact with clients. First, practitioners' primary concern should always be clients' well-being; commitment to a particular therapeutic theory or model that includes physical touch should not supersede concern for clients (Kertay and Reviere 1993). Second, practitioners should obtain clients' informed consent before any touch occurs (K. S. Pope 1994). Third, practitioners should pay close attention to their feelings toward clients to ensure that any physical touch is not self-serving. Fourth, practitioners should never use any form of physical touch that makes clients or themselves feel uncomfortable (Willison and Masson 1986). Fifth, practitioners must be careful to explore with clients the true meaning behind clients' request for their clinician to touch them (Davidson 1991). Finally, practitioners must decide whether their decision to not touch a client in unique circumstances would be inhumane (Maroda 1994).

Many boundary issues involve intimate relationships with clients, former clients, clients' relatives or acquaintances, practitioners' former sexual partners, and individuals with whom practitioners have professional relationships (such as supervisees and students). Boundary issues that do not explicitly involve sexual relationships also arise frequently, often as a result of the practitioner's unique emotional and dependency needs. I will now turn to these issues.

3

EMOTIONAL AND DEPENDENCY NEEDS

BOUNDARY PROBLEMS arising from a practitioner's personal issues can take many forms other than inappropriate intimate relationships. Some manifestations amount to boundary violations that lead to harm or exploitation of clients and others. Other boundary problems constitute boundary crossings, introducing complex issues that do not rise to the level of actual violations but must be managed carefully nonetheless.

What many of these phenomena have in common is that they are rooted in the practitioner's emotional and dependency needs, such as those stemming from childhood experiences, marital issues, aging, career frustrations, or financial or legal problems. Research on impaired professionals provides ample evidence that troubled practitioners sometimes find themselves enmeshed in boundary-related complications (Celenza 2007; Gutheil and Brodsky 2008; Guy, Poelstra, and Stark 1989; Kilburg, Kaslow, and Vanden-Bos 1988; Reamer 1992; Syme 2003; Thoreson, Miller, and Krauskopf 1989). Emotional distress among professionals generally falls into two categories: environmental stress, which is a function of employment conditions (actual working conditions and the broader culture's lack of support or appreciation of the human service mission), and personal stress, caused by problems with marriage, relationships, emotional and physical health, professional education and training, and finances (Reamer 1992). Of course, these two types of stress are often interrelated, as suggested by Freudenberger's illuminating overview of impaired professionals:

> I have worked with at least 60 impaired professionals, psychologists, social workers, dentists, physicians, and attorneys during the past ten years and have found certain personality characteristics to be common. For the most

part, impaired professionals are between 30 and 55 years of age. This is in essential agreement with Farber and Heifetz (1981) who suggested that "suicides of physicians, when they happen, are most likely to occur in the 35–54 age group" (p. 296). Early childhood impoverishment is another common characteristic. This is in agreement with Vaillant, Brighton, and McArthur (1970), who pointed to the "lack of consistent support and concern from their parents" in their study of drug-using physicians.

Most, if not all, of the patients I worked with led consistently unhealthy lifestyles. They tended to be masochistic, to have low self-images, and to be self-destructive in their personal and professional lives. Eighteen of the 60 had been married more than one time, 10 were bachelors, and the remainder were separated or divorced. Those who were married had frequent extramarital affairs. They all worked excessively long hours and, as Pearson and Strecker (1960) suggested, "had poor organizational habits . . . seldom took vacations, lunch hours and [had] few outside interests" (p. 916).

Their masochism made them prone to their patients beyond their own personal limits. All tended to be perfectionists and were usually never pleased with their work. "I know I can be better, I'm not good enough, I could have done more" are frequently heard refrains. They tended to conduct their lives, both at home and in the office, in such a way that they found little, if any, relief from their chores. They had a desperate need to be needed and rationalized, denied and overcompensated to an excessive degree. While expressing a sense of dedication and commitment, they denied that abusing drugs or alcohol or sexually abusing clients might eventually lead to their destruction. As a group they were risk takers with their own as well as their patients' lives.

(1986:137–38)

Of course, practitioners' emotional needs are not always this extreme. As I will discuss shortly, sometimes the issues are much more subtle with respect to both their causes and their manifestation.

Boundary issues arising from a practitioner's emotional and dependency needs assume a variety of forms, including forming friendships with clients or former clients, engaging in self-disclosure to clients, communicating with clients affectionately, and deliberately interacting with clients in the context of community-based groups or activities.

FRIENDSHIPS WITH CLIENTS

Occasionally, human service professionals establish such special rapport with clients that they enter into friendships with them. Sometimes these friendships meet practitioners' deep-seated emotional needs; they may be lonely or in the midst of a personal crisis, and the friendship with a "special client" may provide solace and important support, as in case 3.1.

CASE 3.1

Mark L. was a case manager at an outpatient clinic that provides mental health services to armed forces veterans. One of Mr. L.'s clients was Sam T., fifty-seven, who was being treated for anxiety symptoms associated with posttraumatic stress disorder.

Mr. L. was also a veteran, and he had grown disillusioned with his career. He had been turned down for promotions several times and was feeling alienated from his colleagues. Also, Mr. L.'s twenty-three-year-old marriage had recently ended, and he was estranged from his two adult children. Mr. L. was lonely and isolated and started drinking heavily (he was a recovering alcoholic). In general Mr. L. was feeling burned out.

During their work together Mr. L. and Mr. T. learned they had a number of interests in common. Both were divorced and felt jaded about their jobs. Both felt eager for a fresh start in life—new relationships, new jobs, and a change of scenery. They became Facebook friends and frequently posted comments on each other's Facebook wall. Mr. L. gave Mr. T. his cell phone number, and the two regularly exchanged text messages.

As their professional work together began to wind down, Mr. T. mentioned to Mr. L. that they might enjoy spending some time together socially. Mr. L. responded enthusiastically, and the two first arranged to go to a local football game together. Before long Mr. L. and Mr. T. were spending considerable social time together, having dinner, going to movies, fishing, and taking day trips to local attractions.

All friendships between practitioners and former clients do not necessarily arise from a practitioner's personal struggles, crises, or deep-seated pathology; rather, they may develop because of the practitioner's wish to maintain the close emotional connection established during the professional-client relationship, as in the next example.

CASE 3.2

Mary Anne V. was a counselor at a group psychotherapy practice. One of her clients was a forty-two-year-old woman, Alberta D., who sought counseling to help her decide whether to abandon her long-term career to pursue new interests. Ms. V. identified with Ms. D.'s dilemma, because Ms. V. had gone through a similar process when she had left her career in business to pursue graduate-level education in the counseling field.

Ms. V. and Ms. D. often commented about how they were "on the same wavelength." Ms. D. once told Ms. V., "Gee, I feel like we've known each other for years. Have you noticed how often we're able to finish each other's sentences, as if we're reading each other's minds?" Ms. V. responded by saying she agreed that they seemed to have similar perspectives on life.

At the conclusion of their counseling, Ms. D. asked whether they might be able to stay in touch as friends. In fact, Ms. V. was quite interested in maintaining contact with Ms. D. Although Ms. V. recognized that it was typically unwise for counselors to maintain friendships with former clients, she believed that this particular situation was unique. Ms. V. regarded Ms. D. as an unusually mature client who would not have difficulty handling a shift in their relationship from professional-client to a friendship. Shortly after they terminated their working relationship, the two began exchanging occasional email messages and eventually agreed to meet for lunch.

Attitudes vary among practitioners about entering into friendships with clients. In their survey of a large sample of randomly selected members of the American Psychological Association Division 29 (Psychotherapy), Pope, Tabachnick, and Keith-Spiegel (1995) found that only 6.4 percent believed that developing a social friendship with a former client was "unquestionably not ethical." Nearly half (51.1 percent) stated that such relationships could be ethical "under rare circumstances," and nearly 30 percent stated that such relationships could be ethical "under many circumstances" or were "unquestionably ethical." More than half the sample reported having begun a social friendship with a former client. In contrast, Jayaratne, Croxton, and Mattison (1997) found in their survey of clinical social workers that about one-fifth (21 percent) believed that it is appropriate to develop a friendship with a client; approximately the same percentage (21.2 percent) reported having actually developed such a friendship. In their survey of a sample of New York City social workers, DeJulio and Berkman (2003) found that about three-fourths of their sample (77.1 percent) stated that becoming friends with a former therapy client is never ethical (42.7 percent) or ethical under rare circumstances (34.4 percent).

As with sexual relationships between practitioners and clients, friend-ships between professionals and clients can be harmful. Former clients who become a practitioner's friend may wish to resume counseling to address new or reemerging issues in their lives. The friendship between the parties likely would interfere with the practitioner's ability to provide truly professional, unbiased, and impartial service. Having to locate and initiate counseling with a new practitioner—starting all over again—could be costly to the client both financially and emotionally. In addition, practitioners who develop friendships with clients or former clients expose themselves to significant legal risks. In one case ("Counselor, Counseling Center" 1997), for example, a client and her twin daughters went to a mental health clinic for counsel-ing and family therapy. The client developed a close personal relationship with the counselor that included family trips together. The client eventually sued the counselor and the clinic for harm, alleging that "the defendants had mismanaged her transference phenomenon and that the plaintiff would require future treatment and hospitalization due to the defendants' negli-gence" (6). The parties settled for $315,000.

Even practitioners with the best of intentions, and whose motives are beyond reproach, risk harming clients by confusing the boundaries with a friendship. As Bograd (1993, cited in Corey and Herlihy 1997:185) observes,

> The basic argument against dual relationships goes something like this: the hierarchical nature of the therapist-client or teacher-student relationship, which seems a necessary aspect of the professional encounter, undermines the truly equal consent to the nonprofessional connection. Even an ethical practitioner may unconsciously exploit or damage clients or students, who are inherently vulnerable in the relationship. Once the clarity of professional boundaries has been muddied, there is a good chance for confusion, disap-pointment and disillusionment on both sides.

Practitioners who consider maintaining any kind of relationship with a former client would do well to consider several key questions:

- How much time has passed since termination of the professional-client relationship? Has enough time passed to defuse complex boundary issues?
- What was the nature of the professional-client relationship? Did it involve intense psychotherapy or more concrete services associated with case management?

- To what extent is the client mentally competent and emotionally stable? Is the client able to grasp the nature of subtle and complicated boundary issues?
- What issues were addressed in the professional-client relationship? Did the work focus on complicated boundary issues in the client's personal life that might be brought up by a posttermination relationship?
- How long did the professional-client relationship last? Was it relatively short-term or long-term?
- What circumstances surrounded the termination of the professional-client relationship? Did the relationship end in order to enter into a friend-ship or more personal relationship, or was it a more natural termination?
- To what extent is there foreseeable harm to the client as a result of the relationship? How might a posttermination relationship injure the client emotionally, especially if it is not sustained? Might such a relationship bring up troubling issues for the client related to intimacy, boundaries, and loss?
- Have the practitioner and client engaged in an electronic relationship through social media (for example, email, Facebook, text messaging) that may lead to boundary confusion?

UNCONVENTIONAL INTERVENTIONS

A significant number of ethics complaints and lawsuits filed against human service professionals allege boundary violations arising from a practitioner's use of interventions that are variously described as unconventional, nontraditional, and unorthodox (Austin, Moline, and Williams 1990; Barker and Branson 2000; Reamer 2006b, 2009b). In substantiated cases evidence often shows that the practitioner introduced the unethical or negligent intervention in part to meet her or his own emotional needs. The diverse cases that follow illustrate this phenomenon.

CASE 3.3

The *Daily News-Herald* of Harrisonburg, Virginia, reported that a former client sued a clinical social worker, claiming that the social worker had violated the client's boundaries (Barr 1997). The lawsuit, which sought $400,000 in compensatory damages and $350,000 in punitive damages, alleged that the social worker had used "past life regression" and what the social worker called spiritual "guides and masters" as treatment techniques. The claim also asserted that the client often had been under the influence of medication during clinical sessions, at the social worker's request, and that the social worker had involved the client in nontherapeutic discussion groups in which the social worker was personally involved. The client further claimed that the social worker had taken the client flying in a plane he rented. The state board of social work found that the social worker had not kept "appropriate therapeutic boundaries" with the client because he had invited her to join a nontherapeutic discussion group in which he was personally involved, visited her in the hospital where she was being treated for an unspecified illness, and lent her money.

CASE 3.4

The *New York Times* reported that a child psychiatrist who was a third-year resident disclosed in a therapy session with his own treating psychiatrist that he was a pedophile and had gone to South America to "find a nice child" (Bruni 1998). Four months later, according to the news report, the psychiatric resident molested a ten-year-old boy at a Connecticut hospital. According to court records, the offending psychiatrist would turn out the lights to play hide-and-seek; upon finding the child, the psychiatrist would rub his groin against the boy's buttocks while holding the boy's hands behind his back. The boy testified, "I felt really disgusting. I felt nasty. It changed me so much. I still don't feel like me. I don't know who the hell I am sometimes." A federal jury found the treating psychiatrist negligent for failing to warn anyone that a doctor undergoing psychoanalysis with him had confessed to being a pedophile.

CASE 3.5

Two therapists, Connell Watkins and Julie Ponder, were sentenced to sixteen years in prison after being convicted of reckless child abuse resulting in the death of ten-year-old Candace Newmaker. According to ABC News, Jeane Newmaker, Candace's adoptive mother, brought the child to be treated by Watkins and Ponder for an attachment disorder. Evidence presented in their criminal court trial showed that Candace suffocated during a seventy-minute rebirthing session, part of a two-week intensive program that was supposed to help her bond with Newmaker. The rebirthing session was videotaped and shown to the jury during the trial. It showed Candace pleading for air and for her life. It also showed the therapists disregarding those pleas ("'Rebirthing' Therapists Get Prison Terms" 2011).

CASE 3.6

A forty-two-year-old woman sought counseling from a clinical social worker to address issues stemming from sexual molestation she had experienced as a child. The client reported that recently she had been in therapy with another counselor in the community but felt she had not been making much progress.

About two months into their professional-client relationship, the client disclosed to the social worker that she had terminated her therapy with the counselor for other major reasons. She explained that although the therapy with the counselor began normally, over time the counselor had engaged in a series of behaviors that the client eventually found deeply disturbing. According to the client, the counselor seemed to become more and more attached to her emotionally and wanted to become more involved in her daily life. The client disclosed pertinent details, including allegations that during a six-month period the counselor had several candlelight dinners with the client in the counselor's home, exchanged expensive gifts with the client, traveled with the client to attend a professional continuing education conference that addressed clinical issues relevant to the client, shared a hotel room with the client while attending the conference, went camping with the client and shared a pup tent with her, and watched movies with the client in the counselor's home.

After exploring with the social worker the clinical ramifications of these boundary violations, the client decided to file an ethics complaint against the counselor with the state licensing board and to sue her for professional negligence. The counselor responded to the formal complaints by acknowledging that these various activities had occurred and by stating that they were thoughtfully designed components of a legitimate therapeutic approach that she dubbed "reparenting therapy." In her testimony during the trial, the counselor said that in her professional opinion the client—who had not experienced nurturing parents during her childhood—would benefit from the counselor's assumption of a "parental role," in which she could provide the client with "sustained, supportive, and loving care in the way that a parent should." The counselor acknowledged that she felt emotionally attached to the client but denied that her "therapeutic actions" departed significantly from acceptable standards of care. The court ultimately ruled that the counselor had violated the client's boundaries and was negligent and awarded damages. The counselor's license was revoked by the state licensing board.

CASE 3.7

A fifty-seven-year-old psychologist provided counseling to a sixty-year-old client who sought help with his recent onset of dysthymia symptoms (a mood disorder characterized by feelings of pessimism, sadness, irritability, low self-esteem, and indecisiveness). During their work together the psychologist and client occasionally reminisced about similar life-altering experiences they had during the tumultuous

1960s. The two learned that they had a number of similar experiences with rock music and drug use.

During one clinical session the client told the psychologist that he still enjoyed smoking marijuana as much as he had during the 1960s. The psychologist responded by telling the client that he understood because he too continued to enjoy smoking marijuana and found that "it's a great way to relieve stress and relax." At that moment the client pulled out two marijuana cigarettes, smiled, offered one to the psychologist, and said, "I'd really like to join you for a joint!" Subsequently, on several occasions before the therapy ended, the psychologist and client smoked marijuana together during clinical sessions.

The client disclosed these facts during a licensing board hearing scheduled to address the client's allegations that the psychologist was negligent in his treatment of the client's clinical dysthymia. The psychologist claimed that their marijuana use enhanced the therapeutic alliance.

It is important to note that not all nontraditional interventions create problematic boundary issues. Some nontraditional approaches create ambiguous boundaries, but they do not constitute boundary violations. Outdoor behavioral health programs, also known as wilderness therapy programs, provide a good example. These programs offer highly structured, intensive, short-term (usually seven to eight weeks) therapy in remote locations that remove adolescents from the distractions of their home communities (for example, television, smartphones, music, Facebook, cars, drugs and alcohol, high-risk peer groups). The natural challenges of living outdoors full time and developing wilderness survival skills help teens develop self-confidence, take responsibility for their choices, experience the natural consequences of their behaviors, and develop problem-solving and social skills under the guidance of therapeutic staff.

Typical wilderness therapy programs provide individual and group counseling, education, leadership training, and survival skill challenges that strengthen a teenager's ability to function in a community of people. Programs foster interdependence and seek to enhance teenagers' honesty, awareness, openness, accountability, and responsibility. Common wilderness therapy activities include outdoor education, primitive living, team-building exercises, structured daily activities, individual and group counseling, and expeditions (Reamer and Siegel 2008).

Necessarily, the more formal boundaries that one finds in traditional therapeutic programs for struggling teens (for example, residential treatment programs, outpatient mental health clinics) are not possible in wilderness therapy programs. There are no office walls to contain therapeutic conversations; counseling sessions may occur during a late-evening thunderstorm when a teen is finally eager to talk about his childhood trauma while sitting in a temporary lean-to constructed from a tarp attached to a tree. The clinician may decide to spend the night in the field, relatively close to the client, so they can resume their counseling session in the morning after clients and program staffers have shared a hearty breakfast. That is, what are considered acceptable and appropriate boundaries in one therapeutic context might be considered unacceptable and inappropriate in another (Zur 2007). A behavior therapist working with a client who struggles with an eating disorder might accompany the client to a restaurant for a meal as part of the therapeutic protocol; this would not be appropriate in the more typical office-based psychotherapeutic relationship.

It is important to note that while practitioners may feel comfortable with less formal boundaries in the context of some outside-the-office interventions, some clients nonetheless may feel confused and uneasy. Practitioners would do well to anticipate this possibility and discuss it with clients.

The advent of novel computer-based clinical interventions has created new boundary-related challenges. For example, a growing number of clinicians are providing clinical services using email and Internet-based chat rooms.

This controversial innovation has unleashed a daunting array of complex ethical issues related to client informed consent, confidentiality and privacy, client abandonment, emergency management, termination of services, and, especially, boundaries. Internet counseling has redefined the concept of therapist availability and responsiveness. The idea of a tightly controlled in-office therapeutic hour seems archaic in the context of Internet-based therapy that, in principle, is available twenty-four hours a day, seven days a week. Clinicians and ethicists are actively creating new standards of care regarding ordinary, reasonable, and prudent practice. For example, the International Society for Mental Health Online has developed a comprehensive set of principles identifying challenging ethical issues that clinicians must consider.

Similar ethical and boundary issues accompany clinicians' increased use of telephone therapy with clients they may never meet in person. Some clinicians now provide extensive counseling over the telephone, sometimes to clients who live in other states that are hundreds or thousands of miles away. This trend is especially compelling in light of Simon's strong assertion in

1992, long before the proliferation of formal telephone counseling services, that "psychotherapy cannot be conducted effectively over a telephone" (cited in Gutheil and Brodsky 2008:70).

Another new Internet-based therapeutic protocol, known as cybertherapy and avatar therapy, has created yet another set of complex boundary-related issues. With this approach clients create an avatar—a visual graphic image that clients use to represent themselves—that they use relatively anonymously to interact with a therapist and, possibly, other clients. Therapists using this approach typically use software technology known as Second Life, which is an online environment that allows multiple participants to interact with one another virtually and relatively anonymously. In cybertherapy clinicians may provide therapy to clients they never meet or see in person. Clients can participate in online group therapy sessions without ever seeing the faces of other group members or the therapist; participants know each other only by their graphic avatar characters. In addition to the challenging clinical issues associated with this form of therapy, clinicians must be cognizant of the ambiguous boundaries that accompany this form of intervention, including issues related to clients' identity, privacy, self-disclosure, and clinician availability.

These nontraditional approaches to clinical services require exceedingly skillful management of boundaries by clinicians. Clearly, human service professionals' emotional issues can lead to boundary crossings and violations, especially when they use unorthodox and unconventional interventions. Unscrupulous, self-serving, and possibly impaired practitioners may use these novel treatment approaches to exploit clients. Their actions have a manipulative and coercive quality, for example, when a clinician with poor boundaries convinces his client to participate in the clinician's controversial spiritual activities. Practitioners may believe, typically in a delusional or self-deceptive way, that the nontraditional and unorthodox intervention may be in the client's best interest. The practitioner's lack of insight concerning the likely harmful consequences—both for clients and themselves—is often a clear sign of the depth of their impairment.

Certainly, professionals have differences of opinion about the use of nontraditional and unorthodox treatment approaches, especially with the advent of such novel interventions as online and avatar counseling. For example, years before the emergence of web-based interventions, Jayaratne, Croxton, and Mattison (1997) found that more than two-fifths of their sample of clinical social workers believed that praying with a client is appropriate; nearly one-fifth of the group reported having done so. Three-fifths of the sample stated that using techniques such as tai chi chuan and yoga is appropriate, although only 15 percent reported having used these techniques with clients. In contrast, only 4 percent of the sample said that using psychic readings or astrology as a treatment approach is appropriate; virtually none (0.5 percent) reported having used such techniques. Pope, Tabachnick, and Keith-Spiegel (1995) found that about three-fifths of their sample of psychologists believed that leading nude group therapy or "growth groups" is never ethical; only 7 percent said that such activity is ethical under many circumstances or unquestionably ethical.

SELF-DISCLOSURE: WHOSE NEEDS ARE BEING MET?

When I conduct workshops related to boundary and other ethical issues, I often ask the audience of human service professionals how many of them have disclosed to clients information about themselves or their families. Typically, the overwhelming majority raise their hands. What the subsequent discussion reveals, inevitably, is that despite this common practice, professionals have widely varying opinions about the circumstances under which self-disclosure is appropriate, the extent to which personal details should be shared with clients, the content of appropriate self-disclosures, and the clinical and ethical ramifications.

In general practitioner self-disclosure can occur in a wide variety of ways and for diverse reasons (Barrett and Berman 2001; Bridges 2001; Farber 2006; Gaines 2003; Goldfried, Burckell, and Eubanks-Carter 2003; Goldstein 1997; Hill and Knox 2002; Knox and Hill 2003; Stricker and Fisher 1990). As Zur observes, these disclosures can occur deliberately or accidentally; some disclosures are unavoidable:

> Therapists' self-disclosure refers to therapists' revelations of personal rather than professional information about themselves to their clients. Such self-disclosure has been classified as deliberate, unavoidable, or accidental. Deliberate self-disclosure usually refers to therapists' intentional, verbal disclosure of personal information, but it also applies to other deliberate actions such as an empathic gesture or placing a certain family photo in the office. Unavoidable self-disclosure might include a therapist's tone of voice, foreign accent, and a great range of other cues. . . . Accidental self-disclosure occurs when there are incidental encounters outside the office, spontaneous

verbal or nonverbal reactions, or other unplanned occurrences that happen to reveal therapists' personal information to their clients.

(2007:149)

This diversity of opinion about practitioner self-disclosure is reflected in research data. Pope, Tabachnick, and Keith-Spiegel (1995) found that more than two-thirds of their sample of clinical psychologists (69 percent) reported that using self-disclosure as a therapy technique is ethical under many circumstances or unquestionably ethical. Only 2 percent stated that such self-disclosure is never ethical. Further, nearly three-fourths of the sample reported having used self-disclosure at least sometimes; about one-third stated that they used it fairly or very often. In their survey of New York City social workers, DeJulio and Berkman (2003) found that nearly four-fifths of the sample (78.8 percent) believed that disclosing details of current personal stresses to clients is never ethical (42.9 percent) or ethical under rare conditions (35.9 percent).

In one of the earlier discussions of the ethics of self-disclosure, Senger notes that his thinking has changed over time; he argues that self-disclosure by therapists can sometimes be used deliberately in effective ways:

My 30 years in full-time office practice have led me to some modification of my originally conservative view of self-disclosure. Often I've found that patients have benefited from, more than been burdened by, appropriate discussion of my human response to them including answering some of their questions. To do so models openness, usually facilitating rather than hampering exploration of patients' fantasies. The traditional reply, "Why do you ask?" often provokes sullen or guilty withdrawal.

To say that we therapists have successfully analyzed our idiosyncrasies away is utopian. To believe we can hide our values from observant patients is naïve. To think that we can prevent our biases from influencing therapy is, at best, a hope. To claim that patients cannot process these data often underrates them. If we discuss relevant personal information, then patients can make a more informed decision about whether and how to continue their treatment.

(1994:294)

In principle self-disclosure may occur for a variety of reasons. In some cases—which I will discuss in chapter 5—practitioners may self-disclose in an effort to be helpful, for example, when a clinician attempts to empathize with a grieving client whose parent has just died by making a reference to his own experience when his parent died. A clinician may believe sincerely that the client would benefit from the clinician's carefully constructed and handled disclosure. As Senger asserts,

> Obviously there can be too much therapist openness: disclosure is not for therapist aggrandizement nor to begin the well-known slide down the "slippery slope." Like all tools, disclosure can be abused. Yet I wonder how often we therapists are protecting primarily ourselves when we try so hard to conceal all because that is supposedly "best for the patient." Perhaps we could discuss with (nonanalytic) patients what might be helpful for them to know about us, as well as why they are curious. I do not believe risk management should put the burden of proof on therapists who disclose relevant personal information more than on therapists who conceal it and who thereby limit informed consent.
>
> A second (and more important) reason for exploring countertransference with selected patients is its therapeutic value. To limit patient discussion to an intrapsychic focus sacrifices the rich enlightenment obtained through a mutual interpersonal exploration of the therapeutic relationship. We often wait too long—until provoked to desperation by a borderline patient. Not wanting to "burden" the patient with our countertransference, we use self-disclosure as a last resort—to learn with relief that the patient, too, is relieved and responds. Countertransference disclosures can be of great benefit (if less dramatic) with nonborderline patients as well. Let us not exclude "high level" patients from interpersonal enlightenment as a price they must pay for being healthier.
>
> (1994:294)

Gutheil and Gabbard express a similar sentiment: "Few clinicians would argue that the therapist's self-disclosure is always a boundary crossing. Psychoanalysis and intensive psychotherapy involve intense personal relationships. A useful therapeutic alliance may be forged by the therapist's willingness to acknowledge that a painful experience of the patient is familiar to himself" (1993:194).

In other circumstances, however, self-disclosure may occur inappropriately because of the practitioner's own deep-seated emotional or dependency needs. This may happen because of the clinician's (perhaps unconscious) wish to establish a personal relationship with the client; sharing personal details may be a way to set this process in motion. Practitioners often refer to this as poor "use of self" (Farber 2006; Reupert 2007). As Gutheil and Gabbard observe,

> When a therapist begins to indulge in even mild forms of self-disclosure, it is an indication for careful self-scrutiny regarding the motivations for departure from the usual therapeutic stance. Gorkin observed that many therapists harbor a wish to be known by their patients as a "real person," especially as the termination of the therapy approaches. While it may be technically correct for a therapist to become more spontaneous at the end of the therapeutic process, therapists who become more self-disclosing as the therapy ends must be sure that their reasons for doing so are not related to their own unfulfilled needs in their private lives but, rather, are based on an objective assessment that increased focus on the real relationship is useful for the patient in the termination process.
>
> (1993:194)

In some instances, then, a clinician may be so absorbed or overwhelmed by his or her own personal issues, perhaps as a result of problematic countertransference, that the clinician leaks personal information and details without recognizing that the leak is occurring or without a sense of its inappropriateness. In one case in which I served as an expert witness, a counselor's former client filed a licensing board complaint and lawsuit alleging boundary confusion and violations. Part of the evidence I had to review included email messages sent by the counselor to the client from his personal, nonwork email address during nonworking hours (including several late-night emails). Several of the counselor's email messages included personal information about him and his family. In addition, the counselor sent the client several email attachments that included poems written by the counselor. The poems included references to the counselor's life that, the client asserted, confused her about the nature of her relationship with the counselor. The counselor argued that these personal disclosures were only for therapeutic purposes. The licensing board concluded that the counselor's personal disclosures constituted inappropriate boundary crossings and placed the clinician on probation for three years; the board also levied a significant fine, along with a requirement for extensive continuing education focused on boundary issues. The lawsuit was settled before trial.

The next case also illustrates inappropriate self-disclosure that occurs because of a practitioner's unmet needs.

CASE 3.8

Jim L. was a school social worker who provided counseling services to students enrolled in three urban high schools. Mr. L. worked primarily with students with learning disabilities and significant behavioral problems. He provided one-on-one counseling to students, led several treatment groups, and worked with a number of the students' parents to address home-based issues that might be contributing to the youths' difficulties.

One of Mr. L.'s clients was a sixteen-year-old named Mark, who had been suspended by the school on two occasions for fighting. Mark had also been arrested when a teacher found Mark threatening another student with a knife.

In addition to meeting weekly with Mark, Mr. L. met with Mark's mother, who had divorced Mark's father shortly after Mark's birth. Mark's mother, Ms. M., shared considerable detail with Mr. L. about the family's struggles, including Mark's abandonment by his father, Mark's premature birth (which contributed to his learning disabilities), and Ms. M.'s isolation after recently moving to this community.

Over several months Mr. L., who was single, became attached to Mark and his mother. Mr. L. sensed accurately that he was having a major positive influence on Mark and that Ms. M. was also finding Mr. L.'s advice helpful. Mr. L. was beginning to feel as if he was assuming the role of a father figure in Mark's life; on occasion he fantasized about developing a relationship with Mark's mother and assuming the father role more formally.

Mr. L. was unaware that he spent increasing amounts of time with Ms. M. in sharing personal information, such as his single status and that he enjoyed some of the same kinds of activities that Ms. M. had said she enjoyed (such as ballroom dancing and bird-watching). Unconsciously, Mr. L. was offering Ms. M. personal tidbits somewhat flirtatiously and in an effort to pique Ms. M's. interest in a more intimate relationship. His self-disclosure reflected his own emotional needs more than his client's.

Practitioner self-disclosure is clearly inappropriate in some instances; however, handled carefully and circumspectly—using what I call judicious self-disclosure—self-disclosure may be appropriate in others. Realistically, some circumstances will always fall in a middle range that is difficult to assess; these are the cases in which thoughtful and reasonable practitioners may disagree, in part because of their different training and ideological orientations (Barglow 2005; Cornell 2007; Farber 2006; Gaines 2003; Knox and Hill 2003; Roberts 2005). And, of course, some forms of self-disclosure are inevitable, for example, in the form of the practitioner's speech or accent, personal appearance and clothing, and office decor. Inquisitive clients can also discover a great deal of information about a clinician by perusing web sites that contain details that the clinician has chosen to disclose in other contexts.

Many scholars believe that different forms of clinical intervention warrant different forms and degrees of self-disclosure. Substance abuse treatment programs may permit, and even encourage, staffers to disclose whether they are in recovery. However, more analytically oriented treatment is less accepting of self-disclosure (Zur 2007). Cognitive and behavioral therapists may favor modest self-disclosure to provide clients with constructive role modeling. As Gutheil and Brodsky conclude,

> Different schools of therapy involve different levels of self-disclosure, which in turn serve the needs of different patients. For example, a highly inhibited patient may become uncomfortable with a highly self-disclosing therapist and may change therapists. Another patient who finds an analytically oriented therapist too withholding may do likewise. No therapist or therapy is right for everyone. What is right—and necessary—for every patient is to be able to make an informed choice based on knowing what to expect.
>
> (2008:109)

Thus there is considerable variation among clinicians' patterns of self-disclosure depending upon their theoretical orientations. Traditional analysts may prefer stricter self-disclosure boundaries, whereas humanistic, existential, narrative, and feminist therapists may feel more comfortable with greater self-disclosure as a way to enhance their transparency and promote a more egalitarian, nonhierarchical therapist-client relationship.

Some contemporary clinicians, a minority it appears, have made a deliberate choice to associate with clients on Facebook. In so doing these clinicians have made a deliberate decision to disclose some personal information to clients. Some clients may appreciate this self-disclosure, and some may find it objectionable. Clinicians who choose to self-disclose in this manner would do well to discuss the issue in peer consultation, supervision, and with their clients, focusing especially on the clinical rationale and potential boundary issues and ramifications.

Practitioners who consider any form of self-disclosure should always question their motives and ensure that the self-disclosure is likely to help, not harm, the client. It is useful to keep in mind the Latin phrase *cui bono*—to whose advantage? Smith and Fitzpatrick (1995) convey this instinct about this very complex phenomenon:

> In certain circumstances . . . self-disclosure by the therapist can be a power-ful intervention, and many contemporary schools of psychotherapy encour-age its practice (see Stricker & Fisher, 1990, for a comprehensive review). The hallmark of appropriate self-disclosure is that it is done for the client's benefit within the context of the therapeutic process. Used as a tool to in-struct or illustrate, the therapist's disclosure of some past event or problem can help the client overcome barriers to therapeutic progress (Dryden, 1990; Lane & Hull, 1990). Informing the client about personal conditions that might cause interruptions, such as illness or pregnancy, may also be neces-sary (Lane & Hull, 1990; Simon, 1991). Disclosures by the clinician that are generally not considered suitable include details of current problems or stressors, personal fantasies or dreams, and social, sexual, or financial cir-cumstances (Gutheil & Gabbard, 1993; Simon, 1991).
>
> These distinctions, which seem clear-cut on paper, can become murky in practice. Consider the case of a young graduate student in therapy for 18 months who becomes pregnant by her new boyfriend. She comes to her session trying to resolve the question of whether to have an abortion, which she considers the rational choice given her life circumstances, or to keep the baby, which she wants. Her therapist, a married woman in her early 40's who recently miscarried after trying to conceive for many years, is aware of being too emotionally invested in the decision. In the course of the session, the client says to the therapist, "I feel as if you want me to have this baby." Does the therapist disclose the fact that her professional objectivity has been compromised? Would disclosure help the client by allowing her to weigh the therapist's bias into her decision or would it hinder her by adding another consideration to an already complex problem? Judging what is of benefit to the client is an ideal that can be very difficult to practice.

(1995:503)

Disclosing information about one's religious practices or beliefs is espe-cially complex. Some clients may ask the practitioner about her or his beliefs and practices, because this is a subject that matters to the client. In other situations practitioners may consider volunteering information without wait-ing for a client to ask. Clearly, such disclosures can complicate the boundary issues. Some clients may be upset or confused by a practitioner's disclosures—whether invited or not. Others may be comforted by them. As Zur observes,

Self-disclosure has a unique importance for therapists working with clients who hold particular religious or spiritual beliefs. These clients often ask therapists questions about their spiritual orientations and values as part of the interview process. Clients who are devout Christians, for example, often seem to work with therapists who share their spiritual beliefs whereas they are not likely to feel understood by atheist therapists. Additionally, many clients choose their therapists because they are aware of their spiritual orientation. These clients often meet their future therapists in the context of the church, synagogue, or meditation retreat.

(2007:157–58)

Similar challenges arise when clients seek out clinicians based on their beliefs about the clinicians' sexual orientation, ethnicity, or status as a person in recovery. Clinicians who work with clients in these contexts must be vigilant in their efforts to manage boundaries carefully.

AFFECTIONATE COMMUNICATIONS

I have encountered a number of instances when a human service professional decides to send a client or former client a warm, affectionate note. Typically these messages are sent on personal stationery, not on professional letterhead. In addition, the notes are usually handwritten rather than typed. The practitioner's choice of this informal style of communication in itself often sends a signal that the message is more personal than professional.

Affectionate communications can occur for a variety of reasons, some of which seem quite appropriate and ethical and some of which do not. Sending a client or former client a condolence note following the death of someone close to the client is an example of a warm, informal message that most practitioners would consider appropriate. Sending such a message on agency letterhead may be unnecessarily and insensitively cold and stiff, although the envelope for the more informal note should include the agency's return mailing address rather than the clinician's home address in order to maintain clear boundaries.

In other situations, however, warmly and affectionately worded notes on personal stationery may communicate to a client that the practitioner is interested in something other than a professional-client relationship.

CASE 3.9

Mildred D. was a counselor in a rural family service agency. Most of her clients were referred by the human resources department of the local town in conjunction with its employee assistance program. Town employees who were having job-related problems that might be addressed through counseling—for example, interpersonal conflict with colleagues or declining job performance associated with an employee's substance abuse or marital difficulties—were referred to Mildred D. and one of her colleagues.

One of Mildred D.'s clients was a midlevel administrator in the city's parks and recreation department. The client, Barbara S., was referred by her supervisor because of the supervisor's concerns about Barbara S.'s frequent absences and deterioration in the quality of her work. Ms. S. acknowledged to Ms. D. that indeed she was having some serious problems in her life, associated primarily with her recent divorce and child custody dispute with her former husband. Ms. S. also reported an "up-and-down" relationship she was having with one of her coworkers, Melanie N. It happens that Melanie N. was also a client of Mildred D.'s, having been referred to the employee assistance program by her supervisor because of her problem with alcoholism. When Mildred D. accepted Barbara S. as a client, Mildred D. was not aware that Barbara S. was having difficulty with Melanie N., thus creating a potential conflict of interest.

Mildred D. helped Barbara S. identify counseling goals that might help her function more productively in her personal and professional life. They met weekly for about three months and accomplished a great deal. Barbara S. and Mildred D. then terminated their working relationship; Ms. D. wrote a favorable report to Ms. S.'s supervisor.

By the end of their work together Barbara S. and Mildred D. had developed a close relationship. In fact, Ms. D. told Ms. S. during their last session that she would truly miss their meetings, that Ms. S. had become one of Ms. D.'s "special clients."

For months after the termination of their professional-client relationship, Mildred D. found herself thinking about Barbara S. and fantasizing about having a friendship with her. About six months after their working relationship terminated, Ms. D. decided to write Ms. S. a casual note on informal, decorated stationery, mainly to say hello and to wish Ms. S. well. At the end of the note, Ms. D. wrote, "So, I hope this note finds you well and that you're as content as you were when we last saw each other. I have great faith in your ability to manage life's challenges. You really are very special to me; I hope, somehow, we will be able to share time together in the future. P.S. Last week I saw Melanie. I guess you know she's having a real hard time. I hope this doesn't affect you."

Barbara S. felt honored by Mildred D.'s note and Ms. D.'s willingness to confide in her about one of her other clients, who had been Ms. S.'s friend; however, she also felt somewhat confused about Ms. D.'s intentions. She was not sure whether Ms. D. was reaching out to her in an effort to begin a friendship.

This case illustrates how a practitioner can lose sight of appropriate boundaries with a client to whom she feels emotionally attached. The clinician's informal written communication not only suggested a dual relationship that her former client found confusing (albeit flattering) but also breached the confidentiality of another of the clinician's clients (Melanie N.), an additional indicator of a conflict of interest and the inappropriate breach of boundaries in this case. Moreover, the clinician did not address the potential conflict of interest that arose when she discovered that a new client (Barbara S.) wanted to address issues involving her relationship with another current client (Melanie N.).

A gesture as seemingly innocuous as sending a client a holiday card can also be problematic. On the surface it may appear that the card is sent as a reflection of social custom. However, some clients may interpret such a card in another way—particularly if the return address reveals that the card was sent from the practitioner's home; some clients may assume that the practitioner is treating them as special and that the practitioner is interested in more than a professional relationship. In fact, in some cases this is an accurate conclusion on the client's part. The holiday card may be an indirect and relatively subtle—and not always conscious—way for the clinician to address his or her emotional needs and wish to connect with a former client.

Not surprisingly, practitioners differ in their views of the appropriateness of sending holiday cards to clients. Pope, Tabachnick, and Keith-Spiegel (1995) found considerable variation in the opinions of clinical psychologists. About one-fourth of the sample (23.4 percent) stated that sending holiday greeting cards to clients is unethical (although to varying degrees); however, nearly half the group said that sending holiday greeting cards is ethical under many circumstances or is unquestionably ethical. About two-fifths of the sample (37 percent) said that they had sent clients holiday greeting cards. As Zur notes, it is important to distinguish between appropriate and inappropriate cards: "Appropriate cards by either therapists or clients are boundary crossings and, as such, can enhance the therapeutic alliance and clinical efficacy. Inappropriate or offensive cards are boundary violations" (2007:212).

COMMUNITY-BASED CONTACT WITH CLIENTS

Human service professionals often encounter clients in the community, especially in smaller and rural communities. This may occur by happenstance—for example, when a practitioner and a client encounter each other unexpectedly in the supermarket aisle or at a local athletic event—or, more predictably, for example, when practitioners and clients learn that they are members of the same community-based group or organization and can expect to run into each other at social events or online (for example, as members of an organization's Facebook site). In the remainder of this chapter I will focus on community-based contact that is predictable and that may trigger issues related to a practitioner's emotional and dependency needs (for discussion of unanticipated community-based encounters, see chapter 6).

Certainly, it is reasonable for practitioners to want to pursue community activities without being constrained by their relationships with clients. Ideally, practitioners' and clients' personal worlds would not intersect. Realistically, however, community-based encounters with clients are inevitable for most practitioners, especially in rural and other small communities (for example, military bases). Although such encounters may not occur frequently, they can be laden with meaning and potential repercussions.

CASE 3.10

Marsha R. was a therapist who had been in private practice for fourteen years. Ms. R. is a lesbian and is visible and active in the local lesbian community.

A number of Ms. R.'s clients are lesbians who seek her professional services because of Ms. R.'s strong professional reputation in the lesbian community. Many of her referrals come by word of mouth within the lesbian community.

Over time Ms. R. has grown increasingly uncomfortable with the expanding overlap between her professional and personal worlds. It is not unusual for Ms. R. to attend a party, social gathering, concert, or political event related to gay and lesbian issues and encounter current and former clients. Ms. R. has become much more self-conscious at these events and has had difficulty just being herself. Ms. R. often feels on display, as if her clients are observing her actions and behaviors to see what their therapist is really like.

This sort of dilemma has no simple solution. In principle Ms. R. would not knowingly put herself in a social situation that may generate complicated boundary crossings. Ms. R. understands that such boundary crossings may ultimately be confusing to clients, which could harm them emotionally. Such crossings may also be confusing to Ms. R., which could affect the quality of her work and her ability to be helpful to clients.

At the same time Ms. R. has her own legitimate emotional and social needs. Is it realistic and fair to expect that Ms. R. would avoid all social gatherings where she has reason to believe that she may encounter one or more clients? To do so would mean that Ms. R. would have to abstain from virtually all her meaningful social activity.

How can a practitioner handle this predicament in a way that protects clients and does not require the complete forfeiture of her personal and social life? This set of circumstances contains the core ingredients of an ethical dilemma, where two or more rights and duties conflict. To use the language of the moral philosopher W. D. Ross (1930), this situation entails conflicts between prima facie duties. Prima facie duties entail obligations that people are inclined to meet simultaneously. When prima facie duties clash, people must attempt to determine whether rank-ordering the conflicting obligations, or some other mechanism, will lead to a way to reconcile the conflict.

Such ethical decision making has no simple formula. In such a situation practitioners may find it useful to consult with thoughtful colleagues and supervisors, consult relevant literature and ethical standards, and so on. In some cases a solution will be clear-cut; in other cases practitioners and consultants are likely to disagree about what is ethical. For example, Jayaratne, Croxton, and Mattison (1997) found that about 30 percent of the sample of clinical social workers believed that participating in recreational or social activities with clients is appropriate; one-fourth of this group had engaged in such activity. Nearly three-fifths of this sample (58.7 percent) stated that serving on community boards or committees with clients is appropriate; nearly one-fourth of the sample reported having actually served on community boards or committees with clients.

The overall concern in a situation of this sort is for the practitioner to minimize potential harm to the clients. The language in two standards contained in the NASW *Code of Ethics* (2008) is instructive:

> Social workers should be alert to and avoid conflicts of interest that interfere with the exercise of professional discretion and impartial judgment. Social workers should inform clients when a real or potential conflict of interest arises and take reasonable steps to resolve the issue in a manner that makes

the clients' interests primary and protects clients' interests to the greatest extent possible. In some cases, protecting clients' interests may require termination of the professional relationship with proper referral of the client.

(standard 1.06[a])

Social workers should not engage in dual or multiple relationships with clients or former clients in which there is a risk of exploitation or potential harm to the client. In instances when dual or multiple relationships are unavoidable, social workers should take steps to protect clients and are responsible for setting clear, appropriate, and culturally sensitive boundaries. (Dual or multiple relationships occur when social workers relate to clients in more than one relationship, whether professional, social, or business. Dual or multiple relationships can occur simultaneously or consecutively.)

(standard 1.06[c])

Two standards in the American Psychological Association's *Ethical Principles of Psychologists and Code of Conduct* (2010) are similarly pertinent:

A multiple relationship occurs when a psychologist is in a professional role with a person and (1) at the same time is in another role with the same person, (2) at the same time is in a relationship with a person closely associated with or related to the person with whom the psychologist has the professional relationship, or (3) promises to enter into another relationship in the future with the person or a person closely associated with or related to the person.

A psychologist refrains from entering into a multiple relationship if the multiple relationship could reasonably be expected to impair the psychologist's objectivity, competence, or effectiveness in performing his or her functions as a psychologist, or otherwise risks exploitation or harm to the person with whom the professional relationship exists.

Multiple relationships that would not reasonably be expected to cause impairment or risk exploitation or harm are not unethical.

(standard 3.05[a])

If a psychologist finds that, due to unforeseen factors, a potentially harmful multiple relationship has arisen, the psychologist takes reasonable steps to resolve it with due regard for the best interests of the affected person and maximal compliance with the Ethics Code.

(standard 3.05[b])

The ethics standards for social work and psychology that pertain to dual and multiple relationships suggest that practitioners should approach these circumstances incrementally. Thus in case 3.10, Ms. R., the therapist, should be alert to the possibility that her simultaneous involvement with clients professionally and socially may affect her judgment and pose a risk of harm to clients. Once she becomes aware of potential harm, Ms. R. should take reasonable steps to protect clients to the greatest extent possible. Practically speaking, Ms. R. could take several measures. First, she can prevent problems by referring certain potential clients to other providers, particularly if Ms. R. has already had significant social contact with these individuals or those with whom the potential clients have personal relationships. This step would be consistent with the widely held belief that it is unethical for a practitioner to accept as a client an individual who has been a friend or close acquaintance. Ms. R. can explain to friends or social acquaintances who approach her for psychotherapy services that ethical standards in her profession discourage such arrangements and explain the rationale (the ways in which providing counseling services to a friend or acquaintance could prove to be harmful and not in the client's best interests).

Second, Ms. R. can take preventative steps at the beginning of her professional relationship with clients who are neither friends nor social acquaintances but who, Ms. R. anticipates, she might encounter in the community in various settings or at social events. As a matter of routine, early in the professional-client relationship, Ms. R. can broach the subject of how the two can handle foreseen and unforeseen encounters they might have in the community in a way that minimizes the risk of misunderstandings, inappropriate dual relationships, and hurt feelings. Ms. R. might pose several hypothetical but plausible scenarios or encounters and discuss with the client appropriate ways of handling them. For example, if Ms. R. and her client should encounter each other at a party, in order to avoid a dual relationship and complicated boundaries they might agree that they will not spend time socializing. If Ms. R. and a client find themselves in some ongoing community-based activity—for example as members of a committee sponsored by a social action group—they can agree to discuss the situation to decide whether one of them should withdraw from the activity. Third, Ms. R. can take steps to deal constructively with dual relationships that emerge after the professional-client relationship has begun. For example, Ms. R. might be surprised to learn some time after therapy has commenced that her client is part of the local lesbian community. If Ms. R. then anticipates that this could lead to a complicated dual relationship, she can bring up the subject—and reasonable ways of handling the boundary issues—in the context of a counseling session (Brown 1984; Kessler and Waehler 2005). Although these steps do not provide a simple, guaranteed solution to all challenging circumstances, the process can help minimize harm and help practitioners comply with prevailing ethical standards.

Similar complications can arise for practitioners who are active members of cultural, ethnic, or religious communities. This can occur, for example, if a Cambodian practitioner is actively involved in her community's relatively small and visible Cambodian mutual aid society, or if a therapist who is active on her synagogue's board of directors learns that one of her clients has just been appointed to the board and to the subcommittee that the therapist chairs and that typically meets in the therapist's home. These complicated possibilities are illustrated in the next case.

CASE 3.11

Dianne S. is a therapist in a medium-size city. In her thriving private practice Ms. S. specializes in the treatment of children with behavioral and emotional difficulties. Ms. S. also works extensively with adoptive families, especially in relation to clinical issues pertaining to adoptees' and adoptive parents' relationships with birth parents. Ms. S.'s clinical interests and expertise in adoption-related issues stem in part from her experiences as an adoptive parent. Ms. S. has been active in an adoptive families support group and in an advocacy group that focuses on adoption-related bills introduced in the state legislature.

Because of her clinical expertise, community groups often ask Ms. S. to speak about adoption issues, particularly the emotional issues that can arise among members of adoptive families throughout the life cycle. Members of her various audiences sometimes approach Ms. S. afterward to inquire about the possibility of arranging to see her for clinical services.

Ms. S. knows from experience that some of her clients who seek counseling for adoption-related issues may encounter her in other contexts—for example, at meetings of the adoptive parents' support group or at meetings of the legislative advocacy group in which Ms. S. is active. As a result Ms. S. has been careful to broach the possibility of such dual relationships when embarking on counseling with clients whom she anticipates she will encounter in the community. When she begins working with clients with whom she has had some kind of relatively brief contact in the community such as those who approach Ms. S. following her talks to community groups—Ms. S. speaks with them about how they will handle community-based encounters, should they occur; Ms. S. especially emphasizes this issue with clients who apparently travel in similar social and community circles as Ms. S.

Occasionally Ms. S. receives a request for counseling services from adoptive parents she has come to know well, sometimes socially, through her community-based activities. In these situations Ms. S. typically explains that it would be difficult for her to begin relating to these individuals professionally, in light of their shared social history, and why. Ms. S. then helps these individuals locate an appropriate counselor who may be helpful.

This example illustrates various steps that practitioners can take to minimize any harm that might arise from a dual relationship that develops because of a practitioner's encounters with clients in social, cultural, ethnic, or religious contexts that are meaningful emotionally to the client and practitioner. This risk-management strategy enhances the protection of clients and practitioners alike. As Zur (2007) notes, practitioners who encounter clients in public settings, or anticipate the possibility of such encounters, must consider a variety of factors:

> When encountering a client in public, it is important to take the cue from the client before choosing to ignore or address the client. Discussing incidental encounters with clients in subsequent therapy sessions can be beneficial; however, routine or brief encounters usually may not merit any lengthy discussion. The nature and importance of such discussions depends on the client's personality, presenting problem, and culture; the setting in which therapy takes place; the nature of the therapeutic relationship; the therapeutic orientation used; and the therapist's values and attitude toward such encounters.
>
> (2007:111)

Gutheil and Brodsky offer practical risk-management advice to practitioners who encounter clients in social and community-based settings:

> 1. Behave professionally while together. Do not engage in personal revelations or exchanges that would be inappropriate in the office.
> 2. Do not attempt to conduct therapy outside the office.
> 3. Document the boundary crossing as relevant data.
> 4. At the next office session, debrief the patient and open up the incident for exploration.
> 5. Make note of the boundary crossing in supervision, or obtain a consultation.
>
> (2008:138)

Human service practitioners embark on dual and multiple relationships for a variety of reasons. Some boundary problems reflect clear exploitation and manipulation to satisfy the practitioner's self-centered and prurient interests. Others reflect a practitioner's more subtle emotional and dependency needs, which produce dual relationships characterized by, for example, forming friendships with clients or former clients, interacting inappropriately with clients in the context of community-based groups or activities, engaging in excessive personal self-disclosure to clients, and sending clients affectionate written communications.

Preventing boundary problems associated with a practitioner's emotional and dependency needs requires diligent and sustained efforts by the practitioner to constantly examine her or his motives and intentions when behaving in ways that are not consistent with prevailing clinical and ethical standards. A special risk in the helping professions is that some practitioners may "need to be needed"; they make themselves too available to clients in order to meet their own emotional needs and become involved in their clients' lives in inappropriate ways. Practitioners must be able and willing to examine their actions in a constructively critical way and be open to feedback from colleagues and supervisors. To use the language of the trade, practitioners must be reflective practitioners (Schon 1983) and exceedingly skilled in their "use of self."

4

PERSONAL BENEFIT

SOME BOUNDARY AND DUAL RELATIONSHIP issues emerge because of pragmatic concerns, specifically, the possibility that the practitioner's relationship with the client could produce tangible, material benefits or favors for the practitioner beyond simple monetary payment for services rendered. Some such dual relationships arise from relatively benign motives—for example, when a client with specialized knowledge or expertise offers to help a practitioner with a personal need or challenge—and some arise from more sinister motives—for example, when a practitioner attempts to exploit a client for material gain.

This chapter explores this wide range of circumstances, focusing on issues related to bartering for professional services, entering into business and financial relationships with clients, seeking advice or services from clients, accepting favors or gifts from a client (including client bequests), and engaging in self-interested conflicts of interest (for example, paying for referrals and soliciting clients).

BARTER FOR SERVICES

Most clients (or their insurance providers) pay fees for social services, but in a relatively small number of cases a practitioner participates in a barter arrangement when a client is unable to pay for services and offers goods or services as a substitute. Bartering also occurs in some communities—particularly smaller and rural communities—that have established norms involving such nonmonetary exchange of goods and services.

On the surface barter may not seem to pose ethical problems if the parties participate willingly. In actuality, though, barter may lead to troubling ethical questions (not to mention complicated legal issues when practitioners file their tax returns).

CASE 4.1

A psychologist in private practice provided counseling services to a forty-six-year-old man who had been diagnosed with symptoms of an anxiety disorder. In general the client functioned well; he was married and actively involved in the parenting of his two teenage children. He was concerned, however, about the family's finances; the client's income was derived primarily from his work on construction sites, and construction had been slow in the local area because of a recent economic downturn. During the winter the family sometimes struggled to pay the bills, although the client occasionally earned extra income by plowing snow. With the counselor's help the client embarked on a constructive strategy to manage his anxiety symptoms.

The client's insurer authorized seven counseling sessions. The company was not willing to authorize additional sessions, despite the counselor's detailed explanation of the client's progress and wish for additional assistance. In an effort to be helpful to the client, the counselor offered to work out an arrangement by which the client would perform some badly needed repairs in the practitioner's office (putting up drywall in an unfinished area of the office, putting down ceramic tile, painting and plastering) in exchange for counseling services. The client agreed to the proposal and, after some discussion about the fair market value of the client's services, the two determined the number of counseling sessions that would be bartered for them (the fair market value for the construction services divided by the counselor's customary hourly fee).

About six weeks after the client finished his work, and while the client was still in counseling, the counselor noticed a major defect in the tile floor that the client had laid. The floor was uneven, and several tiles had cracked or were loose. According to a friend of the counselor's, who is in the construction business, the surface had not been prepared properly before the tile was laid.

The counselor, assuming that the client would willingly repair the defect, shared his concerns with the client. The client acknowledged the problem but denied that he was responsible. The client claimed that the subflooring must have had a latent defect that neither party knew about. The client agreed to try to fix the problem but said that he might not be able to do the work for several months because he had recently started work on a new construction site. The counselor grew increasingly frustrated with the client's handling of the situation. In his peer consultation group the counselor acknowledged that his feelings about the client's behavior were affecting the professional relationship.

This case illustrates what can be ethically problematic in barter arrangements. Negotiations about the fair market value of the goods or services to be exchanged and, in particular, about the handling of defects in a product or service can interfere with the professional-client in a way that is harmful to the client. In addition, the services the practitioner provides may be determined in whole or in part by the market value of the goods or services provided by the client rather than by the client's clinical needs. Especially because the client may be dependent on the practitioner, and because of the unequal power in their relationship, the client may be vulnerable to exploitation, conflicts of interest, and coercion. As Peterson notes with regard to ethical standards in psychology, "Bartering exposes the psychologist to all of the potential problems of any nonsexual dual relationship. Psychologists who barter with clients risk exploitation of the client by accepting goods and services that may be worth an undetermined amount or much more than the market value of therapy"(1996, cited in Woody 1998:174).

Practitioners are in some disagreement about the extent to which barter arrangements in the human services should be permitted (Gutheil and Brodsky 2008; Hill 1999). Some practitioners are clearly opposed to barter. Woody, for example, asserts, "Although bartering is not prohibited by ethics or law, I argue against the use of bartering for psychological services. In point of fact, bartering seems so fraught with risks for both parties that it seems illogical even to consider it as an option" (1998:176).

Other practitioners, however, argue that barter can be ethical, particularly in communities where it is an accepted practice (for example, where farmers in rural areas exchange produce for plumbing or electrician services). Zur concludes, "Successful bartering arrangements can enhance the therapeutic alliance and the probability of positive therapeutic outcome" (2007:97). Nearly two-fifths of a sample of clinical social workers (38.3 percent) stated that it is appropriate for clinicians to accept goods or services from clients instead of money; 9.5 percent reported that they had actually accepted goods or services from clients in exchange for professional services (Jayaratne, Croxton, and Mattison 1997). In a study of New York City social workers, DeJulio and Berkman (2003) found that about two-fifths of respondents (41.5 percent) believe that accepting a service or product as payment for therapy is never ethical; about one-fourth of the sample (23.8 percent) believe that accepting a service or product as payment for therapy is always ethical, ethical under most conditions, or ethical under some conditions. Only one-fifth (22.6 percent) of a sample of psychologists who are psychotherapists stated that accepting services from a client in lieu of a fee is unquestionably unethical, and about one-third (31.1 percent) reported having accepted such services (Pope, Tabachnick, and Keith-Spiegel 1995). An even smaller percentage of this group believed that accepting goods, rather than money, for payment is unquestionably unethical, and about one third (31.8 percent) reported having accepted such goods.

Professional ethics codes provide some guidance on this issue. For example, after much discussion the NASW Code of Ethics Revision Committee concluded that categorically prohibiting barter arrangements between social workers and clients would be inappropriate. Rather, the committee took the position that social workers should *avoid* bartering and that they should accept goods or services from clients as payment for professional services only in limited circumstances (Reamer 2006a):

> Social workers should avoid accepting goods or services from clients as payment for professional services. Bartering arrangements, particularly involving services, create the potential for conflicts of interest, exploitation, and inappropriate boundaries in social workers' relationships with clients. Social workers should explore and may participate in bartering only in very limited circumstances when it can be demonstrated that such arrangements are an accepted practice among professionals in the local community, considered to be essential for the provision of services, negotiated without coercion, and entered into at the client's initiative and with the client's informed consent. Social workers who accept goods or services from clients as payment for professional services assume the full burden of demonstrating that this arrangement will not be detrimental to the client or the professional relationship.
>
> (standard 1.13[b])

The American Psychological Association's *Ethical Principles of Psychologists and Code of Conduct* (2010) conveys a similar sentiment: "Barter is the acceptance of goods, services, or other nonmonetary remuneration from clients/patients in return for psychological services. Psychologists may barter only if (1) it is not clinically contraindicated, and (2) the resulting arrangement is not exploitative" (standard 6.05). Further, the American Counseling Association's *Code of Ethics* (2005) states, "Counselors may barter only if the relationship is not exploitive or harmful and does not place the counselor in an unfair advantage, if the client requests it, and if such arrangements are an accepted practice among professionals in the community. Counselors consider the cultural implications of bartering and discuss relevant concerns with clients and document such agreements in a clear written contract" (standard A.10.d).

Practitioners who are considering barter arrangements should carefully address several questions (Reamer 2006a). First, to what extent are such arrangements an accepted practice among professionals in the local community? The widespread local use of barter can strengthen a practitioner's contention that this was an appropriate practice in a particular case. Second, to what extent is barter essential for the provision of services? Is it used merely because it is the most expedient and convenient form of payment available, or is it the only reasonable way for the client to obtain needed services? As a general rule barter should be a last resort, used only when more conventional forms of payment have been ruled out and only when it is essential for the provisions of services. As Woody observes, "The psychologist often believes, at least consciously, that accepting a bartering arrangement is for the benefit of the client. As one psychologist said, 'The client desperately needed treatment but could not afford to pay for it—besides, I needed another car for my teenager'" (1998:174).

Third, is the barter arrangement negotiated without coercion? Human service professionals should not pressure clients to agree to barter. For example, a client may agree reluctantly to give a practitioner a valuable jewelry item that the client's business manufactures primarily because the practitioner has commented on how much he would like to own such an item; in this situation the client may feel pressured. Clients who agree to participate in a barter arrangement must do so freely and willingly, without any direct or indirect coercion from the practitioner. Fourth, was the barter arrangement entered into at the client's initiative and with the client's truly informed consent (Reamer 1987)? To avoid coercing clients or the appearance of impropriety, practitioners typically should not take the initiative to suggest barter as an option. Such suggestions should come from clients. Practitioners who decide to barter should explain the nature and terms of the arrangement in clear and understandable language and discuss potential risks associated with barter (for example, how the professional-client relationship could be adversely affected, particularly if the goods or services provided by the client in exchange for the professional's services prove to be defective), reasonable alternatives for payment (for example, a reduced monthly payment rather than a single payment in full), the client's right to refuse or withdraw consent, and the time frame covered by the consent.

In addition to these broad questions, practitioners should heed Woody's specific risk-management guidelines:

1. Unique financial arrangements should be minimized: that is, terms and conditions for any compensation, including the use of bartering, should be as close to established practices as possible and be consonant with the prevailing standards of the profession.

2. The rationale for any compensation decision, including the use of bartering, should be documented in the case records.

3. Discussions about any financial matters should be detailed in writing, giving equal emphasis to what is said by the practitioner and the client.

4. If bartering is used, there should be a preference for goods instead of services; this will minimize (but not eliminate) the possibility of inappropriate personal interactions. [As Zur (2007:92–93) notes, "Bartering of goods is generally more acceptable and less clinically and ethically problematic than bartering of services. . . . The reason for this is primarily that most often a fair market price or value can be established more easily and more objectively for goods than for services."]

5. The value of the goods (or services) should be verified by an objective source; this may, however, involve additional cost.

6. To guard against any semblance of undue influence, both parties should reach a written agreement for the compensation by bartering.

7. Any new, potentially relevant observations or comments about compensation by bartering should be entered into at the client's records, even though a previous agreement exists.

8. The agreement should contain a provision for how valuations were determined and how any subsequent conflicts will be resolved (e.g., a mediator); this may, however, involve additional cost (and a concern about confidentiality), which will have to be accommodated by the practitioner (i.e., the added expense should not elevate the cost to the client beyond the established fee for service).

9. If a misunderstanding or disagreement begins to develop, the matter should be dealt with by the designated conflict resolution source (e.g., a mediator), not the practitioner and client; again, recall the issues of added cost and concern for confidentiality stated in the preceding guideline.

10. If monitoring by the individualized treatment plan reveals a possible negative effect potentially attributable to the compensation arrangement, it

should be remedied or appropriate termination of the treatment relationship should occur.

(1998:177)

Woody is quick to caution, however, that even if the practitioner "adheres strictly to these guidelines, bartering still imposes a high risk of allegation of misconduct" (1998:178). Zur offers similarly wise advice:

Therapists must weigh the risks-benefits of bartering arrangements very carefully and consider other options besides bartering such as low or no fees. They must avoid situations that are likely to lead to conflict of interest and any arrangement that is likely to negatively affect their clinical judgment, their feelings toward their clients, or therapeutic effectiveness. Therapists must make sure that risks are articulated, that clients are fully informed, and that the arrangement is consensual, fully understood, spelled out in writing, and part of the treatment records. Therapists must attend to and be aware of their own needs through supervision and consultations. Keeping meticulous written records throughout treatment is very important in the event that problems and complications arise with regard to the bartering arrangement. It is just as important that therapists continually reevaluate the appropriateness of the bartering arrangement and change it, if necessary, through discussion with and, it is hoped, consent of the clients. If complications, negative feelings, or disagreements arise as a result of the bartering agreement, the therapist should discuss it with the client, seek consultations, and change it in a way that will be most helpful to the client and conducive to effective therapy.

(2007:97)

Human service professionals must recognize that even when all these conditions have been met, the practitioner assumes the full burden of demonstrating that bartering will not be detrimental to the client or the professional relationship (Gutheil and Gabbard 1993). Their principal responsibility is to protect the client; practitioners must exercise sound judgment when considering the risks associated with barter.

BUSINESS AND FINANCIAL RELATIONSHIPS

In a relatively small percentage of cases, human service professionals are accused of entering into inappropriate business and financial relationships with clients. This can occur in several ways. First, clients sometimes raise issues in counseling about their financial condition and future. Some clients are in financial distress and send out signals that they are eager for assistance. For a practitioner to respond instantaneously with the offer of a loan would be highly unusual, but practitioners who have crossed boundaries with a client for other reasons or in other ways—for example, to pursue a friendship or romantic relationship—may end up lending a client money as part of the broader dual relationship.

CASE 4.2

Sam G. was a psychiatrist who provided medication, advice, and counseling to Anna C., a woman who sought his help because of her symptoms of depression. Over a period of months the relationship between Dr. G. and Ms. C. moved gradually from a purely professional-client relationship to a sexual affair.

During their affair Ms. C. received a notice of foreclosure on her home. Because of her depression Ms. C. had missed a considerable amount of work. As a result she was fired from the insurance company where she had been employed and fell behind on her mortgage payments. Ms. C. owed her bank approximately $7,300. After Ms. C. told Dr. G. about the foreclosure, Dr. G. wrote Ms. C. a check for the amount she owed the bank.

After their intimate relationship fell apart, Ms. C. filed an ethics complaint and lawsuit against Dr. G. One piece of evidence introduced in court by Ms. C.'s attorney, in her effort to demonstrate the psychiatrist's negligent handling of boundary issues, was a photocopy of the canceled check that Dr. G. had made out to Ms. C.

In other situations a practitioner may encounter a client who is in counseling to think through a midlife career change that involves establishing a new business that requires venture capital. From this conversation may come a client's invitation for the counselor, for whom the client feels great appreciation, to invest in this new opportunity with insider information.

CASE 4.3

Diane P. was a counselor in a small group practice. One of Ms. P.'s clients was a fifty-two-year-old man, Allen F., who was coping with what he described as "your all-purpose, predictable midlife crisis." Mr. F. explained to Ms. P. that he was "just plain tired of getting up in the morning and repeating the rhythm of yesterday, and the day before, and the day before, and . . . oh, you get the idea. I really need a fresh challenge, something that would make me want to jump out of bed in the morning." During counseling sessions Mr. F. and Ms. P. spent time talking about what was holding Mr. F. back from pursuing his dream of a major change.

After several months of exploration Mr. F. reported to Ms. P. that he had finally settled on a new and exciting venture. Mr. F. was planning to work with a local consultant he had met to design and inaugurate an Internet-based business that makes books available to college students electronically at a deep discount from printed editions. Mr. F. described how excited he was and the terrific financial returns he expected from this venture. Mr. F. explained that he would need to spend several months recruiting a handful of investors who would likely enjoy an impressive return on their initial investment.

Mr. F. then paused and asked whether Ms. P. might be interested in "getting in on the ground floor of this wonderful opportunity." Ms. P., who was considering partially retiring from clinical practice, said she would like to take some time to think about the offer. In fact, Ms. P. had become quite interested recently in investing some of her money outside the traditional stock market.

Finally, on occasion practitioners who are experiencing personal financial problems have disclosed this fact (inappropriately) to clients of means, hoping—perhaps unconsciously—that the client would offer to help the practitioner out financially.

CASE 4.4

Malcolm A. was a marriage and family therapist. Dr. A. also sponsored monthly "marriage encounter" groups for local couples who were interested in spending "intensive weekends" designed to nurture and strengthen their marriages.

Sarah and John H. signed up for one of Dr. A.'s marriage encounter sessions. During the weekend Dr. A., a widower, and the couple found that they both had children attending the same college about 150 miles away. Shortly after the marriage encounter weekend, the couple called Dr. A. to ask whether they could see him "for several sessions to talk about some issues that emerged during their marriage encounter experience." They saw Dr. A. for six sessions to discuss some issues concerning their communication styles and patterns.

After the fourth session the couple called Dr. A. and asked whether he might want to travel with them when they drove to the parents' weekend at the college their respective children attended. Dr. A., who enjoyed the couple's company, agreed, and the trio spent a lovely weekend traveling to and from the college campus.

During the long drive Dr. A. told the couple how much he enjoyed his work as a marriage and family therapist. He mentioned that the only drawback was that, because of current managed care reimbursement policies, he was having considerable difficulty making ends meet, especially considering his child's college bills. To make matters worse, Dr. A. said, he was in considerable debt because of extraordinary expenses he incurred during the past year when his recently deceased wife was ill and he took a lot of time off from work. Dr. A. said that he was actually thinking of abandoning his career as a therapist, which he loves, in order to pursue more lucrative employment.

One week after the trip the affluent couple called Dr. A. to tell him that they had decided to lend him some money interest free to help him out of his financial bind and to enable him to continue the work he loves. They explained how much they admired Dr. A.'s work and that they found his expertise helpful; they wanted to do whatever they could to help him out. Dr. A. thanked them for their generous offer and said he wanted to take some time to think about it.

Professionals disagree about engaging in financial transactions with clients, although most practitioners appear to oppose the practice as a matter of principle. Pope, Tabachnick, and Keith-Spiegel (1995) report that two-fifths of psychologists in their sample (40.6 percent) believed that lending money to a client is unquestionably unethical; however, a similar proportion (38.8 percent) believed that such a practice is ethical only under rare circumstances. An overwhelming majority of psychologists (86.2 percent) believed that borrowing money from a client is unquestionably unethical; however, 11 percent stated that borrowing money from a client was permissible under rare circumstances. Virtually none of these respondents said that they had ever loaned clients money or borrowed money from them. This pattern is reflected as well in the views of the clinical social workers surveyed by Jayaratne, Croxton, and Mattison (1997)—only 4.4 percent said that lending or borrowing money from clients is appropriate; 6.7 percent acknowledged having engaged in such a practice. (To be fair, these responses do not reveal whether the professionals who reported having engaged in this practice included modest sums—say, several dollars to take public transportation home from an agency—as opposed to lending or borrowing much larger amounts of money. This distinction may be meaningful when assessing the ethics of financial transactions between practitioners and clients.)

The psychologists surveyed by Pope, Tabachnick, and Keith-Spiegel (1995) were somewhat more willing to consider entering into a business relationship with clients, although with former clients. More than one-fourth (28.9 percent) of the psychologists surveyed by Pope, Tabachnick, and Keith-Spiegel stated that going into business with a former client would be ethical under rare circumstances; about 15 percent of the group stated that such a business relationship with a former client would be ethical under many circumstances or unquestionably ethical. Approximately 13 percent of this sample reported having actually gone into business with a former client. In contrast nearly four-fifths of these psychologists (78.5 percent) stated that going into business with a current client is unethical under all circumstances; only 2 percent of the sample reported having actually gone into business with a current client.

What these various scenarios have in common is the inappropriate blurring of boundaries and the possibility of client exploitation. Introducing financial transactions into the professional-client relationship has great potential to distract both practitioners and clients from the social service agenda with which they began their work, compromise clients' interests, and introduce actual or potential conflicts of interest (where the practitioner's judgment and behavior are affected by the business and financial concerns). Such transactions can also expose practitioners to legal risk—for example, when a client files an ethics complaint against the clinician with a licensing board or sues the practitioner, alleging that the professional unduly influenced or manipulated the client for self-interested purposes. In a Massachusetts case, for example, a court affirmed a disciplinary board's decision to sanction a licensed psychiatrist for having engaged in multiple commercial transactions with a patient in a manner that "demonstrated deplorable clinical judgment and deviated from acceptable standards of care" ("Psychiatrist Censured" 1996:6).

In another case ("Therapist Marries Patient" 1996), the former patient married her psychiatrist and sued him six years after the marriage began; the plaintiff, who had been diagnosed with multiple personality disorder, alleged that the psychiatrist had exploited her condition for his personal benefit, staging public lectures where he charged admission and showcased her as a subject (the plaintiff was awarded $350,000 plus interest). In yet another case (Woody 1998:175) a psychologist invested a substantial sum of money in a client's new business. When the business was successful, the attorney for the client demanded that the psychologist accept a refund of the initial investment only (that is, no interest or gain), saying, "Your control of my client's mind was the only thing that got you into the deal." Whether such an allegation is true is almost irrelevant. A panel of peers on an ethics review committee or a jury could very well be influenced by the obvious appearance of impropriety.

Some cases involving clinicians' access to insider information shared by clients are much more complex and do not involve blatant exploitation. In these cases principled clinicians struggle with the nature of their moral duty once they learn of insider information in the confidential psychotherapeutic context. Gutheil and Brodsky share just such a case:

> A clinical psychologist who managed the funds of a large condominium association began to see a patient who, it turned out, had a responsible position in the bank where the funds were invested. During the course of therapy the patient revealed that the bank was in unsound condition and might be forced to close. The psychologist did not see this disturbing situation as an opportunity to profit from insider trading. Rather, as she put it, she felt "as if I've been told that the ground under my house isn't safe anymore." She struggled with the competing claims of her fiduciary responsibility as a psychotherapist to refrain from misusing a patient's confidential disclosures for any purpose outside of therapy. Did the former responsibility extend to acting on information which, being privileged, the psychologist might be said not even to "know" outside the therapy setting? Did the latter responsibility extend to considering specific harms the patient might suffer if his therapist withdrew funds from the bank? Would a large withdrawal cause the patient (as one of a small number of individuals possessing the "insider information") to come under suspicion as the source of the disclosure, which he had made in the expectation of safety and confidentiality? Would the withdrawal make it more likely that the bank would close, or close sooner, thereby costing the patient his job? Finally, if the psychologist's withdrawal of funds were to be traced to her therapeutic relationship with the bank manager, not only would this patient suffer a damaging loss of trust in therapeutic confidentiality, but other patients might be discouraged from speaking openly with therapists. On the other hand, if the psychologist adhered strictly to her ethical duty to her patient and did not make the withdrawal, her distress at her fellow depositors' losses might damage or destroy the very therapeutic alliance she was struggling to protect.
>
> (2008:83)

ADVICE AND SERVICES

Human service professionals sometimes provide services to clients who have expertise that might benefit the practitioners. This can happen under two sets of circumstances. The first occurs when a practitioner faces personal

problems and challenges that might be addressed by using a client's expertise. Relying on the client's position, expertise, or knowledge can lead to serious boundary crossings and violations.

CASE 4.5

Judy C. was a social worker who provided counseling to Miriam R., a nurse who
worked at a local hospital in the maternity unit. Ms. R. sought counseling to address issues related to her recent decision to separate from her husband.

Sometimes Ms. R. would begin counseling sessions by talking about work-
related stress. On several occasions she mentioned how hard it was for her to see
teenagers deliver babies yet how gratifying it was when she was able to help a teenager make an informed decision to place her baby with an adoptive couple eager to
parent.

Ms. C. and her husband had been struggling with infertility for many years.
They were eager to adopt but had several private prospective adoptions fall through
after pregnant women with whom they had developed a relationship changed their
mind about making an adoption plan for their baby. Ms. C. was thinking seriously
about asking Ms. R. whether she might be able to help her and her husband pursue the private adoption of a baby delivered at Ms. R.'s hospital.

CASE 4.6

Sandy M. worked for the state child welfare agency as a foster care and adoption
specialist. Her job included screening and licensing foster parents. In addition,
Ms. M. was responsible for supervising several children placed in foster care.

Ms. M. interviewed and ultimately approved a license for Tom and Nancy J., who
owned a large farm. For years the couple had been eager to provide foster care.

Soon after the license was approved, the state agency placed a thirteen-year-
old runaway girl, who was having serious conflict with her parents, with Tom and
Nancy J. Ms. M. was responsible for supervising the placement.

Shortly after they met, the couple and Ms. M. became good friends. Mr. and
Ms. J. invited Ms. M., a single parent who was experiencing chronic financial
and child-care problems, to join them at their church and invited her to a number of
social functions. On one occasion they provided child care for Ms. M.'s three-year-
old daughter when Ms. M. traveled out of town. In addition, they invited Ms. M. and
her daughter to move into a small cottage on their vast property; Ms. M. accepted
their offer. During this period Ms. M. was still supervising the foster placement in the
couple's home.

Three months after the runaway was placed in the home, she was examined by a doctor retained by the state child welfare agency. The doctor confirmed that the girl was pregnant. The girl then disclosed that for about six weeks she had been involved in a sexual relationship with Tom J., the foster father. A state-appointed lawyer for the girl sued the child welfare agency and the social worker, Ms. M., for negligence. A principal allegation was that Ms. M. had engaged in an inappropriate dual relationship with Mr. and Ms. J—as evidenced by her pursuing a social relationship with them, her allowing the couple to take care of her daughter while they were also functioning as foster parents for a child whose foster care Ms. M. was supervising, and her moving her residence onto their property. The plaintiff's lawyer argued that the dual relationship and boundary crossings and violations were a "proximate cause" of the injury sustained by the foster child as a result of the foster father's sexual abuse—that is, that the dual relationship impaired the social worker's professional judgment and that her failure to supervise the placement properly was a cause of the sexual abuse. The case was ultimately settled for $750,000.

The second circumstance occurs when a practitioner is eager to draw on a client's expertise, not so much to address a personal problem but to enhance the quality of the practitioner's life.

CASE 4.7

A counselor, Sanford B., provided long-term psychotherapy to a married couple, Amanda and Jose L. Ms. L. worked as an accountant, and Mr. L. owned a small wallpapering and painting company. The couple sought counseling because of conflict they were experiencing in their marriage and several challenging parenting issues. Over time the couple improved the quality of their relationship with each other and their children.

At the end of one counseling session Mr. B. asked Mr. L. for some advice about his plans to replace several rooms of wallpaper in his home with paint. Mr. L. offered to stop by Mr. B.'s home to examine the walls and offer advice. Mr. B. accepted the offer and two met at Mr. B.'s home the following evening. Mr. L. suggested several options and then offered to complete the work for a "very favorable price. You've been so helpful to our family; I'd be happy to do this for you. It's my way of saying thanks," Mr. L. said.

Mr. L. removed the wallpaper and prepared and painted the walls. Six weeks later Ms. L. told Mr. L. that she was beginning to feel uncomfortable with Mr. B. "There's something that's not right here. I'm beginning to have a bad feeling," Ms. L. said. Ms. L. then told Mr. L. that she had received several poems from Mr. B. by email and that "a couple of the poems are creepy. I'm not sure what this is all about."

Several weeks later Ms. L. filed a licensing board complaint against Mr. B. alleging a number of boundary-related violations. During the hearing it came out that both Mr. B. and Ms. L. were poetry aficionados and that Mr. B. had decided to share with Ms. L. several poems because, he testified, these poems included images and messages that he thought were quite relevant to some of Ms. L.'s struggles. Ms. L. testified that the poems confused her about the nature of her relationship with Mr. B.: "I thought he was trying to tell me that he was interested in having a relationship with me." Mr. B. denied any such intent.

The licensing board found evidence that Mr. B. mismanaged boundaries in his relationship with Mr. and Ms. L. The board cited Mr. B.'s decision to enter into a business relationship with Mr. L. that included inviting Mr. L. to visit and work in Mr. B.'s home. The board also cited Mr. B.'s use of his personal email account to send poems to a client and noted that the email message was sent late at night, suggesting to Ms. L. that this was a personal, not professional, communication. The board fined Mr. B., placed him on probation, and mandated that he complete continuing education courses on ethical and boundary issues.

Accepting advice or services from clients has the potential to create boundary confusion. Over time human service professionals may begin to feel indebted to their clients or eager for specialized treatment from them; this may cloud the practitioner's judgment and, ultimately, lead to the perception of compromised care and impropriety, actual compromised care and impropriety, conflicts of interest, exploitation, and other forms of ethical misconduct and negligence.

FAVORS AND GIFTS

Unique boundary issues sometimes emerge when clients offer gifts or special favors to human service professionals. A client's presentation of a gift to a practitioner is a particularly complex issue (Knox et al. 2003; Krassner 2004; Smolar 2002). Clearly, some clients offer practitioners gifts—often modest in value—as genuine expressions of appreciation, with no ulterior motive or hidden agenda. Examples include clients who give the practitioner a plate of home-baked cookies at holiday time, an infant's outfit when the counselor has had a baby, a special book, or a handmade coffee mug at the conclusion of treatment. Typically, these gifts represent tokens of appreciation—nothing more and nothing less. The client would likely feel wounded or insulted if the professional rejected such a gift on ethical grounds. In fact, only 5 percent of the sample of psychologists surveyed by Pope, Tabachnick, and Keith-Spiegel (1995) stated that accepting a gift worth less than five dollars is unquestionably unethical; more than half the sample (56.6 percent) said that accepting such a gift is appropriate under many circumstances or unquestionably appropriate. Moreover, only a small minority of the respondents (8.6 percent) stated that they had never accepted this kind of modest gift. Similarly, only 9.3 percent of a sample of New York City social workers stated that accepting a gift worth less than ten dollars is never ethical (DeJulio and Berkman 2003). As Zur (2007:189) says, "Most psychotherapists do not view clients' gifts of small value, such as home-baked cookies or bread, books, CDs, or a potted plant as clinically or ethically problematic."

In contrast, however, are more complicated situations, involving clients who offer practitioners gifts of considerable value or gifts that represent a more complex practitioner-client relationship (sometimes from the client's view, sometimes from the practitioner's, and sometimes from both). According to Zur :

> The meaning and appropriateness of clients' gifts have been central to discussion of gifts. Most common, small, well-timed gifts have simply been viewed as a normal and healthy expression of gratitude. However, other gifts by clients have been fueled by motivations other than, or in addition to, gratitude. These may include attempts to express negative feelings, manipulate, or sexually seduce the therapists and similar behaviors. An important concern regarding gifts is whether a client's gift-giving is an effort to "buy" love. Many clients seek therapy because they do not feel appreciated, loved, or cared for. Others feel generally undeserving and have low self-esteem. One way that people who feel unworthy and not lovable can try to increase the chance of people, including therapists, liking them is through gift-giving. These clients often repeat such patterns with their lovers, friends, teachers, supervisors, employers, and other significant people in their lives.
>
> (2007:190)

Consider the cases 4.8 to 4.10.

CASE 4.8

Aaron C. was a case manager in a residential program that provides services to people with substance abuse problems. One of his clients, Marie Y., was being treated for her cocaine addiction. Ms. Y and Mr. C. met weekly to address a variety of pertinent issues, including her sexual abuse history. Mr. C. helped Ms. Y.

understand more clearly how her early-life trauma contributed to her initial drug abuse.

Toward the end of their work together, Ms. Y. was having fantasies of dating Mr. C.; she had been attracted to him for months. During their last session Ms. Y. gave Mr. C. an expensive watch engraved with his name, told him how much he meant to her, and said she hoped that they would be able to spend some time together once she returned to the "free world" and was no longer his client.

CASE 4.9

Melinda G., a social worker in a high school, was the internship supervisor for Alexandra P., an MSW student from a nearby school of social work. They developed a rich working relationship. According to Ms. P., "Melinda is a fabulous mentor. I can't believe how much I'm learning from her."

Several months after they began working together, Ms. G. was diagnosed with kidney failure. She was in desperate need of a kidney transplant. Ms. G. had difficulty finding a satisfactory donor match based on widely accepted blood type, tissue, and cross-matching criteria. Ms. G. explained her dilemma to Ms. P. because of its possible implications for their future work together as mentor and student.

Unbeknown to Ms. G., Ms. P. went to the nearest kidney transplant center to be evaluated as a possible donor. In fact, Ms. P. was a suitable match. She shared this remarkable news with Ms. G. and told her how happy it made her that she would be able to donate a kidney to her beloved mentor. Ms. G. was overwhelmed by Ms. P.'s generosity but uncertain about how to manage the boundary issues. Ms. G. consulted with colleagues to address the potential conflict of interest. Together they agreed that Ms. G. could accept Ms. P.'s kidney; however, because of the dual relationship Ms. G. would not be able to continue supervising Ms. P.'s internship. Ms. G. arranged for a qualified colleague to take over as Ms. P.'s supervisor; Ms. G. and Ms. P. talked at length about the boundary issues and the best way to address them.

These two cases raise much different boundary issues. In the case involving Dr. C. and Ms. Y. (case 4.8) the gift giving appeared to have an ulterior motive involving a hoped-for intimate relationship; her having had the watch engraved added a complication beyond those ordinarily involved in receiving an expensive gift from a client. In the second case involving the field instructor and student (case 4.9), the student had no ulterior motive; the supervisor and student simply needed to manage the boundaries carefully to ensure there was no conflict of interest going forward.

Clients of means—and even clients with modest assets—will sometimes feel moved to give a practitioner a gift as a gesture of pure, unadulterated generosity.

CASE 4.10

Don S. was a case manager in a day program for senior citizens. One of his clients, Mildred N., was a spry eighty-seven-year-old who had attended the program for six years. Ms. N. often told her children how special and helpful Mr. S. was to her. Mr. S. and Ms. N. sometimes talked about their shared love of art; Ms. N. was known locally for her large and valuable art collection.

Ms. N.'s health deteriorated badly, and it became clear to her and her two adult children that she would need a nursing home placement. Mr. S. helped Ms. N.'s children locate and assess the suitability of several local facilities. He went above and beyond the call of duty to spend time with Ms. N. and her children as they made their decision.

Several days after Ms. N. entered a nursing home, Mr. S. received a large special-delivery package. He was surprised to find that the N. family had sent him a small sculpture by an internationally famous artist as a token of their heartfelt appreciation. The art had been in Ms. N.'s personal collection. Mr. S. had the sculpture appraised and estimated that the market value was about $9,000.

Most practitioners agree that in many instances—when there is no evidence of ulterior motives that might lead to egregious boundary violations—human service professionals may keep gifts of modest value. Some social service agencies permit staff to do so, although they may stipulate that staff members must thank the clients on behalf of the agency, that is, make it clear that the gift will be shared with the agency's staff at large. This procedure can defuse the interpersonal dynamic and potential boundary confusion between the client and practitioner; depersonalizing the transaction may help staff members to avoid complicated boundary issues.

In contrast the psychologists surveyed by Pope, Tabachnick, and Keith-Spiegel (1995) were generally inclined to believe that accepting expensive gifts was unethical. About one-third of the group (34.2 percent) stated that accepting a client's gift worth at least fifty dollars was unquestionably unethical, and a similar portion (36.2 percent) stated that doing so was ethical only under rare circumstances. Only about 12 percent of the sample stated that accepting a gift of this sort was ethical under many circumstances or unquestionably ethical; nearly three-fourths of the sample (72.1 percent) stated that they had never accepted this kind of gift. Similarly, only a small fraction (2.3 percent) of the clinical social workers surveyed by Jayaratne, Croxton, and Mattison (1997) stated that accepting expensive gifts from clients was appropriate, and few (1.9 percent) reported having ever accepted such gifts. In their survey of New York City social workers DeJulio and Berkman (2003) found that only 2.2 percent of the sample believed that accepting a gift worth more than fifty dollars was always ethical or ethical under most conditions.

Practitioners face unique challenges when they receive gifts that appear to have no ulterior motive but could introduce complex boundary issues. Sometimes clients may not be consciously aware of the emotional meaning and significance—and the mixed messages and complications—that may be attached to a gift. Practitioners sometimes face double-edged swords in these situations: a decision to reject a gift can have significant clinical repercussions—because the client may feel hurt, wounded, humiliated, or guilty—and a decision to accept a gift may trigger boundary issues that complicate and reverberate throughout the clinical relationship. In such circumstances practitioners are wise to obtain sound consultation and supervision to think through how best to handle the client's gesture, including assessing the apparent (and perhaps not so apparent) meaning behind the gift, ethical and clinical implications, potential responses and related consequences, and any risk-management issues (related to potential ethics complaints and lawsuits). It is critically important to document the client's gift and any related consultation and supervision to protect both the client and clinician. As Zur (2007:198) observes, "As with any risk management concern, therapists should consider documentation of any gifts as a way to protect themselves from misinterpretation of conduct." Gutheil and Brodsky (2008) encourage practitioners to carefully consider several key criteria when deciding whether to accept a gift from a client:

- Monetary value of the gift: "Inexpensive gifts are more likely than expensive gifts to be mere expressions of appreciation or personal consideration, although their potential symbolic meanings must still be considered" (91).
- Handmade versus purchased gifts: "If a patient makes you a ceramic bowl while in the hospital as an expression of appreciation, it may be best to accept the gift while exploring its meaning. A patient may be all the more

disturbed by the rejection of his or her own handiwork. At the same time, the clinical significance of such a gift is that it was made with the therapist in mind and therefore tends to be loaded with personal meanings and active fantasies—including perhaps the assumption that the gift would be accepted, coupled with fear that it would not be. Thus, a handmade gift is all the more to be appreciated and all the more to be understood" (91).

■ Characteristics of the client: "Clearly the clinical and ethical calculus with respect to giving or receiving gifts is different when the patient is a child. Likewise, since gifts have different meanings in different cultures, the patient's cultural background is another contextual factor to be evaluated. The nature of the patient's disorder is also a factor" (91–92).

■ Type of therapy: "Where the contract between clinician and patient does not limit their interaction to words, as may be the case with a social worker or case manager, a gift is not necessarily a breach of contract" (92).

■ Appropriateness of the type of gift: "A homemade Christmas fruitcake is generally regarded as innocuous. Likewise, books or articles relevant to the therapy can be accepted when offered in a spirit of mutual investigation or simply goodwill. . . . At the other extreme, sexually suggestive gifts are obviously inappropriate." (92–93). (As in case 4.8, a practitioner would need to explore the clinical significance of a client's decision to give the clinician an expensive engraved watch. What does the gift signify? Did the client have the watch engraved to prevent the clinician from returning it?)

■ Stage of therapy: "Early in therapy, considerations of trust and alliance building may argue for accepting a gift, at least provisionally, in marginal cases. On the other hand, early in therapy it is also critical to establish and maintain a therapeutic frame strong enough to withstand the patient's wishes, fantasies, or bribes. . . . Gifts at termination also raise special issues" (93).

■ Red-flag contexts: "Anything out of the ordinary about the situation in which a patient offers a gift should be documented and explored, and usually will rule out accepting the gift. . . . Any circumstances indicating an expectation of a quid pro quo also change the nature of the gift" (93).

Similar issues can arise when clients offer meals to practitioners who provide in-home services. Typical examples include practitioners employed by home health-care agencies and programs that provide in-home services for high-risk families (for example, family preservation programs that provide intensive in-home services for families following allegations of child abuse or neglect). It is not unusual in these situations for practitioners to visit a home at mealtime and to be invited to join the family at the table. In many cultures, however, sharing a meal—breaking bread—is a meaningful social, and sometimes intimate, event. Some family members may view the sharing of a meal as a signal that their relationship with the practitioner has moved to a new plane, one that entails social as well as professional purposes. For example, a family that has resisted the practitioner's efforts to provide services may communicate willingness to finally accept services by inviting the practitioner to join them at a meal.

The dynamics can be especially complicated when the family belongs to a cultural or ethnic group that attaches great meaning and symbolic significance to such invitations; that is, norms related to boundaries differ among cultural and ethnic groups. Members of some cultural and ethnic groups may be hesitant to trust a practitioner who is unwilling to break bread with the family; the practitioner's willingness to eat with family members may be an important signal that the practitioner accepts them. A practitioner who (presumably politely and diplomatically) rejects the family's meal invitation risks insulting the family, hurting its members' feelings, and so on. According to Zur (2007:210), "Refusing an offer to share food with the family during a home visit is likely to be perceived as insulting or, at least, discourteous, and is very likely to negatively affect the therapeutic alliance, trust, and clinical efficacy." Here too discussion with colleagues and staff in advance and in anticipation of such invitations can provide critically important preventative maintenance. Role playing such scenarios as part of agency in-service training can be valuable. In one family preservation program, for example, staff members concluded that in some instances they could finesse the situation by saying they were not particularly hungry but would be happy to have a cup of tea or coffee, a gesture that tends to be far less culturally significant but that may help establish and preserve comfortable relationships with clients. With families that are more insistent, practitioners may need to explain that their employer or their profession's ethical standards prohibit this kind of activity.

In some contexts sharing a meal with a client may be entirely acceptable. This would occur in programs where staff are expected, as part of their intervention protocol, to provide services to people outside a formal office setting, perhaps in a residential facility, home, or restaurant (for example, when working with clients on the development of independent-living skills). In these instances widely accepted standards and practices in the human services would permit sharing meals with clients.

CASE 4.11

Connie T. was an outreach worker in a program in a southern state that provided social services to homeless youths. Because of its warm climate, the area attracts many teenagers who have run away from home. Many of these youths get involved in drug-related activity and prostitution once they arrive in the area.

Ms. T. spent much of her time walking the streets where these teenagers tend to congregate in an effort to develop relationships with them. In fact, Ms. T was provided with money so she could offer meals to these youths in local fast-food restaurants. Ms. T. and her staff understood that they were much more likely to reach and connect with these youths by sitting down with them in a fast-food restaurant than by inviting youths to come to the agency's offices for more formal meetings. That is, having meals with these youths was part of the program design.

Clearly, some practitioners believe that under some circumstances it is acceptable to go out to eat with a client. For example, DeJulio and Berkman (2003) found that 30.1 percent of their sample of New York City social workers stated that going out to eat with a client is ethical under some circumstances.

CASE 4.12

Wayne D. was a psychologist at a community mental health center. He specialized in the treatment of anxiety disorders. One of his clients was Ms. L., forty-seven, who had been diagnosed with agoraphobia. Ms. L. lived with a sister and rarely left her home. Her symptoms had become more severe after the sisters' parents died in an automobile accident.

Ms. L. was being treated with a combination of psychotropic medication, prescribed by the mental health center's psychiatrist, and psychotherapy. One technique Mr. D. was using with Ms. L. involved systematic desensitization, where over a period of time Mr. D. helped Ms. L. gradually leave the house—first by opening the front door, then by moving onto the sidewalk, then out to the street, then into the car, and so on—working closely with Ms. L. at each step to help her manage her anxiety symptoms. Ms. L. had made considerable progress. As part of the treatment Ms. L. and Mr. D. agreed that they would try to visit a nearby restaurant together for lunch.

Sometimes clients offer practitioners intangible favors, as opposed to intangible gifts. Examples include an invitation for the practitioner to attend the client's holiday party or to contact the client's relative who specializes in repairing the kind of automobile transmission trouble that the practitioner mentioned when he or she was late for a scheduled appointment. The clinical and ethical issues are similar, with one significant exception: tangible gifts that the practitioner and her or his colleagues are inclined to accept—because of the negative clinical ramifications their refusal might entail—can be accepted by the agency instead, to minimize boundary complications between the client and the individual practitioner. Typically, this is not possible with offers that involve intangible benefits.

CASE 4.13

Sally N. was a counselor with an early intervention program that provides services for children younger than three who show some signs of failure to thrive or other developmental delays. Ms. N.'s job required her to visit clients' homes, consult with them about their parenting techniques, provide crisis intervention, and offer other supportive services.

Ms. N. was scheduled to visit a client, Amy C., at 2:00 p.m. However, on her way to Ms. C.'s home, Ms. N.'s car would not shift gears. Ms. N. used her cell phone to call for roadside assistance. She also called Ms. C., told her about her car problems, and said she would get to her home as soon as possible.

It turned out that Ms. N. had major transmission trouble. Ms. N. had her car towed to the garage and took a taxi to Ms. C.'s home, arriving about an hour late. When she arrived, Ms. C. told Ms. N. that her sister owns an automotive repair shop that specializes in transmissions. Ms. C. then told Ms. N. that she had already asked her sister whether she could help Ms. N. and give her a "special rate" since Ms. N. had been so helpful to Ms. C. Ms. C. was very excited that she was able to arrange this kind of assistance for her counselor.

CASE 4.14

Paul G. was a caseworker in a vocational training program that provides services to people who have major disabilities. Mr. G. coordinates and facilitates a variety of social services—such as counseling, food and housing subsidies, and health care—for the program's clients.

One of Mr. G.'s clients was Daniel M., a forty-two-year-old who was recovering from a major stroke. Mr. G. had spent many hours helping Mr. M.'s parents identify and coordinate benefits for their son. The parents deeply appreciated Mr. G.'s efforts. As a token of their appreciation, they offered Mr. G. and his family use of a guest apartment at their oceanfront vacation home during the upcoming Fourth of July weekend.

As in any case in which a client offers a practitioner a gift or favor, human service professionals must carefully examine the potential for significant boundary problems, in the form of either boundary violations or boundary crossings. Most practitioners are likely to agree that if a client offers to get her relative to provide the practitioner with a "special deal" on his automobile repair, the practitioner should thank the client and explain that he or she has a regular mechanic who will address the problem (assuming that is true). If the client persists, the practitioner might consider explaining why his or her profession discourages practitioners from doing business with clients' relatives or close acquaintances. As with barter arrangements, practitioners who conduct business transactions with clients' relatives or close acquaintances open the door for boundary problems, particularly if any dispute arises in regard to the goods or services involved in the transaction. Most clients will accept these responses and explanations.

Similarly, practitioners expose themselves to considerable risk if they accept a client's invitation to attend a social event or to use a client's personal property for vacation or other social purposes. Although in rare instances a practitioner's attendance at a social event (an issue I will address more fully in chapter 5) may offer therapeutic benefits for the client, in general practitioners are likely to introduce significant boundary complications if they accept. A client can easily misconstrue the practitioner's attendance. Most psychologists surveyed on the issue agreed that generally it is a mistake to accept a client's invitation to a party, although professionals disagree about where to draw the line. Pope, Tabachnick, and Keith-Spiegel (1995) found that about one-fourth of their sample (25.7 percent) believed that it is never appropriate to accept such an invitation. Slightly less than half (46.1 percent) believed that it is ethical to accept a client's invitation to a party only under rare circumstances. Three-fifths of the sample (59.6 percent) said that they have never accepted such an invitation. In contrast DeJulio and Beckman (2003) found that 9.3 percent of their sample of New York City social workers believed that accepting an invitation to a special occasion is never ethical; about one-third (34.0 percent) believed that accepting an invitation is ethical under rare circumstances, and nearly half (45.2 percent) believed that accepting an invitation is ethical under some conditions.

Whenever a practitioner seriously considers accepting a gift or favor from a client—of whatever value or tangibility—the practitioner should consult with thoughtful colleagues and supervisors, when feasible, and critically examine the clinical and ethical implications (including current ethical standards and agency policy), the client's and practitioner's motives, any alternatives, and so on. The practitioner should carefully document in the case record the client's offers, the process the practitioner used to make the decision (for example, relevant consultation), the nature of the decision, and the rationale. This documentation can prove to be enormously helpful if the client or some other party raises questions about the appropriateness of the practitioner's decision.

CONFLICTS OF INTEREST: SELF-SERVING MOTIVES

Clearly, one principal risk associated with dual and multiple relationships concerns conflicts of interest from which practitioners may benefit. Conflicts of interest occur when a professional's services to or relationship with a client (or former client, or other pertinent party) are compromised, or might be compromised, because of decisions or actions in relation to another client, a colleague, the professional, or some other third party. Using more formal language, a conflict of interest involves "a situation in which regard for one duty leads to disregard of another . . . or might reasonably be expected to do so" (Gifis 1991:88).

All the codes of ethics in the human service professions prohibit conflicts of interest. Typical is the standard in the NASW (2008) code:

> Social workers should be alert to and avoid conflicts of interest that interfere with the exercise of professional discretion and impartial judgment. Social workers should inform clients when a real or potential conflict of interest arises and take reasonable steps to resolve the issue in a manner that makes the clients' interests primary and protects clients' interests to the greatest extent possible. In some cases, protecting clients' interests may require termination of the professional relationship with proper referral of the client.
>
> (standard 1.06[a])

According to the ethics code of the American Psychological Association (2010), "Psychologists refrain from taking on a professional role when personal, scientific, professional, legal, financial, or other interests or relationships could reasonably be expected to (1) impair their objectivity, competence, or effectiveness in performing their functions as psychologists or (2) expose the person or organization with whom the professional relationship exists to harm or exploitation" (standard 3.06).

Conflicts of interest in the human services can take several forms. They may occur in the context of practitioners' relationships with clients or in their roles as community advocates, supervisors, consultants, colleagues, administrators, policy officials, educators, researchers, or program evaluators. Practitioners must be careful to avoid conflicts of interest that, because of their decisions or actions involving other clients, colleagues, other third parties, or themselves, might harm clients or other parties with whom the practitioners have a professional or personal relationship. Examples—illustrated in the cases that follow—include practitioners who are named in a client's will, have a financial interest in other service providers to which they refer clients, pay referral fees to colleagues, accept a referral fee, sell goods to clients, and solicit clients.

CASE 4.15

A social worker employed in a hospice program, Allan S., counseled an elderly man, Sam V., who had been diagnosed with liver cancer. Mr. V., a widower, looked forward to Mr. S.'s weekly visits and over time grew close to him. Mr. V. told Mr. S. on several occasions how important their conversations were, especially because so few of Mr. V.'s friends and relatives felt comfortable talking about death and dying.

Shortly after Mr. V. died, Mr. S. received a notice from Mr. V.'s lawyer. The notice said that Mr. V. had named Mr. S. in his will, specifying that Mr. S. should receive $50,000 from Mr. V.'s estate.

CASE 4.16

A case manager employed by a state department of corrections, Alma L., administered the prison system's substance abuse treatment program. Ms. L. conducted treatment groups for inmates who were serving sentences for drug-related offenses, such as sale or possession of narcotics or other illegal drugs. When inmates were eligible for parole, Ms. L. made recommendations to the parole board concerning each inmate's readiness for release and, for those deemed ready, suggestions for follow-up substance abuse treatment services that the board should mandate as a condition of release.

In addition to her duties with the state department of corrections, Ms. L. was a part-time employee of a community-based substance abuse treatment program; Ms. L. usually worked weekends in this part-time position. In her job with the department of corrections, she recommended to the state parole board that parolees be referred to the community-based treatment program with which she was affiliated; however, Ms. L. did not disclose her own affiliation with, and financial stake in, the program.

CASE 4.17

Sandra T. was a psychologist in private practice. Her practice included five other clinicians who worked on a fee-for-service basis. One of the clinicians was Molly B., who had been affiliated with Dr. T. for nearly six years.

Ms. B. decided to leave Dr. T.'s group practice to begin her own solo practice. When she told Dr. T. about her plans, Dr. T. reminded Ms. B. that when they began working together, Ms. B. had signed a noncompete agreement. Dr. T. told Ms. B. that she wished her well but that Ms. B. would not be able to take any of her existing clients with her to the new practice. Ms. B. told Dr. T. that she thought it was unethical for Dr. T. to stand in the way of any client who wished to continue working with Ms. B. in her new practice. Dr. T. threatened to sue Ms. B. if Ms. B. did not honor the noncompete agreement.

CASE 4.18

Pam K. was a counselor in a group practice. After obtaining her master's degree and working in the field for several years, Ms. K. became interested in the use of herbal remedies to alleviate stress and promote mental health. She eventually became affiliated with a national herb distributor; in her spare time Ms. K. recruited and supervised local sales representatives. Ms. K. provided her clients with brochures and literature on various herbal products and sold them to clients who wished to purchase them. Ms. K. earned commissions on the products she sold to clients.

These cases broach a diverse set of issues pertaining to actual or potential conflicts of interest. As with most ethical issues, no single standard provides clear-cut guidance. In some instances conflicts of interest are so blatant that they leave little or no room for discussion—for example, when practitioners refer clients to, or accept referrals from, colleagues based on financial incentives; encourage clients to purchase profitable products from them; or extend treatment beyond what is clinically necessary in order to enhance their income from clients or third-party payers. Also, it would be unethical for a clinician who owns a group private practice to enforce a noncompete agreement that prohibits fee-for-service clinicians' clients from continuing to work with them in a new practice setting. The owner of the group private practice would be violating clients' right to seek services wherever they wish. These clients may not want to start with a new clinician; assuming their current clinician did not try to convince them to follow the clinician to a new practice setting and only helped the client think through the possible benefits and risks of all her options (for example, finding another clinician in the group practice, following the current clinician to her new office, or seeking services in some other setting), no one should constrain clients' choices.

The matter of the clinician who is named in a client's will poses a unique challenge that has attracted explicit discussion in the professional literature. Accepting a client's bequest, spelled out in the client's will, is usually problematic because of the possible appearance of impropriety and undue influence. Even though the clinician may not have known about the bequest, it is difficult to prove that. Out of an abundance of caution, most professionals agree that the clinician would be obligated to donate the proceeds to a charity or philanthropic organization. Zur has commented on this phenomenon:

> If a client expresses a wish to include the therapist in her or his will or trust, as a first step the therapist should reiterate that the clinical fee is all the compensation expected. Then, discussions should take place in which the meaning of this gift to the client is clarified and articulated. One solution for a client who insists on including his or her therapist in a will or trust is to have the client bequeath the money to a charity that is supported by both client and therapist.
>
> When a therapist realizes after the fact that she or he was bequeathed money or assets by a client who died, it is necessary to seek consultation and navigate with caution around the concerns of confidentiality. A legal concern is that once the client is dead, it is too easy for relatives to claim

undue influence. At that point, the therapist may, unfortunately, need to respond to civil malpractice lawsuits or to licensing board complaints initiated by the heirs. Without the client to set the record straight, the therapist is in an extremely vulnerable position. In a case in which the therapist's identity was not known to the relatives, confidentiality issues become highly relevant, which complicates the matter further and increases the therapist's vulnerability significantly. Another option for a therapist who is surprised by the gift is, if appropriate, to consider relinquishing or refusing the gift.

(2007:200)

Other instances leave room for legitimate debate. For example, should practitioners employed in an agency be permitted to establish a part-time private practice within the same city or county that serves clients with similar clinical challenges? Should practitioners be permitted to refer clients to a relative whose specialized expertise is likely to benefit the client? To what extent is it appropriate for practitioners to rely on clients for research that is not likely to benefit the clients themselves or invite clients to participate in presentations at professional conferences that address the clients' clinical issues? Should staffers at a family services agency be permitted to adopt foster children served by the agency who are not in the staffers' caseloads? Might clinicians encounter boundary crossings and a potential conflict of interest if they accept referrals from current clients?

Several professional codes of ethics comment on phenomena germane to conflicts of interest. For example, with regard to the issue of referrals and fees, the ethics code of the American Psychological Association (2010) states, "When psychologists pay, receive payment from, or divide fees with another professional, other than in an employer-employee relationship, the payment to each is based on the services provided (clinical, consultative, administrative, or other) and is not based on the referral itself" (standard 6.07). Similarly, the NASW (2008) ethics code states that "social workers are prohibited from giving or receiving payment for a referral when no professional service is provided by the referring social worker" (standard 2.06[c]). The code of the American Association for Marriage and Family Therapy (2001) states, "Marriage and family therapists do not offer or accept kickbacks, rebates, bonuses, or other remuneration for referrals; fee-for-service arrangements are not prohibited" (standard 7.1).

Professional codes also comment on conflict-of-interest issues involving solicitation of clients. The American Psychological Association (2010) code states, "Psychologists do not engage, directly or through agents, in uninvited in-person solicitation of business from actual or potential therapy clients/ patients or other persons who because of their particular circumstances are vulnerable to undue influence. However, this prohibition does not preclude (1) attempting to implement appropriate collateral contacts for the purpose of benefiting an already engaged therapy client/patient or (2) providing disaster or community outreach services" (standard 5.06). The American Counseling Association (2005) states, "Counselors do not use their places of employment or institutional affiliation to recruit or gain clients, supervisees, or consultees for their private practices" (standard C.3.d). The NASW ethics code (2008) says, "Social workers should not engage in uninvited solicitation of potential clients who, because of their circumstances, are vulnerable to undue influence, manipulation, or coercion" (standard 4.07[a]).

Another conflict-of-interest issue on which several ethics codes comment concerns the use of confidential client information for practitioners' own purposes (such as for research, public presentations, and media interviews). According to the code of the American Psychological Association (2010), "Psychologists do not disclose in their writings, lectures, or other public media, confidential, personally identifiable information concerning their clients/patients, students, research participants, organizational clients, or other recipients of their services that they obtained during the course of their work, unless (1) they take reasonable steps to disguise the person or organization, (2) the person or organization has consented in writing, or (3) there is legal authorization for doing so" (standard 4.07).

The American Counseling Association's code (2005) states, "Identification of clients, students, or supervisees in a presentation or publication is permissible only when they have reviewed the material and agreed to its presentation or publication" (standard B.7.e). Similarly, the NASW code (2008) states, "Social workers should not disclose identifying information when discussing clients for teaching or training purposes unless the client has consented to disclosure of confidential information" (standard 1.07[p]). It adds, "Social workers who report evaluation and research results should protect participants' confidentiality by omitting identifying information unless proper consent has been obtained authorizing disclosure" (standard 5.02[m]).

Clearly, the spirit of the ethical standards concerning conflicts of interest is similar in the codes of the various human service professions, as are practitioners' opinions about how to handle various conflicts of interest. For example, only about 15 percent of the psychologists surveyed by Pope, Tabachnick, and Keith-Spiegel (1995) believed that it is ethical to ask favors (for example, a ride home) from clients or give gifts to those who refer clients; about 18 percent believed it is ethical to accept a client's invitation to a party, less than 1 percent believed that it is ethical to get paid to refer clients to someone, about 5 percent believed that it is ethical to sell goods to clients, and only about 3 percent believed that it is ethical to directly solicit a person to be a client. In their survey of New York City social workers, DeJulio and Berkman (2003) found that only 1.3 percent of respondents believed that it is always ethical to sell a product to a client or ethical to do so under most conditions, only 2.6 percent believed that is always ethical to provide therapy to an employee or ethical to do so under most conditions, only 3.2 percent believed that it is always ethical to employ a client or ethical to do so under most conditions, and only 1 percent believed that it is always ethical to invite a client to a personal or social event or ethical to do so under most conditions.

In summary, when potential conflicts of interest arise, professionals have an obligation to be alert to and avoid actual or potential conflicts of interest that might interfere with the exercise of their professional judgment. Practitioners should resolve the conflict in a manner that makes the client's (or potential client's) interests primary and protects the client's interests to the greatest extent possible.

5

ALTRUISM

A NUMBER OF BOUNDARY issues arise because of practitioners' genuinely altruistic instincts and gestures. The vast majority of human service professionals are caring, dedicated, and honorable people who would never knowingly take advantage of clients. Ironically, practitioners who are remarkably generous and giving may unwittingly foster dual and multiple relationships that are counterproductive and harmful to the parties involved.

Boundary issues related to altruism fall into several conceptual categories: giving gifts to clients; meetings clients in social or community settings; offering clients and other parties favors; accommodating clients' unique needs and circumstances; and disclosing personal information to clients.

GIVING GIFTS TO CLIENTS

At first blush it may appear that human service professionals should not give clients gifts under any circumstances, even with the most altruistic of motives. After all, clients may easily misinterpret even a modest gift as a message that they are in some special, perhaps exalted, relationship with the practitioner that entails some nonprofessional and personal dimension. Gifts often imply friendship and, at times, intimacy. Gifts can lead to confusion about the nature of the client-professional relationship. As I noted earlier, in some rare instances a practitioner may give a client a gift as a way to communicate the practitioner's interest in developing an intimate relationship. In other instances gifts from a practitioner to a client may reflect the practitioner's inappropriate emotional dependency on the client. Survey data clearly show that few mental health professionals (in this case psychologists) believe that giving clients valuable gifts is ethical or have engaged in this practice (Pope, Tabachnick, and Keith-Spiegel 1995).

A practitioner may, however, encounter occasional circumstances where a modest gift seems appropriate, perhaps as a humane gesture in response to a client's illness or a major life-altering event that was addressed in treatment (Smolar 2003). In such situations, especially when the client may be relatively alone in the world, a modest get-well card or socially appropriate gift may seem innocuous. Gutheil and Gabbard offer the following illustration and comment:

> A patient in long-term therapy had struggled for years with apparent infertility and eventually, with great difficulty, arranged for adoption of a child. Two years later she unexpectedly conceived and finally gave birth. Her therapist, appreciating the power and meaning of this event, sent congratulatory flowers to the hospital.
>
> In this case, the therapist followed social convention in a way that—though technically a boundary crossing—represented a response appropriate to the real relationship. Offering a tissue to a crying patient and expressing condolences to a bereaved one are similar examples of appropriate responses outside the classic boundaries of the therapeutic relationship.
>
> (1993:193)

Recently, I encountered my own "tear-related" boundary issue. As I mentioned earlier, for many years I have served on my state's parole board. My duties include presiding at hearings in various state prisons where inmates and their attorneys petition the board for the inmates' release. I review each inmate's record (including the seriousness of the offense, the inmate's insight and remorse, prison treatment and disciplinary record, employment and housing plans, social supports, mental health and substance abuse treatment needs, and so on) and decide whether to release the inmate and under what conditions (such as residential treatment for substance abuse, sex offender treatment, or electronic monitoring).

I conducted a hearing for a thirty-four-year-old female inmate who was serving a six-year sentence for narcotics distribution. I knew from the inmate's prison record that she had been sexually molested as a child and eventually began self-medicating by abusing alcohol, cocaine, and heroin. The inmate began selling drugs in order to support her own addiction; one of her customers, who had been arrested on drug possession charges, disclosed the name of his dealer, who was the inmate.

Two days before the inmate's parole hearing, she was disciplined for possession of contraband; she had horded some of her prescription medication, which is a violation of prison regulations. As a result the inmate was placed in a segregation cell for thirty days and required to wear an orange prison uniform, rather than the customary green uniform worn by female inmates who are in "general population." Consistent with prison rules and regulations pertaining to inmates housed in the segregation unit, the inmate was handcuffed behind her back when she was escorted to the parole board hearing room. During the hearing I asked the inmate several questions about the connection between her horrific trauma history and her substance abuse. The inmate acknowledged the connection and began to cry copiously. Because she was handcuffed behind her back, the inmate was not able to wipe her tears. She tried desperately and in vain to touch her cheeks to her shoulder in order to wipe her tears with the blouse of her inmate uniform; she simply could not make physical contact. I felt acutely uncomfortable watching the inmate struggle to control her tears. In the moment I considered wiping her tears with tissues but was keenly aware of the boundary issue; I was a parole board official who was in a position of authority and about to decide her fate. I was aware that the inmate might feel uncomfortable having someone in my position touch her physically under these circumstances, especially considering her trauma history, which involved inappropriate physical touch. The unusual circumstances did not permit me to consult with a colleague or summon another prison staffer; I had to decide in the moment how to handle the awkward predicament. I was not comfortable ignoring the inmate's plight. Because of my awareness of the boundary issue and the inmate's trauma history, I made a spontaneous decision to acknowledge the inmate's tears and ask her whether she wanted me to wipe the tears. My thinking was that this gesture would allow the inmate to consent to the boundary crossing and give her some control over a difficult situation. The inmate smiled at my offer and gave me permission to wipe her tears. The hearing lasted about a half hour; every few minutes I wiped her tears. At the end of the hearing she thanked me for being considerate.

This scenario illustrates the sometimes complicated nature of boundary issues that involve giving gifts and favors, some of which are not tangible. Human service professionals have no rule book to guide them in these circumstances. Rather, the unique circumstances require thoughtful reflection about the nature of boundary-related challenges and application of ethical principles related to boundaries, dual relationships, conflicts of interest, informed consent, confidentiality, privacy, and so on. In the end, of course, reasonable minds may differ on the best way to handle these situations.

Even though many altruistic gestures in the form of a modest gift or favor are completely benign on the surface, practitioners should always consider potential ramifications, particularly with respect to the possibility that the client will misinterpret their meaning. The next case, presented by Gutheil and Brodsky, illustrates this phenomenon:

> A young woman who had had great difficulty with relationships with men was seeing a male therapist for depression. Early in the therapy she gave the therapist a pair of socks for Christmas. The therapist accepted the socks (but did not wear them) to help the patient engage with treatment at that early stage—a reasonable rationale if properly documented. Subsequently the patient asked the therapist to give her a pair of his socks. The therapist quite properly declined to do so. But the request, in retrospect, should have prompted further exploration of her reasons for giving him socks.
>
> A few months later, in an effort to give her life more structure, the patient started a used clothing store just when the therapist's wife was giving away some ill-fitting men's shirts she had purchased abroad. In what he regarded as a gesture of encouragement, the therapist gave one of the shirts to this patient to add to her inventory. To his dismay, the therapist later discovered that the patient was sleeping with the shirt, which he had never worn.
>
> (2008:100)

When practitioners sense confusion could arise from giving a client a gift, they should seek collegial consultation and supervision and consider constructive risk-management strategies designed to protect both client and practitioner. Case 5.1 provides an example of a sound risk-management approach to a seemingly problem-free situation.

CASE 5.1

Allison P., seventeen, was a client in a residential program for youths and in the custody of the county child welfare department. Allison was placed in the program after her single mother was sentenced to a long prison term for selling drugs. Allison did not have other relatives with whom she could live. The program was designed to provide youths in similar circumstances with a variety of educational and social services, including preparation for independent living.

After ten months in the program Allison was ready to move into her own subsidized apartment. Staff members had worked diligently with her so that she would have the knowledge and skills to live on her own. Allison was proud of her accomplishments; she invited her caseworker at the program, Melanie N., to come to her new apartment during the open house Allison had scheduled for the following weekend. Ms. N. very much wanted to go to Allison's new house but was unsure whether such a visit would be appropriate. In addition, Ms. N. was unsure whether she should give Allison a modest housewarming gift (for example, a scented candle or kitchen utensils).

In this case—which in a variety of ways is typical of situations in which practitioners are tempted to give a client a modest gift—the counselor was torn between her instinct to accept the invitation and bring a small gift and her awareness that the client might misinterpret such a gesture. It happens that this client, who did not have an ongoing, constructive relationship with her parents, found the counselor's nurturing support very appealing. In some respects the counselor functioned as the client's surrogate parent. The counselor worried that visiting the client's new home—which would be remarkably unusual—might reinforce whatever fantasies the client might have about an ongoing, posttermination relationship or friendship she might have with the counselor. At the same time the counselor wanted to be supportive and understood fully how meaningful it would be to the client to show the counselor her new home, particularly in light of all the hard therapeutic work they had done together. Also, the counselor understood how devastated and hurt Allison was likely to feel if Ms. N. turned down the invitation.

Wisely, the caseworker shared her dilemma with her immediate supervisor, who suggested that Ms. N. present the scenario at the next day's weekly group supervision meeting. As a result of this consultation, which entailed thorough examination and discussion of the clinical and ethical aspects of the situation (including review of relevant ethics code standards and agency policies), the caseworker devised a sound risk-management strategy designed to enhance protection of the client (the central priority), the caseworker's program, and the caseworker herself. The plan included three key elements: first, both Ms. N. and several colleagues concluded that sound clinical reasons to accept Allison's invitation existed, primarily those related to bolstering her self-esteem, reinforcing her sustained and diligent efforts to achieve independence, and avoiding hurting her emotionally. To minimize any confusion or misunderstanding, Ms. N. planned to talk to Allison explicitly about why she accepted the invitation and what her visit would represent (that is, helping the client celebrate this remarkable achievement) and about how important it was that Allison understand the need for appropriate boundaries in their relationship. Second, to protect the program and herself, Ms. N. decided to briefly document in Allison's case record the invitation to the open house, Ms. N.'s consultation with her supervisor and colleagues, and the rationale for her decision to accept the invitation. This documentation makes it clear, in the event that any party should raise questions about what happened, that the caseworker's actions were the product of careful deliberation, sound decision making, and professional judgment. That is, the record provides ample evidence that the caseworker did not visit the client's new home in an effort to pursue a friendship or some other type of inappropriate relationship.

The final element of this risk-management strategy specifically concerned the gift. The caseworker and her colleagues agreed that a modest gift, consistent with social custom, would be appropriate. The case record also would document the gift. However, rather than sign a card saying that the gift was from Ms. N., the card would make it clear that the gift was from the *agency and its staff.* Ms. N. and her colleagues agreed that this apparently subtle adjustment could have profound meaning; instead of suggesting that Ms. N. was giving the gift personally—which could be misinterpreted—the card's message would defuse and depersonalize the situation by making it clear that the entire staff and the program itself were giving the gift. This thoughtful, comprehensive approach increases the likelihood that the client's legitimate and understandable needs and wishes will be met *and* that the gift will not trigger boundary-related complications and confusion.

This case illustrates the benefit of thinking creatively about how to address challenging boundary issues. Recently, I consulted on a case that also required creative problem solving related to boundaries and altruistic gestures. The colleague who called me worked in a program that provides services to parents who have children with severe disabilities. The mother was a recent immigrant to the United States; she received notice from the U.S. Immigration and Customs Enforcement agency (ICE) informing her that she was required to visit the district office located in a major city about an hour away by car or bus. The mother did not drive a car and was so new to the United States that she was completely unfamiliar with public transportation. She told her social worker that she was overwhelmed by the mandate from ICE.

The social worker was eager to help the woman find her way to the ICE office; she asked her supervisor for permission to take a personal day in order to drive the mother to the ICE office. However, the supervisor wisely asked the social worker about possible boundary issues, that is, whether this personal favor, though admirable, might confuse the mother about the nature of their relationship, particularly if they were to travel together in the social worker's personal car and spend a day together. The supervisor suggested that they think about ways for the social worker to assist the mother without introducing complicated boundary issues. After I consulted with the social worker and the supervisor, we agreed that the social worker and client could identify learning how to use public transportation as one of her goals in the agency's program. The social worker would teach the woman how to find the bus station, buy a ticket, board the bus, travel to the nearby city, take a subway to the neighborhood where the regional ICE office is located, walk to the office, and complete necessary ICE paperwork. The client agreed and the experience was successful. The outcome was ideal: the boundaries were kept clean, the client learned new skills and completed the mandated tasks, the social worker assisted the client, and the entire experience was viewed as an important and appropriate element of their professional-client relationship. The social worker's initial altruistic instinct, which may have led to complex boundary issues, was transformed into professional management of boundaries.

In another case that called for creative problem solving involving altruistic gestures and boundary management, my wife and our two daughters volunteered at a local shelter for people who are homeless. One cold winter night a woman arrived without a winter coat; she carried all her possessions in a flimsy plastic bag and shivered as she walked through the door. Another volunteer, a middle-aged woman, asked the client whether she had a winter coat. The client explained that her one winter coat had been stolen at another shelter and that she was eager to find a new one but did not have any money.

The volunteer expressed her dismay in light of the fierce weather conditions; she immediately took out her cell phone and called her husband. "Jerry," she said. "I'm at the shelter and there's a woman here who doesn't have a winter coat. Listen, please go to the closet by the front door; in the back there's that brown coat I haven't worn in a couple of years. I'd like to give it to this woman. Can you bring it over?" About twenty minutes later the volunteer's husband arrived with the coat. The volunteer offered it to the client, who was elated. The client wrapped her arms around the volunteer and showered her with kisses. The client, who struggled with mental illness, began asking the volunteer questions about her husband, where they live, and how often the woman volunteers at the shelter. The volunteer, who was well meaning but largely untrained and not a human service professional, quickly realized that the client was eager to develop a close relationship. The volunteer became quite uncomfortable but was unsure how to extricate herself from the situation. To complicate matters, two other clients were seated nearby and witnessed this encounter. The two other women asked the volunteer whether she had coats for them. By the end of her shift the volunteer realized that her good intentions were spiraling out of control.

Shortly thereafter the director of the shelter, who was familiar with my work related to ethics, asked whether I would consult with her about how to train volunteers about boundary issues. We used this opportunity to introduce the concept of boundaries and dual relationships and to talk about reasonable guidelines to protect both clients and volunteers. Together we engaged in creative problem solving; by the end of the training session everyone agreed that an ideal solution was to solicit clothing contributions and to create a clothes closet for clients who stay at the shelter. Volunteers were welcome to contribute their personal items, such as winter coats. Clients who need clothing items could be encouraged by volunteers to visit the clothes closet. In this respect everyone wins. Volunteers are able to donate clothing to people in need; clients can receive much-needed clothing, but to avoid complicated boundary issues clients would not know who donated the clothing. Thus creative problem solving can manage complicated boundaries without depriving people of the services they need.

MEETING CLIENTS IN SOCIAL OR COMMUNITY SETTINGS

Earlier I discussed how human service professionals might become involved in dual relationships with clients in community settings and social circumstances as a result of their emotional and dependency needs. These situations involve boundary issues that arise when practitioners have difficulty separating their professional duties from their personal relationship needs and wishes (for example, when practitioners accept a client's invitation to a social event because the event fills a void in the practitioner's personal life or provides the practitioner with an opportunity to pursue a personal relationship with the client).

In contrast practitioners are sometimes inclined to have contact with clients in social or community settings for more genuinely altruistic reasons. In these situations the practitioner's motivation is a sincere wish to be helpful to and supportive of the client. Yet this admirable altruism may trigger complicated boundary issues. Skillful handling of these circumstances is necessary to avoid harming the client and exposing the practitioner to ethical and liability risks.

CASE 5.2

Ivy E. was a psychologist at a community mental health center. Her client, Karen R., was in recovery following years of cocaine abuse. Ms. R. had lost custody of her two children after the county child welfare agency investigated her for child neglect. In her earnest effort to turn her life around, Ms. R. sought counseling from Dr. E. and enrolled in an ambitious outpatient drug treatment program. Ms. R. also resumed her studies at a local community college, from which she had dropped out after her drug use escalated.

One day Ms. R. handed Dr. E. an envelope and asked her to open it. "I've been looking forward to this day for months," she said. Dr. E. opened the envelope and found an invitation from Ms. R. to attend her community college graduation and a reception at her home that evening. "You're one of the only people in my life who stuck with me. You've believed in me. I never could have done this without you," Karen R. told Ivy E. "It will mean so much to me to see you in the audience when I walk across that stage at graduation."

The psychologist in this case understood why her client was eager for her to attend the graduation ceremony. Ivy E. had been a major influence in Karen R.'s life and had provided her with unique sustained support. The psychologist was inclined to attend the graduation to provide her client with the emotional support she was requesting. Ivy E. understood the potential therapeutic benefit of her attendance at the graduation. She also sensed how hurt and disappointed Ms. R. would be if she declined the invitation and how that might undermine their therapeutic relationship.

At the same time the psychologist was concerned about potential boundary issues. Although the client had not manifested major symptoms of boundary confusion in their relationship—which may be more likely to occur with some clinical syndromes than others, such as borderline personality disorder—Dr. E. was concerned that going to the graduation might communicate to Karen R. that their relationship, including their posttermination relationship, was moving in the direction of a friendship.

The psychologist raised her concerns with her peer consultation group. The group members agreed that the arguments in both directions were compelling. One colleague encouraged Dr. E. to think about Karen R.'s clinical issues and to speculate about the extent to which she had a history of boundary-related challenges—for example, in Ms. R.'s relationships with family members or previous mental health counselors—that might be exacerbated by any boundary confusion in her relationship with the psychologist. Dr. E. truly believed, however, that this client had no such history and that, in this respect, attending the graduation was relatively low risk. After their lengthy consultations the psychologist and her colleagues agreed that attending the graduation was reasonable. One colleague, however, encouraged Dr. E. to take several steps to minimize the possibility of boundary-related problems. First, the colleague encouraged her to document the client's invitation to attend her graduation ceremony in the client's case record, the consultation process that Dr. E. engaged in concerning her decision about attendance (including collegial discussion and review of relevant ethics code standards), and the reasons she decided to attend the graduation. The colleague told Dr. E. that the documentation would provide protection in the unlikely event that questions were raised about her decision to attend the graduation (for example, subsequent allegations that the psychologist was interested in having a personal relationship with the client). Such documentation would clearly show that Dr. E.'s decision was the product of professional judgment and decision making.

Second, the colleague encouraged the psychologist to talk with Karen R. about her reasons for accepting the invitation—that the psychologist was eager to be supportive and believed that attending the graduation would be consistent with their therapeutic work together. The psychologist would ensure that the client did not misunderstand the meaning and significance of her attendance. The psychologist would also explain that she would need to avoid meeting and chatting with any of Karen R.'s friends or relatives who would be attending the graduation ceremony, so she could avoid compromising her client's privacy and any confusion regarding the nature of their relationship.

Finally, the psychologist would explain to the client that while she appreciates Ms. R.'s invitation to the graduation party, accepting it would not be appropriate. The psychologist would explain how the ethical standards in her profession discourage social relationships with clients and why. She would also document this conversation as further evidence of her attention to pertinent boundary issues.

Practitioners face comparable challenges when clients invite them to any social event, such as a wedding, baptism, confirmation, or bar mitzvah. We have ample evidence that practitioners disagree about the appropriateness of attending such events. Some are concerned that attendance will unnecessarily complicate the boundary issues in the professional-client relationship. Others, such as Zur (2007:108), believe that attendance can be appropriate and have rich therapeutic value: "Celebrating and otherwise affirming clients' lives and accomplishments may be an important attestation for those clients who experience low self-esteem and have lacked external validation or the experience of celebrations throughout their lives." Nearly half (46 percent) of the psychotherapists in the survey by Pope, Tabachnick, and Keith-Spiegel

(1995) stated that attending a client's special event, such as a wedding, is ethical under many circumstances or unquestionably ethical. However, two-fifths of this group (39 percent) stated that doing so is unquestionably unethical or appropriate only under rare circumstances. Three-fourths of the sample (76 percent) reported having gone to a client's special event at least once. As I noted earlier, nearly half (45 percent) of New York City social workers surveyed by DeJulio and Berkman (2003) believed it is ethical to accept a client's invitation to a special event, 8.7 percent stated it is ethical to do so under most conditions, and 1.3 percent reported that it is always ethical. In these circumstances practitioners must be vigilant in their efforts to avoid confusing the boundaries in their professional-client relationships.

Boundary issues that emerge because of practitioners' altruistic instincts are especially likely in programs that provide home-based services. Examples include intensive home-based intervention programs for families facing crises (for instance, as a result of substance abuse or allegations of child neglect) as well as those provided by home health agencies and hospice programs. In these situations practitioners must be careful to avoid boundary problems and inappropriate dual relationships, because they are working with clients in personal, casual, somewhat intimate, and informal surroundings. Although formal office settings may have some drawbacks, they do convey to clients that what takes place within the office walls has a professional purpose and structure, and this can help to reduce boundary crossings and violations. Home settings, however, do not automatically convey this message; the informality and intimacy of these settings can be the incubator for boundary confusion and problems. Some clients may experience any interactions in their homes as more personal than professional. The provision of services in clients' homes—within their "comfort zone"—may lead to unusually relaxed boundaries. For these reasons home-based programs can serve as Petri dishes for complex boundary challenges that require practitioners' vigilance and careful monitoring. As Gutheil and Brodsky (2008:69–70) assert, "A home visit may be perceived by the patient, and subsequently by licensing boards or courts, as an unwelcome advance on the therapist's part or as intentionally or unintentionally encouraging the patient's fantasies of nontherapeutic intimacy." They wisely encourage practitioners to consider several key issues before heading down this path: "The criteria for determining the legitimacy of a home visit are the same as for any other treatment intervention. Is it an exploitive intrusion on a patient's personal space or an attempt to deal with an issue clinically? This assessment is most usefully viewed in four dimensions: (1) the therapist's intentions (clinical rationale); (2) foreseeable impact on the patient; (3) consistency with therapy contract or informed-consent process; (4) appearance to third parties" (69).

Case 5.3 illustrates how these challenges can arise when practitioners who provide home-based services try to be helpful.

CASE 5.3

Malcolm B. was a caseworker at a large family service agency. The agency sponsored a variety of programs, including services for families referred by the city child welfare agency following allegations of child abuse or neglect. Mr. B. worked in the family preservation program, which was designed to provide crisis intervention and supportive services to parents seeking to retain custody of their children.

Ordinarily Mr. B. visited families in his caseload three to four times each week to monitor their status and respond to crises. One day Mr. B. arrived at a family's home at noon on a Saturday and discovered that the family was hosting a backyard cookout with several neighbors. The father told Mr. B. that they had forgotten about his scheduled visit and invited Mr. B. to join the group for lunch. When Mr. B. hesitated, the father politely insisted that Mr. B. spend at least a few minutes with the family before leaving.

In this situation the caseworker had to be concerned about confidentiality and privacy issues, as well as boundary issues. In addition to deciding whether to accept the father's invitation to socialize briefly—clearly a boundary issue—the caseworker had to be concerned about protecting the family's confidentiality and privacy in the presence of the family's neighbors. The caseworker did not want to offend the family and wanted to respond to the warm offer in a courteous way that signifies his regard for them. Ultimately, the caseworker may think, this will strengthen the therapeutic relationship and the effectiveness of his intervention approach.

At the same time sitting with a family and breaking bread, as I noted earlier, may communicate to the family that its relationship with the social worker has moved to a new plane, one that involves a social as well as a professional relationship. This may be particularly problematic because the caseworker's report and recommendations about the family's progress in treatment will have a direct bearing on the parents' ability to maintain custody of their children. Confusion about boundaries in this set of circumstances can

be especially consequential, because the family may be upset with the caseworker's recommendations. Family members may feel especially betrayed if
they had begun to sense that the caseworker was their friend, in part because the caseworker attended the backyard cookout and, from their point
of view (not the caseworker's), socialized with them. This is another example
of a situation in which the practitioner may need to use great finesse to avoid
insulting the family and avoid boundary confusion. As always, the practitioner should be careful to document the family's invitation and his management of the boundaries.

OFFERING CLIENTS FAVORS

Now I will extend this example in order to make an additional point about
the untoward consequences of altruistic actions that can result when practitioners offer clients favors. Suppose that about fifteen minutes before Mr.
B.'s planned departure from the clients' home, the mother takes a telephone
call and finds out that her employer is insisting that she immediately come
to work at her job at a nearby hospital to fill in for a colleague who called in
sick. The family does not have a working car and, aware that the social
worker is planning to head back to his agency, which happens to be located
two blocks from the hospital, the mother asks the social worker whether he
would be willing to give her a ride. The social worker wants to be helpful,
yet he is also uncomfortable about establishing a precedent that involves
spending informal time with a client outside the treatment context. This
encounter would occur in the practitioner's personal space (car), which
adds boundary-related complexity. The social worker is concerned that the
mother—and perhaps other family members—will interpret the altruistic
gesture as a sign that the social worker has a special relationship, elements of
which resemble a friendship, with the family. The family's struggles with
boundary issues—which are evident in the clinical issues that led to the court-
ordered referral to the agency—increase the ethical risks. Given the circumstances, the social worker is not in a position to consult with colleagues or a
supervisor. He has to make a spontaneous decision.

   Clearly, refusing the woman's request could be awkward and, in fact, doing
so could ultimately undermine the social worker's therapeutic relationship
with the family. In addition, the social worker's agency may prohibit staff
members from transporting clients (for clinical, ethical, and liability reasons),

which would provide the social worker with a convenient way out of the predicament. Absent this convenient explanation and weighing all the competing factors, the social worker may feel the need to provide the woman with the ride. To prevent misunderstanding and to protect himself, however, the social worker should talk with the client about how this is an unusual situation and not a precedent. The social worker should enter a note along these lines in the case record, so his motives and reasons for offering the client a ride are clear. According to Zur (2007:109), "Such considerate acts fall under the aegis of common courtesy and probably do not require therapeutic examination despite the fact that a boundary is being crossed, unless, of course, such favors become problematic (e.g., demanded, expected, viewed as a sexual advance, etc.)."

Human service professionals may be tempted in a variety of circumstances to offer a client a favor for altruistic reasons. Some of the examples that follow raise red flags.

CASE 5.4

David A., a counselor in private practice, provided psychotherapy to a twenty-nine-year-old man who had a history of relationship problems. Over time the client resolved a number of emotional issues that helped him sustain a long-term relationship for the first time in his adult life. One day the client informed Mr. A. that he was planning to marry and wanted Mr. A. to be in his wedding party. The client said to Mr. A., with heartfelt emotion, "I know there's no way I'd be getting married without the help you've given me. You've been a lifeline."

CASE 5.5

A psychiatrist in a mental health clinic, Dr. P., provided counseling services to a forty-two-year-old woman who had attempted to commit suicide. The woman was despondent after being accosted and raped by a stranger. After more than two years of therapy the client decided to terminate her treatment. She told Dr. P. that she felt able to live her life without sustained psychiatric treatment. Two months after termination the client stopped by Dr. P.'s office unannounced and said she simply wanted to say hello and let her know that she was doing okay. Dr. P. was inclined to accommodate the client's wish for a brief conversation as a benevolent gesture but was unsure whether this informal encounter would set a precedent that would be in neither the client's nor Dr. P.'s best interest.

CASE 5.6

Adam K., a social worker in a residential program for struggling adolescents, provided services to a seventeen-year-old boy who had been abandoned by his parents, both of whom had serious substance abuse problems. Mr. K. helped the boy develop independent living skills. When the boy reached the age of majority, state regulations required that he move out of the residential program. The boy moved to a distant state to live with his mother's brother, whom he barely knew. About six months later the boy—now a young man—contacted Mr. K. to explain "things just aren't working out with my uncle. This isn't the right place for me, but I have nowhere else to go." After a lengthy discussion Mr. K., who had a large house, offered to let his former client stay in a spare room until he found a more permanent residence. Mr. K. also fantasized about the possibility of adopting the young man.

CASE 5.7

Anna F., a counseling psychologist who specialized in the treatment of anxiety disorders, received a telephone call from a former neighbor whom she did not know well. The acquaintance explained to Dr. F. that he had been having some problems lately, specifically related to feeling anxious when in a crowd. The acquaintance explained that he felt uneasy talking about his problem with a complete stranger and wanted to know whether Dr. F. would be willing to provide him with counseling.

CASE 5.8

Tessa L., a social worker in private practice, provided counseling services to a college student who reported feeling depressed after the death of her parents in a plane crash. The counseling lasted for about seventeen months while the client was in college. Following her graduation, the former client accepted a position as a case manager at a local domestic violence shelter. One year later the client applied to graduate school in social work and eventually received her master's degree. Shortly thereafter the former client contacted her former therapist, Ms. L., and asked whether she would be willing to provide the weekly supervision that the former client needed as she worked toward obtaining her license as a clinical social worker.

CASE 5.9

Maria D., a marriage and family therapist, provided counseling to a couple who were having difficulty coping with their infertility. Several months after the counseling began, the wife was hospitalized following a miscarriage with serious complications. Ms. D. wanted to visit her client in the hospital to offer emotional support but was unsure about whether this would be a problematic boundary crossing.

CASE 5.10

Danielle M., a social worker, provided group counseling to clients who are dealing with anxiety. The group had been meeting weekly for about three months. One client asked to speak with Dr. M. after a group session. The client then explained that she had been thinking for some time about converting to Judaism, knew that Dr. M. was Jewish, and wanted to know whether Dr. M. would be willing to talk with her about some aspects of the religion and help her find a local rabbi who might help her start the conversion process.

CASE 5.11

Alma B., a psychiatrist, provided counseling and medication consultation to a ten-year-old boy with Tourette's syndrome. The client and his father arrived for their appointment one day, and the boy asked Dr. B. whether she wanted to purchase wrapping paper that he was selling to raise money for his school.

Each of these scenarios raises questions about the ways in which a human service professional's altruistic instincts may generate boundary issues. Some altruistic gestures toward clients are unlikely to create significant or problematic boundary problems. For example, the psychiatrist who decides to purchase a roll of wrapping paper from her client is not likely to stir up complex boundary problems that would harm the client or lead to an inappropriate dual relationship. Formulating an ambitious risk-management strategy in this situation would be gratuitous. In contrast, however, several of these situations are much more likely to lead to boundary problems.

A counselor who agrees to be in his client's wedding party, a social worker who permits a former client to live in his home and contemplates the possibility of adopting him, a psychologist who agrees to counsel an acquaintance who is a former neighbor, and a social worker who agrees to actively help her client explore the social worker's religion are practitioners who are—perhaps inadvertently—creating greenhouse-like conditions for what could well become complex boundary problems. The clients in these scenarios could easily become confused about the nature of their relationship with their practitioner. The line between professional and friend or social acquaintance is likely to seem blurry to both client and practitioner. In turn, this confusion could undermine the practitioner's ability to provide competent care and the client's ability to benefit maximally from the professional's services. Clients in these circumstances are likely to perceive and relate to their practitioners differently because of the extraprofessional contact. The former client who lives in the practitioner's home may see sides of the practitioner that are unnerving or disturbingly inconsistent with the client's earlier perception of the practitioner—for example, if the client were to observe the practitioner having difficulty handling conflict with his spouse or children. The social worker who counsels an acquaintance may unwittingly harm the client because of the social worker's reluctance to constructively confront an acquaintance on an important issue related to the therapy. The counselor who joins his client's wedding party may stimulate all manner of counterproductive fantasies in the client about their budding friendship.

Although some altruistic gestures are clearly benign or harmful, others are ambiguous, like many ethical dilemmas. Practitioners may disagree, for example, about the appropriateness of a marriage counselor's decision to visit his hospitalized client, a psychiatrist's decision to meet briefly and informally with a former client who stopped by the office to reconnect, a social worker's decision to provide supervision to a former client who is now a colleague, and a caseworker's wish to adopt a former client who is in need of a home and family (Brenner, Kindler, and Freundlich 2010). Some would argue, for example, that a brief visit to a hospitalized client, or a brief informal encounter with a former client, could have profoundly beneficial therapeutic consequences that far outweigh any associated risks. At the same time others would argue that these apparently innocuous, altruistic gestures could be harmful. In these more ambiguous circumstances, practitioners should think carefully about the factors that may increase the risk of misunderstanding, such as the client's clinical profile, the client's ability to handle boundary issues, the practitioner's personality, the strength of the therapeutic alliance, and the practitioner's experience (Simon 1999).

ACCOMMODATING CLIENTS

In some instances human service professionals encounter boundary issues because of their earnest attempt to accommodate a client's unique request or circumstances. These accommodations typically take the form of providing extraordinary service to the client (or former client) in an effort to be helpful. The cases that follow provide several examples.

CASE 5.12

Nora C., a caseworker in a shelter for teenagers who have run away from home, was concerned about a particular client, a sixteen-year-old whose step-brother apparently had sexually assaulted her. The client had talked with Ms. C. about her profound despair. Ms. C. told the young woman that she (Ms. C.) would be on vacation for one week. Ms. C. gave the client her cell phone number and encouraged her to call if she was feeling desperate to talk.

CASE 5.13

Bob K., a marriage and family therapist, provided counseling to a single man, a construction worker, who felt depressed after breaking up with his long-time partner. After eight counseling sessions the client's insurer refused to authorize payment for additional sessions. The client told Mr. K. how eager he was to continue counseling, which he was finding quite helpful, but that he had no money to pay for the sessions out of pocket. For about a year the client had been using all his extra money to pay off an unusually large credit card debt and avoid having to declare personal bankruptcy. Mr. K., who was eager to be helpful to this remarkably earnest client, agreed to provide the client with a six additional counseling sessions in exchange for construction work (bathroom remodeling) the client was willing to perform at the clinician's office.

CASE 5.14

Eric W., a social worker in a grade school and nearby middle school, provided counseling services to a twelve-year-old boy. The student's teacher referred him to Mr. W. because the boy seemed withdrawn and socially isolated. Mr. W. spent time working with the student on self-esteem issues and relationship skills. In his spare time Mr. W. volunteered to coach a youth basketball team affiliated with a local recreation center. Mr. W.'s son played on the team. Mr. W. considered inviting his client to join the team he coached, in an effort to help the boy make friends and have a positive social experience.

CASE 5.15

Fran G., a counselor at Lutheran Family Service, was married to a prominent local minister. The minister occasionally referred church members to Ms. G. for counseling when members wanted to locate a mental health counselor who would understand and be sensitive to their religious values and beliefs. Ms. G. provided services to these individuals, many of whom she knew from the church.

As with offering clients favors, efforts to accommodate a client's unique circumstances require that human service professionals critically examine whether doing so is advisable. Some accommodations are clearly inappropriate, and some are relatively benign. For example, most practitioners would not object if a colleague agreed to provide a terminally ill, bedridden client with counseling in the client's home, even though all previous counseling sessions had occurred in the professional's office. This accommodation seems reasonable in light of the client's unfortunate medical circumstances. In contrast accommodating clients who are acquaintances and members of the church of the practitioner's husband could easily lead to harmful boundary issues. Circumstances may arise where the practitioner and her husband are unsure whether to share with each other critically relevant confidential information about the client—for instance, if the client, a church employee, shares information with the wife about illegal activities taking place in the church's business office. Also, clients who share deeply personal information with the minister's spouse may feel overexposed and worried about whether their minister will learn of these sensitive details.

Similarly, the sixth grader who plays on the basketball team coached by his social worker may encounter boundary problems. For example, suppose the boy and the coach's son, who also plays on the team, become friends, and the coach's son—who is not aware that his new friend is his father's client—invites the client to sleep over at his house during a holiday weekend. The social worker may end up in a situation in which one of his clients spends considerable social time at the social worker's home and participates in family events. This scenario is likely to confuse the client about the nature of his relationship with the social worker and could undermine his counseling experience. One might also wonder whether detrimental consequences might result if, for instance, the basketball team is not playing well and the coach (the social worker) benches his client for the good of the team. The boy could feel deeply wounded by being pulled out of the starting lineup and may experience this as a form of rejection by his social worker. Clearly, these situations can produce conflicts of interest for the parties involved.

Unique issues can also arise in relation to accommodating *former* clients. One particularly challenging case I encountered involved debate among community mental health center staff members about whether to hire former clients to work in their agency as case aides.

CASE 5.16

The clinical director at the Lincoln County Community Mental Health Center decided that she wanted to create three new case aide positions. Her plan was to hire three former clients of the agency's outpatient counseling program for people with persistent and chronic mental illness. The three new staff members—all of whom were functioning at a high level—would receive special training and be assigned to provide supportive and concrete services to current clients.

Several clinical staff members at the agency had concerns about this plan. They admired the clinical director's wish to empower former clients but believed that this initiative might create boundary problems that would be difficult for the former clients and staff to manage. The clinical director and her immediate assistant, however, strongly believed in empowering people with histories of mental illness and that this hiring plan was consistent with that goal. Staff members agreed to schedule a meeting to provide an opportunity for all of the agency's professional staff to discuss the issue.

This agency's staff members asked me to facilitate their meeting and discussion about the ethical dimensions of their disagreement. This experience provided me with an opportunity to explore for myself the pertinent boundary issues and the arguments for and against hiring former clients. The process the staff and I went through provides a good example of the benefits of sound procedures and decision making. At the beginning of the meeting the staff was almost evenly divided on the issue—about half were opposed to hiring former clients, largely because of potential boundary problems, and half favored hiring former clients, mainly because of the agency's empowerment approach to the delivery of mental health services. A handful of staff were on the fence.

In an effort to address the issue thoroughly and comprehensively, I acquainted staffers with the concepts of boundaries and dual relationships, and described prevailing ethical standards in the relevant human service professions (psychology, social work, marriage and family therapy, counseling, psychiatry, psychiatric nursing). I then helped them identify arguments in favor of hiring former clients. First, as I mentioned earlier, hiring former clients is a way to empower people with mental illness and acknowledge the unique and valuable contributions they can make to others who are coping with somewhat similar issues; after all, who can better understand what current clients are experiencing in their efforts to cope with mental illness? Also, recognizing clients with mental illness as equals is a less elitist, paternalistic, and hierarchical way to provide mental health services and is more likely to promote client growth, self-esteem, and self-confidence than more traditional top-down intervention models. In addition, hiring former clients can provide current clients with valuable role models—that is, constructive examples of people who have struggled and coped well with their mental illness. Finally, staffers could not ignore the implications of the Americans with Disabilities Act, which prohibits discrimination in the workplace; certainly staff members would not want to refuse to hire former clients in a way that violated their legal rights.

The mental health agency staff and I then turned our collective attention to a variety of concerns associated with hiring former clients, related primarily to potential—although admittedly not inevitable—dual relationship and boundary problems. For example, staffers wondered whether former clients might encounter problematic transference issues as they attempted to relate to former treatment providers who are now colleagues. Would it be difficult for the former clients to relate to their former treatment providers as genuine colleagues, in light of their previous professional-client relationships? Of course, staff members might experience a comparable challenge, finding it difficult to relate to former clients as colleagues and, for instance, being unsure how candid they should be when expressing their views in staff meetings. In addition, how would former clients who are employees manage relationships with current clients whom they know from their days when both were clients? Former clients who are now staffers would need to manage confidential information carefully.

Also, what would it mean for former clients to learn, as a result of their new employment status in the agency, that some staff members, including their former treatment providers, are not well respected or are involved in complex political feuds within the agency—that is, that the agency idealized by the clients is flawed in some important respects? Might this undermine the former clients' confidence in the services they had received? Also, what if personnel issues involving the former clients emerge that warrant critical feedback or discipline? What would it mean for the former clients to be chastised by their former treatment providers? As Doyle notes,

> If a former client indeed begins work in the program in which a counselor treated him or her, issues relating to supervision, promotion, performance evaluation, and confidentiality may arise that can be problematic for one or both parties. For example, if the counselor were to become the former client's supervisor, objective supervision could be compromised by the circumstances of the previous relationship. Either positively or negatively, the counselor might find himself or herself recalling the new employee's previous behavior and responding accordingly to current situations.
>
> (1997:431)

Further, what would happen if former clients who are now staff relapsed and wanted or needed to become active clients again? How would they, and their treatment providers, handle the shift away from a collegial relationship and back to a professional-client relationship? Would the clients find this disconcerting and humiliating? Would they have difficulty resuming the role of client, and would this interfere with their therapeutic progress? While referral of the former client to another agency or outside service provider would be appropriate to minimize boundary challenges, this is not always feasible, especially in small and rural communities where options may be limited.

In addition, the mental health center staff and I discussed in what ways hiring former clients could have a detrimental effect on other clients, who might be discouraged when they realize they were not selected to become staff members and perhaps conclude that they have not progressed as well clinically. Current clients may also feel overexposed, fearing (perhaps unrealistically) that the former clients would have access to confidential information about them.

By the end of this protracted discussion and careful analysis of potential dual relationship and boundary issues, staff opinion clearly had shifted. Nearly all the staff had concluded that the potential risks outweighed potential benefits from hiring former clients. Although the staff generally embraced the virtues of empowering former clients, they concluded that the potential harm to them, and to the agency's smooth functioning, was a risk not worth taking. Instead, the staffers realized, they could accomplish much the same goal by working assertively with other social service agencies in the region in an effort to find comparable jobs for their former clients, perhaps in exchange for hiring other agencies' former clients. In the staffers' opinion finding jobs in other agencies for former clients would reduce the likelihood of boundary problems while achieving all the benefits associated with hiring former clients to work with active clients.

One other unique boundary-related circumstance that surfaces with some regularity in the human services involves accommodating the wishes of relatives or acquaintances of deceased clients. In one unusual case on which I consulted, the parents of a deceased client asked the social worker to deliver a eulogy at the client's funeral. The parents understood how important the social worker had been to their son. After giving the parents' request considerable thought, the social worker was inclined to deliver the eulogy. The social worker consulted with her supervisor and several colleagues, all of whom supported her inclination; all the parties agreed, however, that the social worker should deliver the eulogy in a way that did not disclose the nature of her relationship with the deceased client. In addition, the social worker decided to obtain a signed, formal release authorizing her to speak at the funeral; the parents had been named executors of the deceased client's estate and personal representatives for legal purposes. The social worker also documented the parents' request, the social worker's consultation with colleagues, and the reasons for the social worker's decision to deliver the eulogy.

Special boundary issues can arise as well when relatives of deceased clients contact a practitioner to discuss confidential issues (for example, related to the former client's suicide). Practitioners should know that clients' confidentiality rights do not end in death; they should release confidential information about deceased clients only when proper releases have been executed or in response to a court order (Reamer 2003a).

As always, the most challenging circumstances involving dual relationships are those that are ambiguous, where practitioners can advance reasonable arguments both for and against accommodating clients' unique circumstances or requests. As with all ambiguous boundary issues, practitioners must weigh the competing arguments, being mindful of their ultimate responsibility to protect clients from harm.

SELF-DISCLOSING TO CLIENTS: THE RISKS OF ALTRUISM

In chapter 3, I discussed how a practitioner's inappropriate self-disclosure to a client often reflects the practitioner's unresolved emotional and dependency needs. In these situations self-disclosure is often associated with the practitioner's unethical and harmful efforts to cultivate intimate relationships or friendships with clients.

In other circumstances practitioners may self-disclose for more altruistic purposes, deliberately and *judiciously* choosing to share personal details—usually modest in scope—in an effort to empathize with clients, offer clients support, align with clients, and provide a constructive role model that clients may use in their efforts to address their own issues. Further, in some cultural or ethnic groups a client may view the practitioner's self-disclosure as an important sign that the practitioner accepts the client and will not be patronizing. Cases 5.17, 5.18, and 5.19 involve practitioner self-disclosure for altruistic purposes.

CASE 5.17

Astrid D., a counselor at a community mental health center, provided counseling to parents of a six-year-old boy whose teacher complained that his behavior in school was difficult to manage. According to the teacher, the boy behaved provocatively with other children by teasing and taunting them. The boy's classmates did not want to play with him, which increased the boy's negative attention–getting behavior. Ms. D., who was knowledgeable about child behavior management techniques and strategies, taught the parents how to use positive reinforcers at home and used role-playing techniques to help the parents learn how to communicate with their child effectively.

Ms. D. first learned many of these techniques when her own child was about six, and she and the child's teacher were having difficulty managing behaviors of his that were similar to those engaged in by the child of the counselor's current clients. After explaining some of the rudimentary features of the behavior management protocol, Ms. D. told the parents that she has found them to be effective with many children, including her own child when he was much younger. Ms. D. decided to share this personal detail as a way to let the parents know that she was able to genuinely appreciate their experience and frustration, that she had encountered similar challenges, and that hard work can produce positive results. In the counselor's judgment this modest form of self-disclosure was likely to help her strengthen her therapeutic alliance with the parents and provide them with much-needed reassurance. Ms. D. did not feel overexposed and did not think this disclosure would compromise the professional-client relationship. In fact, toward the end of their successful work together, the parents told Ms. D. that her brief description of her experience with her own son was a turning point for them, that at that moment they began to have hope and knew that Ms. D. understood their frustration.

CASE 5.18

Len J. was a psychologist at a student mental health center at a large university. One of Dr. J.'s clients was a student who sought counseling because her parents had just informed her they were divorcing. The student told Dr. J. that she felt deeply depressed and was falling way behind in her schoolwork. The student also explained that for weeks she had not felt like eating and had not been sleeping well. For about a month Dr. J. provided the student with supportive counseling and referred her to the center's consulting psychiatrist to determine whether psychotropic medication would be helpful. Despite these efforts the student did not seem to progress.

Dr. J. was concerned about the student and consulted with colleagues about alternative treatment strategies. Dr. J. told his colleagues that the student often commented that no one, including Dr. J., could ever understand the intensity of what she was experiencing. In an effort to align with his client, Dr. J. told her that when he was in college, his parents also divorced and he found it difficult to concentrate on his work and lead the life of a normal college student. Dr. J. disclosed this information deliberately and in a limited way. Almost immediately, the student seemed more responsive and eager to listen to Dr. J.'s comments during their counseling sessions. Dr. J. subsequently told his colleagues about the effectiveness of his strategy. Three of his four colleagues were complimentary; one, however, thought that Dr. J. may have crossed a line, that such self-disclosure—even for altruistic purposes—could confuse the client and lead to boundary complications. The one colleague was especially concerned that transference and countertransference could prove problematic in this case. Dr. J. assured his colleague that he was well aware of these risks but felt that he had them under control. In the end Dr. J. and his colleague agreed to disagree.

CASE 5.19

Bob W. was a caseworker in an outpatient substance abuse treatment program. Many of Mr. W.'s clients were alcoholic or addicted to cocaine. In addition to their treatment in the program, these clients typically attended meetings of Alcoholics Anonymous or Narcotics Anonymous.

Mr. W. was also a recovering alcoholic. He had been sober for twelve years, and he attended AA meetings faithfully. One evening Mr. W. went to his customary AA meeting in a neighboring town; on the way into the building he encountered one of his current clients, who, coincidentally, was also attending the meeting. Mr. W. had to make a quick decision about what to say to his client, and whether to attend the meeting or leave. Mr. W. was concerned that his presence at the meeting might confuse the boundaries in his relationship with his client. At the same time Mr. W. realized that he could also serve as a constructive role model for his client—that he might actually perform a helpful service to his client by remaining at the meeting.

This last case involving a practitioner in recovery provides a valuable illustration of the complex issues related to a practitioner's self-disclosure for altruistic purposes. In fact, this is one of the relatively few dual relationship issues unrelated to sexual relationships that has generated significant discussion in the professional literature. This debate provides a valuable illustration of the complicated boundary issues that can emerge when professionals decide to disclose personal information about themselves to clients for apparently altruistic purposes.

Clearly, professionals in the substance abuse field disagree vehemently about the wisdom and appropriateness of self-disclosure when practitioners are in recovery, particularly when practitioners who are in recovery attend AA and NA meetings that clients also attend (Doyle 1997). One side argues that a practitioner's self-disclosure in this form provides a remarkably valuable service to clients who have substance abuse problems. The clients can view their counselors as role models who practice what they preach about the need to be earnest about recovery, attend AA and NA meetings, and so forth. This argument is especially significant in light of one survey showing that nearly three-fifths of the membership of the National Association of Alcoholism and Drug Abuse Counselors were in recovery themselves (Doyle 1997). In addition, practitioners who disclose their recovery status to their clients may establish instant credibility, particularly among clients who might be skeptical of counselors who have not experienced substance abuse and the challenges of recovery first hand.

In contrast are those who argue with equal passion that the blending of the personal struggles of practitioners with those of their clients—in the context of AA or NA meetings, for example—is likely to have profoundly detrimental consequences. Clients may have difficulty separating their practitioner's professional and personal roles. In addition, some clients may lose confidence in practitioners who display their own vulnerabilities, personal struggles, and personal failures; the result may be an undermining of the practitioner's authority and influence. Further, practitioners in recovery— like all people in recovery—run the risk of relapsing, at least in principle. Should relapse occur, the practitioner's clients may be devastated, disheartened, and disappointed, and this could jeopardize their recovery efforts. As Doyle notes,

> The issue of self-disclosure in the counseling session itself also raises dual relationship issues. If the counselor discloses that he or she is in recovery, a new element in the counseling relationship may be unwittingly introduced. Not only is the counselor's anonymity broken, but also, with this disclosure the relationship between the counselor and client now may become one in which they are co-members of the same A.A. group. The risk here is that the counseling relationship may no longer be an exclusively professional one, but one that has other features as well. The sharing of private information about one's recovery, its challenges, and its successes, while conceivably therapeutic, also may lead to the relationship becoming more personal rather than professional if caution is not used.
>
> Self-help group meetings provide attendees the opportunity to share their "experience, strength, and hope" (Alcoholics Anonymous, 1984) with one another. Meetings typically last for an hour and may consist of one or two speakers or of a rotating discussion among those in attendance. Sharing such private information as the state of one's personal recovery program is certainly a risky proposition in any group setting. For the substance abuse counselor at a meeting with current (or former or future) clients in attendance, the ability to share fully might be compromised, thus lessening the benefit of attending at all. For example, what would be the impact on the counseling relationship if the counselor shared that he or she had nearly relapsed in the past week? Or, what if the counselor had relapsed recently and the client then realized that he or she had more time in recovery than the counselor? Other less dramatic examples exist as well that could include clinical considerations or dilemmas for the counselor. It is not difficult to

imagine situations such as a counselor sharing dissatisfaction with his or her coworkers in the presence of clients of that facility, a counselor discussing thoughts of leaving the field, or a counselor revealing that he or she has difficulty maintaining positive feelings towards his or her clients. Each of these hypothetical scenarios could significantly affect the counseling relationship should clients be in attendance at the self-help group meeting in which it was shared.

(1997:430)

In addition to these potentially detrimental clinical consequences, substance abuse counselors who are in recovery, who exercise some degree of control over their clients' lives—for example, providing progress reports to probation or parole counselors—and who interact with clients at AA and NA meetings may create conditions in which clients may feel exploited. According to Doyle,

The greatest potential for harm from a dual relationship, however, may result from the power held, or perceived as being held, by the counselor. Whereas the counseling relationship will eventually come to an end, the power differential may remain indefinitely, adversely affecting any future, nontherapeutic relationship between counselor and client (Haas & Malouf, 1989). In the substance abuse field, the counselor often holds a substantial amount of power over the client because of the frequency with which clients are involved with the court system. Often clients are required to participate in counseling as a condition of probation or parole, and violation of this requirement could result in their incarceration (Milam & Ketcham, 1981). Counselors thus hold a great deal of power over clients, power that can lead to exploitation. When exploitation appears in the personal interaction between counselor and client, serious dual relationship problems can arise.

(1997:429)

In the end the debate about practitioners' altruistic self-disclosure to clients in recovery illustrates the difficulty of reaching consensus about some boundary and dual relationship issues. Because of the legitimate and complex debate that can arise—as this one issue demonstrates—practitioners would do well to grasp the critical importance of the *process* they should use to make sound decisions, recognizing that in the end reasonable minds may differ. This decision-making process should entail the elements outlined in chapter 1, especially the steps involving examination of conflicting professional obligations; identification of the individuals, groups, and organizations likely to be affected by the decision; identification of all viable courses of action and the participants involved in each, along with the potential benefits and risks for each; examination of the reasons in favor of and opposed to each course of action, considering relevant ethical principles and standards, practice theory and guidelines, ethical standards, agency policies, statutes, regulations, and personal values; consultation with colleagues and appropriate experts (such as agency staffers, supervisors, ethics committees, and when warranted, legal counsel); and appropriate documentation of these various steps.

6

UNAVOIDABLE AND UNANTICIPATED CIRCUMSTANCES

ANOTHER TYPE OF DUAL RELATIONSHIP involves circumstances that practitioners cannot easily anticipate or prevent—circumstances that, in most respects, are difficult to avoid or unavoidable. In these situations practitioners encounter boundary crossings and dual relationships unexpectedly and need to manage the circumstances in a way that protects clients, colleagues, and practitioners to the greatest extent possible.

Boundary issues involving unavoidable and unanticipated circumstances fall into four major categories, including those that involve geographic proximity, conflicts of interest, professional encounters, and social encounters.

GEOGRAPHIC PROXIMITY: SMALL AND RURAL COMMUNITIES

The likelihood of unanticipated boundary issues increases in geographically small communities, such as rural areas and military bases. Human service professionals in these settings often report how challenging it is when they encounter clients in, for instance, the local supermarket, community center, neighborhood gathering, or house of worship (Campbell and Gordon 2003; Ebert 1997; Faulkner and Faulkner 1997; Helbok, Marinelli, and Walls 2006; Johnson 2008; Johnson and Koocher 2011). Practitioners often describe how they walk through their day wondering when—not if—they will encounter clients outside their work settings. They devote considerable effort to managing these encounters in a way that minimizes potential boundary confusion (Helbok 2003; Nickel 2004; Schank and Skovholt 2006). As Smith and Fitzpatrick observe,

That dual relationships are inevitable in certain circumstances adds to the complexity of the issue. In small towns and rural communities, dual relationships are often unavoidable; denying help to a potential client because of a preexisting relationship could mean that the person gets no help at all. Moreover, in rural settings where mental health professionals might be regarded with suspicion, heightening one's visibility by way of involvement in community activities may defuse the suspicion and make the clinician appear more approachable (Gates & Speare, 1990).

(1995:502)

Military communities—especially on aircraft carriers, bases on small islands, and heavily guarded bases in foreign countries—are particularly challenging. Adding to the inevitable boundary challenges that accompany geographic proximity is the challenge associated with military rank; active-duty clinicians and their clients may be ordered to engage in activities together that create complex dual relationships, and active-duty clinicians might provide therapeutic services to clients who outrank them (Hines et al. 1998; Johnson, Ralph, and Johnson 2005; Staal and King 2000). Because of military orders, clients and therapists may become shipmates or share living quarters, and active-duty clinicians may be ordered to conduct fitness-for-duty evaluations of their commanders and military superiors. As Zur (2007:30) notes, "The result of such regulations is that military therapists have neither control over whom they consult or evaluate nor ways to prevent dual relationships and conflicts of interest. . . . Because of the inherent duality in the military, informed consent should always be used. Clients in these settings must be fully informed of the potential eventualities that they may face as a result of engaging in a dual relationship; and, when possible, therapists can leave it to clients to decide if they want to engage in the dual relationship."

The cases that follow illustrate boundary issues and dual relationships that arise in small communities and rural areas.

CASE 6.1

Alice S. was the only child psychiatrist in a rural county. Dr. S.'s daughter, who was in the third grade at the local school, became friendly with a classmate who, unbeknown to her, was one of Dr. S.'s patients. Dr. S.'s daughter invited her new friend to her home to play. Dr. S. was unsure how to handle this predicament, particularly because she could not disclose to her daughter that her friend was Dr. S.'s patient.

CASE 6.2

Brad O. was a social worker in a small rural community. Mr. O. had a contract with the county to provide mental health services for local police officers, firefighters, and other employees as part of the county's employee assistance program. One of Mr. O.'s clients was a police officer who has having marital difficulties. One day Mr. O. was late for a dinner engagement and exceeded the speed limit on his way to the restaurant. The police officer who pulled Mr. O. over was his client.

CASE 6.3

Melinda D. was a substance abuse counselor on a military base. She provided clinical services to military personnel and their families. In her spare time Ms. D. coached a soccer team for children of military personnel. One boy on her team was the son of one of her clients. The child's father was recently charged with child abuse. Ms. D. was ordered to prepare a report concerning the family, including details concerning the relationship between the father and the son.

In geographically small communities some unanticipated encounters between practitioners and clients are innocuous and unlikely to pose significant problems. For example, practitioners and clients who encounter each other in the local supermarket or at the pharmacy may feel awkward, but these brief, unplanned encounters are not likely to have significant, lasting repercussions. In contrast the practitioner whose child becomes friendly with the practitioner's client faces a more daunting challenge. As Brownlee notes,

> In almost all cases, living in a rural area means greater distances between people and communities. The relative isolation increases interdependence between residents and leads to multiple levels of relationships.
>
> Multiple levels of relationships in rural areas are often a significant factor affecting the services provided by mental health professionals (Brownlee, 1992). Such relationships are almost impossible to avoid when there is no choice but to shop at a client's store or when one's children are in school with or even friends with clients' children (Fenby, 1978).

(1996:499)

Dual relationships in small communities and rural areas take several forms, most commonly overlapping social relationships and overlapping business or professional relationships. An unusually ambitious study conducted by Schank and Skovholt (1997) explored these issues. The researchers interviewed sixteen psychologists in Minnesota and Wisconsin who lived at least fifty miles from major metropolitan areas. Ten participants were in private practice, four were affiliated with community mental health centers, one was in a multidisciplinary group practice, and one worked in a hospital setting. These interviews produced rich qualitative data related to dual and multiple relationships in rural areas. The respondents had a great deal to say about overlapping social relationships that occurred in such settings as the practitioner's church, parties and social gatherings, local restaurants, cultural events, school functions, and volunteer activities. The following are noteworthy and illuminating excerpts from the research interviews:

> One of the things we have done in our church for the last 6 years is that we have taken a group of kids to Colorado skiing as part of the youth program. I feel some kind of tension about that sometimes. For example, one of my clients happened to be on the ski trip 3 or 4 years ago. Well, I thought, "Okay, we don't do anything socially with this family." But I don't think these pressures are so unusual. It's just that you have to keep those dual relationships clear in your mind.
>
> (Schank and Skovholt 1997:46).

> When I moved here, I got a membership to the YMCA to go to exercise classes. After running into a couple of clients in the locker room, I decided that this was just so uncomfortable for me. So I'm not going to continue my membership in the YMCA. It was just really awkward. It's not like there are a huge number of athletic clubs here that you can have a choice of which one you go to.
>
> (46)

Respondents in this study described three criteria they use to determine whether they provide services to clients who pose potential boundary challenges: practitioners' own comfort level in traversing the overlapping relationships with clients; clients' opinions about the boundary issues and their ability to handle them; and the type and severity of clients' presenting prob-

lems. One respondent handled boundary issues this way: "I have this wonderful habit of just simply looking straight ahead when I go to the grocery
store, and half the time I don't see people. So that has protected me"
(Schank and Skovholt 1997:47). Another told the researchers:

> It is always [about] establishing boundaries. I live on a very busy street in
> town and was doing some landscaping and working out in the front yard.
> One of my clients must have seen me and later said, "Oh, is that where you
> live? I saw you." I said yes, and she said, "Well, I noticed that the house next
> to you is for sale. Wouldn't that be cool? You know, my parents are thinking
> of helping me buy a house." I said, "No, that would not be cool because you
> are my client—you are not a friend. If you moved in next door to me, it
> would be extremely uncomfortable. I know what you are saying—I listen to
> you, I care about you—but friends know about one another. You don't
> come in, and I sit and tell you about my problems and my life. I don't call
> you when I am hurting or need a friend for support." . . . She said, "Oh,
> yeah. I didn't even think about that." And so it's continually having to estab-
> lish boundaries with a number of clients.
>
> (Schank and Skovholt 1997:47)

The psychologists in Schank and Skovholt's sample also commented on
unanticipated or unavoidable overlapping business or professional relationships with clients. The respondents said that while traveling to neighboring
communities to transact business might be appealing, often this is not feasible; in such instances practitioners must devise practical ways to manage
the boundary issues.

> I have clients who are locksmiths or electricians that come to my house, with
> me not knowing that I was calling the electrical company that they work
> for. . . . It is hard to make small talk with someone who the day before was
> in your office talking about really powerful things. Sometimes clients will
> joke about it, which is kind of nice. They will break the ice.
>
> (Schank and Skovholt 1997:47)

> When you do have business dealings with someone, I find it really hard. I
> won't bargain with them. Recently someone [who was a former client]
> worked on my car, and I thought the price was a little high. I trust the guy,

but I felt awkward in asking him what the charges were for. If it were someone else, I would have had no problem asking.

(47)

We have a nice, isolated building here in a beautiful, quiet place. So professionals many times will come here. Now, I have seen a lot of professionals in town [as clients], either for personal counseling or for their
children. Then I refer [clients] to [those same professionals] because there
is no one else. . . . If you read the rules about dual relationships, that is not
allowed.

(47)

I do consulting at a fair number of group homes. Sometimes I'm in that
dilemma where there is someone [working there] that I've seen as a client.
In fact, I can think of two instances where I currently was seeing people
as clients and subsequently discovered that they had just obtained employment at one of the group homes. So I was dealing with them as clients, as well as in a professional relationship in terms of some of the
counseling.

(47)

Practitioners in small towns and rural areas often comment on the ways
in which their professional relationships overlap, and sometimes interfere,
with their family relationships. In these situations practitioners typically
find that their clients have independent relationships with members of the
practitioner's family, which produces complex boundary issues. Here are
several first-person accounts:

I think there are a lot of variables. If I can avoid a situation, I will. Let's say
it is a function like a hockey party. My kids are on the hockey team. The
kids want to go, and they want the parents to go. So you are at this function
[with clients]. You're not going to say to the kids, "Gee, I can't go to the
hockey banquet." So you just go. . . . Sometimes you just kind of live with
it. My older kids have friends who have been my patients in the past. I prefer that they not come over to our house, but you can't say to your kids,
"Don't invite so and so."

(Schank and Skovholt 1997:47)

Young people that I've seen are becoming friends with my daughter through the school system. I was so surprised—one night I came home from work to discover that one of my clients was a good friend of my daughter's through school and was staying overnight with her.

(47–48)

I think the more difficult situation is interaction that my daughter has had. She is now away at college, but when she was here she would end up dating clients—only to find out and just be absolutely horrified and angry. That is probably the most difficult circumstance that we have been in. The confidentiality piece is really difficult because she would confront me with, "Is so and so your client?" She is real glad to be done with that.

(48)

My husband met another [colleague's] wife who wanted to socialize, and I had to say that I can't go to their house for dinner. . . . He was understanding but was still feeling curtailed by my practice because we couldn't socialize with people that he would have enjoyed because they had come to me for family counseling.

(48)

Based on their extensive exploration of dual relationships that psychologists face in small communities and rural settings, Schank and Skovholt formulated a set of practical guidelines to help human service professionals manage boundary issues:

1. Nonsexual, overlapping relationships are not a matter of "if" as much as "when" in the daily lives of small-community psychologists (Barnett & Yutrzenka, 1995). Ethical codes or standards are necessary but not sufficient and are tempered by experience and context (Barnett & Yutrzenka, 1995). Although it may seem obvious, knowledge of these codes and of state laws is essential in framing the background for small-community application. Continuing education in ethical issues adds to this framework.

2. Clear expectations and boundaries, whenever possible, strengthen the therapeutic relationship. This is especially important in situations where out-of-therapy contact cannot be closely controlled. Obtaining informed consent, sticking to time limits, protecting confidentiality (and explaining its limits), and documenting case progress (including being explicit about

any overlapping relationships) diminishes the risk of misunderstanding between client and psychologist.

3. Ongoing consultations and discussion of cases, especially those involving dual roles, provide a context for psychologists to get additional perspectives and decrease the isolation that sometimes accompanies rural and small-community practice. Each of us has blind spots—trusted colleagues can help us constructively examine them.

4. Self-knowledge and having a life outside of work lessens the chances that we as psychologists will use, even unknowingly, our clients for our own gratification. This also involves what Barnett and Yutrzenka (1995) have recommended in maintaining a constant interpersonal style and authentic presence with clients.

(1997:48–49)

Gottlieb (1995) offers a useful decision-making model designed to help practitioners conceptualize the degree of risk associated with such boundary challenges. The model focuses on three key dimensions: power, duration, and termination. According to Gottlieb, power refers to the amount or degree of influence that a practitioner has in relation to a client. Duration of the professional-client relationship is important because power increases over time. Clarity of termination refers to the likelihood that the client and the practitioner will have further professional contact. Gottlieb argues that dual relationships become more problematic as power increases and the length of treatment or services increases. In addition, vague or ambiguous criteria for termination of the professional-client relationship tend to complicate boundary issues.

Keeping these important dimensions in mind, human service professionals in small communities, including the deaf community (Guthmann and Sandberg 2002) and small ethnic communities, would do well to anticipate the ways in which their professional lives may intersect with their personal and family lives and, where appropriate, talk with clients about how they might best handle these challenging circumstances. In some instances practitioners and their clients can come up with relatively straightforward ways to manage the boundary issues. For example, a practitioner whose client works for the sole local plumber in town might talk about why it would be best for one of the client's colleagues in the plumbing company to handle visits to the practitioner's home. A practitioner who has an opportunity to chaperone an overnight class trip that includes both the practitioner's teenage child and the practitioner's client (that is, a classmate of the practitioner's child) can decide not to sign up to chaperone in order to avoid potential boundary confusion. Also, practitioners can talk with clients ahead of time about how they—the practitioners—will not approach clients they encounter in local stores in order to avoid boundary complications.

In contrast, however, are situations in which the potential or actual boundary issues are more difficult to manage. The practitioner whose client is employed at the same company as the practitioner's spouse may not be able to avoid encountering the client at a holiday party sponsored by the company for employees and their families. The practitioner whose client moves into a house near the practitioner's home cannot be expected to resolve the problem by moving to another location. The practitioner whose client is the one automobile mechanic in town cannot be expected to drive thirty-five miles to another mechanic, especially if her car is disabled. In these circumstances it behooves the practitioner to broach the boundary issues with the client as early in their relationship as possible and discuss reasonable ways of handling potentially awkward circumstances in a manner that both find comfortable and in a way that protects the client's interests to the greatest extent possible. Practitioners should document these conversations to demonstrate their earnest efforts to handle these situations responsibly and ethically. In some situations practitioners may feel the need to consult colleagues for advice or refer clients to other providers—if feasible—in an effort to avoid inappropriate or harmful dual relationships.

In light of the unique boundary challenges in small and rural communities, Zur encourages clinicians to share the following statement with clients as part of the informed consent process:

> *Dual relationships:* Dual relationships (or multiple relationships) in psychotherapy refer to any situation in which therapists and clients have another relationship in addition to that of therapist-client, such as a social or business relationship. Not all dual relationships are unethical or avoidable. Therapy never involves sexual or any other dual relationship that impairs Dr. XX's objectivity, clinical judgment, or therapeutic effectiveness or can be exploitative in nature. Dr. XX will assess carefully before entering into nonsexual and nonexploitative dual relationships with clients. XX is a small community in which many clients know each other and Dr. XX. Consequently, you may encounter someone you know in Dr. XX's waiting room or Dr. XX out in the community. Dr. XX will never acknowledge working with anyone

without his/her written permission. Many clients chose Dr. XX as their therapist because they knew him/her before they entered into therapy with him/her and/or because they are aware of his/her stance on the topic of dual relationships. Nevertheless, Dr. XX will discuss with you, his/her client/s, the often-existing complexities, potential benefits, and difficulties that may be involved in such relationships. Dual or multiple relationships can enhance therapeutic effectiveness but can also detract from it, and often it is impossible to know that ahead of time. It is your responsibility to communicate to Dr. XX if the dual relationship becomes uncomfortable for you in any way. Dr. XX will always listen carefully and respond accordingly to your feedback and will discontinue the dual relationship if he/she finds it interfering with the effectiveness of the therapy or the welfare of the client, and, of course, you can do the same at any time.

(2007:41–42)

CONFLICTS OF INTEREST: UNEXPECTED CHALLENGES

A constant theme in discussions of dual relationships and boundary issues is the concept of conflicts of interest. As I discussed earlier, some conflicts of interest arise when human service professionals knowingly enter into dual relationships—for example, when a practitioner receives a fee from a colleague to whom the practitioner refers clients or when a practitioner receives professional assistance from a client (such as a car mechanic, stockbroker, doctor, lawyer, or house painter) who has specialized expertise from which the practitioner can benefit. However, in some instances conflicts of interest arise because of circumstances that are unavoidable or that practitioners could not have reasonably anticipated.

In my experience, many such conflicts involve adversarial circumstances, in which practitioners unexpectedly find themselves caught between parties who are engaged in a dispute.

CASE 6.4

Laura C. was a counselor who provided psychotherapy services to a twelve-year-old girl who was having difficulty maintaining friendships. During the counseling the girl told Ms. C. about problems that her parents—both of whom were high school teachers—were having at home. The girl talked at length about her parents' incessant arguing and fighting. With the girl's consent Ms. C. met with the parents and talked about their daughter's distress concerning her parents' relationship. The girl's mother became enraged with Ms. C. and blamed her for meddling in the family's personal matters and upsetting her daughter. The mother then terminated the girl's counseling with Ms. C., despite the father's objections.

About five months later, when the next school year began, Ms. C. learned that the school had placed her son in a science class taught by the former client's mother. Ms. C. was concerned that the mother would feel vindictive toward the boy and that his schooling would suffer as a result.

A common scenario with adversarial features involves practitioners who provide marital counseling. In some situations the couple are unable to resolve their differences and decide to divorce. If the couple are not able to agree on child custody issues (for example, one spouse alleges that the other is abusive or neglectful), the lawyer for one parent may subpoena the practitioner's clinical records and request that the practitioner testify about the emotional or psychological problems of the other parent that allegedly render the latter parent unfit. That is, one parent's lawyer may attempt to use the practitioner's records and testimony to impeach the other parent. Such practitioners, who would prefer to remain neutral and uninvolved in the legal dispute, then find themselves facing a subpoena that places them in a conflict-of-interest situation.

CASE 6.5

Lorna S., a family therapist, provided counseling to Janice and Bob P., the parents of eight-year-old twins. Janice and Bob P. sought counseling to help them address chronic conflict in their relationship. After nearly a year of on-again, off-again counseling, the couple decided to divorce. Ms. P. was adamant that Mr. P. was emotionally unfit to parent their children. Ms. P. alleged that Mr. P. was a neglectful and emotionally abusive parent.

Ms. P.'s lawyer subpoenaed Dr. S. and her records in an effort to produce evidence of Mr. P.'s emotional and psychological impairment. Dr. S. felt uncomfortable because she was being forced to testify for one client against the other.

Practitioners who provide couples or marital counseling should always anticipate the possibility (although not necessarily the probability) that the therapy will not resolve the couple's problems, that a serious legal dispute may continue after or arise during the therapy, and that one or both parties may try to involve the practitioner in the dispute. The practitioner should alert the clients to this possibility and of the practitioner's wish to avoid a conflict of interest; some practitioners have a written policy that they share with clients explaining that their role is to be of help to both parties and that they will not serve as a witness for one against the other. In fact, the NASW *Code of Ethics* (2008) highlights this specific phenomenon:

> When social workers provide services to two or more people who have a relationship with each other (for example, couples, family members), social workers should clarify with all parties which individuals will be considered clients and the nature of social workers' professional obligations to the various individuals who are receiving services. Social workers who anticipate a conflict of interest among the individuals receiving services or who anticipate having to perform in potentially conflicting roles (for example, when a social worker is asked to testify in a child custody dispute or divorce proceedings involving clients) should clarify their role with the parties involved and take appropriate action to minimize any conflict of interest.
>
> (standard 1.06[d])

Similar guidance appears in the comparable standards in the American Psychological Association's *Ethical Principles of Psychologists and Code of Conduct* (2010):

> When psychologists agree to provide services to several persons who have a relationship (such as spouses, significant others, or parents and children), they take reasonable steps to clarify at the outset (1) which of the individuals are clients/patients and (2) the relationship the psychologist will have with each person. This clarification includes the psychologist's role and the probable uses of the services provided or the information obtained.
>
> (standard 10.02[a])

> If it becomes apparent that psychologists may be called on to perform potentially conflicting roles (such as family therapist and then witness for one party in divorce proceedings), psychologists take reasonable steps to clarify and modify, or withdraw from, roles appropriately.
>
> (standard 10.02[b])

Human service professionals occasionally receive subpoenas that place them in untenable conflicts of interest. In these situations practitioners must understand the nature of subpoenas and specific strategies they can use in their effort to extricate themselves from these conflicts. Practitioners who are subpoenaed may face a special conflict-of-interest dilemma concerning the disclosure of confidential or privileged information. If the professional practices in a state in which laws grant clients the right of privileged communication, avoiding compliance with the subpoena may be easier because the legislature has formally acknowledged the importance of the privilege. Also, contrary to many practitioners' understanding, a legitimate response to a subpoena is to argue that the requested information should not be disclosed or can be obtained from some other source. A subpoena itself does not require a practitioner to disclose information. Instead, a subpoena is essentially a request for information, and it may be without merit. As Grossman (1973) has said, "If the recipient knew how easy it was to have a subpoena issued; if he knew how readily the subpoena could demand information when there actually was no legal right to command the disclosure of information; if he knew how often an individual releases information that legally he had no right to release because of intimidation—he would view the threat of the subpoena with less fear and greater skepticism" (245). Further, Grossman says, "In private discussion attorneys admit that the harassing tactic of using these writs is as important in court contests as the legal 'right to the truth'" (245).

Resisting disclosure of confidential information is appropriate, particularly when practitioners believe that the information is not essential or if they can argue that the information can be obtained from other sources. According to Wilson:

> When data sought by the court can be obtained through some other source, a professional who has been subpoenaed may not have to disclose his confidential data. If the practitioner freely relinquishes his confidential though non-privileged data with little or no objection, the courts may not even check to see if the information can be obtained elsewhere. If the professional resists disclosure, however, the court may investigate to see if it can get the data from some other source.
>
> (1978:138)

In fact, the NASW *Code of Ethics* (2008) requires social workers to challenge subpoenas if they do not have client consent or a court order mandating disclosure of confidential information: "Social workers should protect the confidentiality of clients during legal proceedings to the extent permitted by law. When a court of law or other legally authorized body orders social workers to disclose confidential or privileged information without a client's consent and such disclosure could cause harm to the client, social workers should request that the court withdraw the order or limit the order as narrowly as possible or maintain the records under seal, unavailable for public inspection" (standard 1.07[j]). Polowy and Gorenberg outline specific steps practitioners can take to manage conflict-of-interest situations involving disclosure of confidential information:

1. Prepare a letter to the requester advising that the information is confidential and privileged and that absent the client's consent or a court order, the requested material cannot be released. Copies of any correspondence should be maintained in the file and may be necessary to present in a hearing on the matter.

2. File a motion to quash or objections to the subpoena based on the privileged nature of the communication between the client and practitioner. A request for a protective order may also be filed seeking to limit access to the records.

3. After writing a letter to the relevant parties in the case advising that the requested materials are confidential and privileged, it may be necessary to follow such a letter with written objections that would be filed with the court or with a motion for a protective order that asks the court to deny access to the file because it contains privileged client information. Finally, a motion to quash the subpoena could also be filed.

(1997:7)

Unanticipated conflicts of interest involving adversarial circumstances can also arise in nonclinical contexts. For example, human service administrators, researchers, or community organizers can find themselves in complicated boundary situations.

CASE 6.6

Melinda T. was a caseworker employed by a local community action program. Ms. T. was in charge of a grant-funded program to work with community residents and area developers to expand the supply of affordable housing for low- and moderate-income residents. Ms. T. also served on the board of the regional United Way, which provided partial funding for Ms. T.'s agency; to avoid a conflict of interest Ms. T. did not participate in any United Way discussions or funding decisions pertaining to her agency.

In her job as a program coordinator at the community action agency, Ms. T. learned that agency staff members were misspending United Way funds. She learned that approximately $62,000 of United Way money that was supposed to support staff salaries had been spent for unauthorized purposes unrelated to the affordable housing program. Ms. T. was unsure how to resolve her conflicting loyalties; she did not want to blow the whistle on her agency in a way that would jeopardize its viability, but she felt obligated to notify United Way officials of her agency's misappropriation of funds.

CASE 6.7

Bonnie F. was the director of research in a large community mental health center. Her office was responsible for maintaining the facility's management information system and conducting program evaluations. The community mental health center received most of its funding from the state mental health department. Ms. F.'s husband was the assistant director of the division within the state mental health department that was responsible for funding her center and others throughout the state.

Ms. F. was reviewing agency data and was concerned about statistics showing a steady, although fluctuating, decline during the previous six months in the number of clients served by the agency. Ms. F. knew that these data would pose a problem for the financially troubled agency, because the decline in clients served would translate into a reduction of state funding. Ms. F. decided to falsify some data about program use to inflate the service delivery statistics. Ms. F.'s husband read his wife's report and realized that she had falsified the data. He felt caught between his loyalty to his wife and to his agency.

As these examples illustrate, some conflict-of-interest situations involve allegations or evidence of wrongdoing. In these dual relationship scenarios practitioners feel caught between their duty to disclose ethical misconduct of some sort and their loyalty to employers, acquaintances, or relatives. As Barry observes with regard to whistle-blowing in agency settings,

Truthfulness, noninjury, and fairness are the ordinary categories of obligations that employees have to third parties, but we can still ask: How are workers to reconcile obligations to employers or organizations and others? Should the employee ensure the welfare of the organization by reporting the fellow worker using drugs, or should she be loyal to the fellow worker and say nothing? Should the secretary carry out her boss's instructions, or should she tell his wife the truth? Should the accountant say nothing about the building code violations, or should she inform authorities? In each case the employee experiences divided loyalties. Resolving such conflict calls for a careful weighing of the obligations to the employer or firm, on the one hand, and of those to the third party, on the other. The process is never easy.

(1986:239)

The circumstances surrounding collegial misconduct and pertinent boundary issues are rarely clear-cut. The evidence of wrongdoing may be questionable, the effect of the misconduct may be equivocal, and the likelihood of resolving the problem satisfactorily may be small. Deciding whether to blow the whistle must be approached deliberately and cautiously. Human service professionals first should carefully consider the severity of the harm and misconduct involved; the quality of the evidence of wrongdoing; the effect of the decision on colleagues and the agency involved; the whistle-blower's motives (that is, whether revenge or a more noble purpose motivates the whistle-blowing); and the viability of alternative, intermediate courses of action (whether other, less drastic means might address the problem—for example, directly confronting the alleged wrongdoer). As Fleishman and Payne (1980) have argued, "There may be other ways to do right . . . than by blowing a whistle on a friend. A direct personal confrontation may serve both public interest and personal loyalty, if the corrupt practice can be ended and adequate restitution made" (43).

Codes of ethics can also provide conceptual guidance when practitioners find themselves in the midst of dual relationships and evidence of collegial misconduct. The NASW *Code of Ethics* (1996) provides a particularly good example of relevant standards that suggest an incremental approach, beginning with constructive collegial confrontation and ending, if necessary, with more formal notification of appropriate authorities:

Social workers who believe that a colleague has acted unethically should seek resolution by discussing their concerns with the colleague when feasible and when such discussion is likely to be productive.

(standard 2.11[c])

When necessary, social workers who believe that a colleague has acted unethically should take action through appropriate formal channels (such as contacting a state licensing board or regulatory body, an NASW committee on inquiry, or other professional ethics committees).

(standard 2.11[d])

Of course, not all dual relationships involving conflicts of interest contain adversarial dimensions or ethical misconduct. Some conflict-of-interest situations involve people of goodwill who have only noble intentions, as in the cases that follow.

CASE 6.8

Gary L. was a professor in a graduate program in counseling. He also served on the state parole board and several days per month conducted hearings for inmates eligible for parole.

One hearing Dr. L. conducted was for an inmate who was serving a seven-year sentence for drug possession and distribution (sales). Dr. L. and his colleagues voted to parole the inmate, a college graduate who had been an earnest and diligent participant in the prison's demanding substance abuse treatment program.

Eighteen months after the inmate's parole Dr. L. was surprised to find the man enrolled as a student in one of Dr. L.'s courses. The former inmate told Dr. L., with pride, that he was now working in the substance abuse treatment field as a residential case manager and was pursuing part time a master's degree in counseling. Because the former inmate was still on parole—and was technically under Dr. L.'s jurisdiction during this period—Dr. L. was uncomfortable having the student in his class. Dr. L. talked with the student about the problematic dual relationship and suggested that he transfer to another section of the course in order to avoid the potential conflict of interest.

CASE 6.9

Cynthia W. was the executive director of a large psychiatric hospital that recently had merged with a nearby residential substance abuse treatment program. At the time of the merger Ms. W.'s husband was the chief financial officer for the substance abuse treatment program. Under the terms of the merger Ms. W. would retain her position as executive director of the new corporate entity. In principle Mr. W. would have been appointed the new entity's chief financial officer. The new board was concerned, however, about nepotism and a conflict of interest, because Ms. W. would have direct supervisory responsibility for her husband.

Whatever form unanticipated conflicts of interests take, human service professionals must take steps to minimize harm. As in the last case example, sometimes practitioners must be concerned about potential harm to colleagues and their employing organizations. In such instances practitioners must take steps to protect these parties to the greatest extent possible. In case 6.9, for instance, Mr. and Ms. W. decided that the administration of the new corporate entity that resulted from the merger needed to be beyond reproach and avoid any appearance of impropriety. Together they decided that Mr. W. would look for a new job in another organization.

Practitioners involved in potential or actual conflicts of interest that were unanticipated or unavoidable need to focus primarily on the need to protect their clients, whether the clients are individuals, couples, families, organizations, or communities. As the NASW *Code of Ethics* (2008) states,

> Social workers should be alert to and avoid conflicts of interest that interfere with the exercise of professional discretion and impartial judgment. Social workers should inform clients when a real or potential conflict of interest arises and take reasonable steps to resolve the issue in a manner that makes the clients' interests primary and protects clients' interests to the greatest extent possible. In some cases, protecting clients' interests may require termination of the professional relationship with proper referral of the client.
>
> (standard 1.06[a])

PROFESSIONAL ENCOUNTERS

The discussion of dual relationships in small communities and rural areas showed that professional relationships sometimes produce overlapping and problematic boundaries. Such situations are not limited to small communities and rural areas, however. Dual relationships among professionals can occur even in the largest metropolitan areas. On occasion practitioners who are involved in a professional relationship with a colleague will encounter that colleague unexpectedly in another professional context in a way that produces boundary issues. As with all dual relationships, practitioners must address the boundary issues in a manner designed to minimize potential harm.

CASE 6.10

Professor S. was on the faculty of the graduate school of social work. She also served as a volunteer on a committee established by a prominent regional foundation with a large endowment to allocate funds for a wide range of human service endeavors. Twice each year the foundation solicited and reviewed grant applications.

The committee reviewed applications from two of Professor S.'s colleagues at the university. The colleagues applied for funds from two different grant programs sponsored by the foundation and thus were not competing with each other. One application was submitted by a colleague with whom Professor S. had worked closely on another large research project. The second application was submitted by a colleague in the psychology department with whom Professor S. had only brief and superficial contact. In her effort to address the boundary issues, Professor S. informed the chair of the foundation's grant review committee that she had decided it would be best to recuse herself from the deliberations concerning her research partner. Professor S. explained that she wanted to avoid any appearance of impropriety. However, Professor S. did not feel a need to recuse herself from the committee's deliberations about the application from her colleague in the university's psychology department, since her relationship with this colleague was superficial.

CASE 6.11

A counselor, Margaret D., served on the ethics committee of her state's professional association. This committee reviewed and, when necessary, adjudicated ethics complaints filed against colleagues.

A long-standing client of Ms. D.'s, also a counselor in the community, was appointed to the ethics committee by the association's board of directors. Ms. D. was not comfortable serving on the ethics committee with her client, who was also her colleague. Ms. D. knew from experience that ethics committee members must engage in frank, sensitive discussion and debate about complicated ethical matters. On occasion ethics committee members disagree with one another's judgments, sometimes vehemently. Ms. D. was concerned about the potentially harmful clinical implications for her client if they experienced conflict on the ethics committee. Ms. D. was also concerned that they might find dealing with each other in these two different contexts awkward and taxing. Ms. D. broached the issue with her client-colleague; together they decided that the potential downside was too great, and that Ms. D.'s client-colleague would not accept appointment to the association's ethics committee. Ms. D. was careful not to pressure her client-colleague to decline the appointment; rather, the two spent considerable time exploring the pertinent issues and reached a mutually satisfactory conclusion.

SOCIAL ENCOUNTERS

One other form of unanticipated or unavoidable dual relationship involves social encounters with clients. Earlier I discussed practitioners' decisions when clients invite them to social events (such as a wedding, graduation, confirmation, or bar mitzvah) or when practitioners can reasonably anticipate encountering clients at community-based social events (for example, when a lesbian therapist in a relatively small community fully expects she will encounter a lesbian client at local social events).

In addition to these circumstances, human service professionals must also anticipate the possibility that they will encounter clients completely unexpectedly, in contexts in which neither party ever expected to encounter the other. Recognizing how frequently such unanticipated and unavoidable encounters occur, practitioners should have in mind how they will respond. In addition, practitioners would do well to raise the issue with clients as soon as is feasible, in order to manage the situation as professionally and smoothly as possible, minimize harm that may result from the boundary crossing, and avoid bruising clients' feelings.

CASE 6.12

A psychiatrist, Dr. F., had just begun providing clinical services to a thirty-two-year-old woman who had been diagnosed with posttraumatic stress disorder; she had been sexually abused as a child. Dr. F. prescribed psychotropic medication and consulted with a clinical social worker who provided the woman with psychotherapy.

On Thanksgiving Day, Dr. F. and her family went to her brother's home for their annual daylong get-together. Dr. F. was stunned to find that her brother's current girlfriend, whom he had invited to the Thanksgiving Day gathering, was Dr. F.'s patient. Dr. F.'s brother had just started dating the woman; she had not realized that her new boyfriend was Dr. F.'s brother, because they had different surnames and the identity of the woman's psychiatrist had not come up in conversation with her boyfriend.

During the Thanksgiving Day event Dr. F. tried tactfully to avoid sustained social conversation with her patient. She also cut her visit short in an effort to avoid the awkward social encounter. During her next regularly scheduled appointment with the patient the following week, Dr. F. broached the boundary issue in an effort to explore the various implications. The patient said that she too felt uncomfortable, particularly because it appeared that she would continue to date Dr. F.'s brother. Dr. F. and the patient explored several options, including avoiding social contact at family events and the more drastic option of terminating their professional relationship. The patient decided that because they had been working together for only a short period, it would not be too traumatic for her to begin seeing a new psychiatrist. Dr. F. agreed with the plan and helped the woman find a new psychiatrist. Dr. F. also reassured the patient that she would protect her privacy and confidentiality in any conversations Dr. F. might have with her brother.

CASE 6.13

Kim T. was a clinical social worker. In her spare time Ms. T. was a long-distance runner. She also worked out regularly at a local health club.

Ms. T. went to her health club one day and discovered that one of her long-standing clients, David R., was working out in the weight room that Ms. T. frequently used. Ms. T. was uncomfortable working out along with her client. She felt overexposed and was concerned that casual encounters with Mr. R. in this setting would complicate their professional-client relationship. When they bumped into each other at the club, Mr. R. told Ms. T. how delighted he was to see her outside the office.

Ms. T. was especially concerned about clinical ramifications because for several weeks she had wondered whether Mr. R. was feeling attracted to her; on a number of occasions Mr. R. had made comments about how he wished he could find a partner who was as sensitive and understanding as Ms. T. On two recent occasions Mr. R. had asked Ms. T. whether she needed an escort to her car after their late-evening appointment, which was Ms. T.'s last appointment of the day.

Ms. T. discussed the issue with her peer consultation group. She and her colleagues decided that the situation was too uncomfortable and the clinical risks were too great for Ms. T. to continue encountering the client at the health club. Ms. T. considered switching health clubs without discussing this with Mr. R., but she and the peer consultation group concluded that he would be offended and that it would be best for Ms. T. to discuss the boundary issues with her client. Ms. T. explained to Mr. R. that she was concerned about the boundary issues and the reasons why she had decided to switch to another health club. Mr. R. denied that a problem existed and felt hurt by Ms. T.'s explanation and course of action. Ms. T. was not able to address the issue to Mr. R.'s satisfaction. Mr. R. eventually terminated the counseling.

This last case illustrates how even the most principled, conscientious, and thoughtful approach to boundary issues may not produce an entirely satisfactory outcome. Clearly, practitioners must do what they can to prevent and manage boundary issues in the most effective, sensitive, and ethical way possible. This includes discussing with clients, toward the beginning of their working relationship, how they will handle unexpected or unavoidable social encounters in the community. This approach does not guarantee satisfactory and uncomplicated results, of course; however, a thoughtful, planned approach can substantially increase the likelihood that clients and other concerned parties will not be harmed.

7

RISK MANAGEMENT

Guidelines and Strategies

I HAVE EXAMINED a diverse array of dual relationship and boundary issues, both those that are relatively uncomplicated and some that are complex. Some involve practitioners who are motivated primarily by altruism, and some involve practitioners who violate clients' boundaries because of their own deep-seated pathology, emotional needs, or greed. Some boundary crossings serve a constructive purpose, whereas boundary violations are uniformly destructive.

Despite the remarkable variety, dual relationship and boundary issues share several key features. First, they contain the seeds of potential harm to others. Although serious harm is not inevitable—except in the most egregious violations, such as sexual exploitation of a client—it is an ever-present possibility. Human service professionals must be vigilant in their efforts to minimize potential and actual harm to others.

Second, dual relationship and boundary issues pose risks to professionals themselves. At one extreme, practitioners who violate clients' boundaries and exploit their relationships with them run the very real risk of losing their license and destroying their career. Although some boundary violations occur in and remain in the dark, many eventually come to light. Even less egregious boundary crossings can sometimes trigger lawsuits and ethics complaints filed with licensing boards and professional associations, thus disrupting the careers of even the most noble practitioners. Given these possibilities, it behooves human service professionals to understand and follow sound risk-management strategies—primarily to protect clients but also to protect themselves.

EMERGING ISSUES: THE CHALLENGE OF ELECTRONIC BOUNDARIES

Many boundary issues I have discussed have loomed large ever since the creation of the human service professions. Practitioners have always had to use their judgment concerning relationships with former clients, self-disclosure, clients' invitations and gifts, unanticipated encounters in the community, conflicts of interest, and so on. Yet practitioners should be vigilant in their efforts to identify novel and emerging boundary issues that previous generations of practitioners could not have anticipated. As I discussed earlier, among the most significant contemporary challenges involve practitioners' and clients' use of social media (for example, Facebook and Twitter) and electronic communications and services (such as online counseling, cybertherapy, telephone counseling, and email therapy). These electronic options have created previously unknown boundary and dual relationship challenges, particularly with respect to self-disclosure, privacy, confidentiality, and practitioner availability (Gutheil and Simon 2005).

Human service professionals would do well to develop comprehensive policies and guidelines that address relevant boundary issues. Discussing these with clients at the beginning of the working relationship can help avoid boundary confusion and misunderstanding. Kolmes (2011) offers a useful template that addresses policies concerning practitioners' use of diverse social media sites and services, including Facebook, Twitter, text messaging, email, Google and other search engines, business review sites, and electronic location-based services. Kolmes routinely informs clients that she does not accept friend or contact requests on social media sites such as Facebook, Twitter, and LinkedIn. Kolmes also informs clients that she will not search for them using search technology such as Google and Facebook unless there is a genuine emergency or crisis (for example, if the client is at risk of harm). In addition, Kolmes explains, she will use email only to arrange or modify appointments; clients are instructed to not use email to correspond about clinical matters.

Zur encourages practitioners to make the following disclosure to clients regarding their use of email, cell phones, computers, and faxes:

It is very important to be aware that computers, e-mail, and cell phone communication can be relatively easily accessed by unauthorized people and hence can compromise the privacy and confidentiality of such communication. E-mails, in particular, are vulnerable to such unauthorized access because servers have unlimited and direct access to all e-mails that go through them. Additionally, Dr. XX's e-mails are not encrypted. Dr. XX's computers are equipped and regularly updated with a firewall, virus protection, and a password. He also backs up all confidential information from his computers on CDs on a regular basis. The CDs are stored securely offsite. Please notify Dr. XX if you decide to avoid or limit in any way the use of any or all communication devices such as e-mail, cell phone, or faxes. Unless Dr. XX hears from you otherwise, he will continue to communicate with you via e-mail when necessary or appropriate. Please do not use e-mail or faxes for emergencies. Although Dr. XX checks phone messages frequently during the day when he is in town, he does not always check his e-mails daily.

(2007:141)

Zur offers a series of practical guidelines to prevent boundary problems when using technology to provide clinical services:

1. Identify the client and obtain basic information such as full name, address, age, gender, phone, fax, emergency contacts, and so on.

2. Provide clients with a clear informed consent form detailing the limitations of telehealth [the delivery of health-related services using telecommunication technology, such as email, social media, videoconferencing, telephone], in general, and confidentiality and privacy, in particular.

3. Inform the clients of potential limitations of telehealth when it comes to crisis intervention and dealing with dangerous situations.

4. Practice within your limits of clinical and technological competence.

5. Have a crisis intervention plan in place, including ways to reach local emergency services and make referrals to local psychotherapists, psychiatrists, and psychiatric hospitals in the client's vicinity.

6. Provide thorough screening when considering which clients may not be suited to this kind of medium.

7. Have a clear agreement with regard to what is being charged, how it is being charged, and the rates and method of payment.

8. Do not render medical or psychiatric advice by giving a diagnosis or proposing a course of treatment except to those with whom you have established professional psychotherapeutic relationships.

9. Follow your state laws, your licensing board rules, and your state and

national professional association guidelines and practice within the standard of care.

10. Screen clients for technical and clinical suitability for telehealth.

11. Telehealth is one of the fastest growing fields in medicine. Update yourself on the latest research on telehealth.

(2007:144–45)

Practitioners who provide clinical services electronically using online counseling, cybertherapy, email, and telephone should develop clear guidelines that draw on emerging ethical standards. For example, the International Society for Mental Health Online, American Distance Counseling Association, and Association for Counseling and Therapy Online have developed useful ethics standards. In addition, literature is beginning to emerge that addresses boundary and other ethical issues associated with online counseling (Jones and Stokes 2009; Kraus, Stricker, and Speyer 2011).

RISK-MANAGEMENT GUIDELINES

Effective risk management concerning dual relationship and boundary issues should provide both conceptual guidance and practical steps that enhance protection of all parties involved. The following is a decision-making model, based on several available frameworks (Corey and Herlihy 1997; Gottlieb 1993; Reamer 1990, 2003, 2005, 2006c, 2008b–c; Gutheil 2005; Younggren and Gottlieb 2004; Zur 2007), that practitioners can use when they encounter potential or actual dual relationships and boundary issues. This model incorporates various factors I highlighted throughout this discussion:

1. Attempt to set unambiguous boundaries at the beginning of all professional relationships. Document relevant discussions.

2. Evaluate potential dual relationships and boundary issues by considering (a) the amount of power the practitioner holds over the client, (b) the duration and intensity of the relationship, (c) the clarity of conditions surrounding planned or actual termination, (d) the client's clinical profile (when involved in clinical work), and (e) prevailing ethical standards as reflected in relevant codes of ethics. How much power does the professional have over the client? How long has the relationship lasted? How likely is it that the client will return for additional services? In clinical relationships, to

what extent do the client's clinical needs, issues, vulnerabilities, and symptoms increase the risk that the client will be harmed? To what extent does the dual relationship, boundary crossing, or boundary violation breach prevailing ethical standards? Is the dual relationship avoidable? Relationships that entail considerable practitioner power, are long lasting, do not involve clear-cut termination, involve clinical issues that render clients vulnerable, and are not consistent with pertinent ethical standards are especially problematic and risky.

3. Consider, based on these criteria, whether a dual relationship in any form is warranted or justifiable. Some dual relationships, or elements of dual relationships, may be constructive and helpful, while others are harmful. Recognize that gradations exist between the extreme options of a full-fledged dual relationship and no dual relationship. For example, a practitioner may decide that attending a client's graduation from a substance abuse treatment program is permissible but attending the postgraduation party at the client's home is not. A practitioner may decide to disclose to a particular client that he is a new parent without disclosing intimate details concerning his struggle with infertility. A human service grant administrator may decide to collaborate on a joint service delivery project with a private agency headed by her husband but recuse herself from all decisions at her agency concerning funding of her husband's program.

4. Pay special attention to potentially conflicting roles in the relationship, or what Kitchener (1988) calls "role incompatibility." For instance, a clinical social worker should not agree to counsel her secretary and the secretary's troubled family. An administrator should not supervise her spouse. A seasoned clinician should not supervise her partner who is seeking licensure as a mental health professional. Of course, sometimes professionals do not agree about the extent of the role incompatibility, which entails divergent expectations and power differentials; among the best examples is the debate among professionals concerning whether practitioners in recovery should attend twelve-step meetings (such as Alcoholics Anonymous and Narcotics Anonymous) at which a client is present and whether community-based treatment programs should hire former clients as staff members.

5. Whenever there is any degree of doubt about dual relationships or boundary issues, consult thoughtful, principled, and trusted colleagues (Reamer 1995a). It is important to consult with colleagues who understand one's work, particularly in relation to services provided, clientele served, and relevant ethical standards.

6. Discuss the relevant issues with all the parties involved, especially clients. Clients should be actively and deliberately involved in these judgments, in part as a sign of respect and in part to promote informed consent. Fully inform clients of any potential risks.

7. Work under supervision whenever boundary issues are complex and the related risk is high. Be sure to develop an exit strategy in the event that a dual relationship proves to be harmful.

8. If necessary, refer the client to another professional in order to minimize risk and prevent harm.

9. Document key aspects of the decision-making process, for example, colleagues consulted, documents reviewed (codes of ethics, agency policies, statutes, regulations), and discussions with clients. As Gutheil and Gabbard (1993) observe in reviewing the findings of Lipton (1977) with regard to clinical contexts, "It is ultimately impossible to codify or prescribe a personal relationship between therapist and patient in a precise manner. Perhaps the best risk management involves careful consideration of any departures from one's usual practice accompanied by careful documentation of the reasons for the departure" (195–96).

To prevent inappropriate dual relationships and to help practitioners manage complex boundary issues, human service professionals must mount an ambitious education and training agenda. This agenda should include four principal components (Reamer 2001a–b; Reamer and Abramson 1982). First, professional education programs in social work, psychology, marriage and family therapy, psychiatry, psychiatric nursing, and counseling must address these issues vigorously and comprehensively, in the context of both classroom education and internships. Discrete classroom courses devoted to professional ethics, and portions of other courses that include ethics as a key topic (for example, courses on clinical practice, administration, supervision), should incorporate readings about and discussions of dual relationships and boundary issues. Supervisors in internship settings should address this issue deliberately as well, with respect to interns' relationships with clients and with their supervisors and other staff.

Second, continuing education programs should highlight these issues regularly. Annual conferences of professional associations and continuing education seminars should routinely provide participants with workshops and seminars on dual relationships and boundary issues.

Third, human service administrators and supervisors should offer staff members sustained in-service training on these issues. In addition to traditional didactic presentations, the training should include opportunities for staff members to wrestle with complex case scenarios. In-service training facilitators can help staff members apply various guidelines—code of ethics standards, agency policies, pertinent statutes, regulations, and case law—to this case material to help sharpen the staff's ethical judgment.

Finally, human service administrators and supervisors should develop and continually refine agency-based policies designed to provide staff with constructive guidance regarding boundary issues. Although formulating crystal clear, unequivocal guidelines that address all boundary-related permutations is impossible, thoughtful, conceptually rigorous guidelines can communicate to staff members the core values and concepts they need to consider and help them enhance their critical thinking skills. Smith and Fitzpatrick's astute conclusion about the ambiguity of many boundary issues in clinical contexts has broad implications for the human services in general:

> In summary, boundary issues regularly pose complex challenges to clinicians. The effects of crossing commonly recognized boundaries range from significant therapeutic progress to serious, indelible harm. The issues are further complicated by the wide range of individual variation that exists in a field where what is normal practice for one clinician may be considered a boundary violation by another. Although setting appropriate boundaries is a professional imperative, flexibility in their maintenance is equally important. Clinicians should avoid setting simplistic standards that may create barriers to therapeutic progress. In the final analysis, ethical practice is governed less by proscriptions than by sound clinical judgment bearing on the therapeutic interventions that will advance the client's welfare. Given the individual differences among clients, fine adjustments are required in every case.
>
> (1995:505)

In the end human service professionals who face difficult and challenging boundary issues must draw on their finely honed ethical instincts. Conceptual guidance is fine and important, but practitioners' handling of daunting circumstances ultimately must depend on their genuine and passionate determination to make ethically sound judgments.

Appendix

EXCERPTS FROM CODES OF ETHICS: BOUNDARIES, DUAL RELATIONSHIPS, CONFLICTS OF INTEREST

AMERICAN ASSOCIATION FOR MARRIAGE AND FAMILY THERAPY, *CODE OF ETHICS* (2001)

1.3 Marriage and family therapists are aware of their influential positions with respect to clients, and they avoid exploiting the trust and dependency of such persons. Therapists, therefore, make every effort to avoid conditions and multiple relationships with clients that could impair professional judgment or increase the risk of exploitation. Such relationships include, but are not limited to, business or close personal relationships with a client or the client's immediate family. When the risk of impairment or exploitation exists due to conditions or multiple roles, therapists take appropriate precautions.

1.4 Sexual intimacy with clients is prohibited.

1.5 Sexual intimacy with former clients is likely to be harmful and is therefore prohibited for two years following the termination of therapy or last professional contact. In an effort to avoid exploiting the trust and dependency of clients, marriage and family therapists should not engage in sexual intimacy with former clients after the two years following termination or last professional contact. Should therapists engage in sexual intimacy with former clients following two years after termination or last professional contact, the burden shifts to the therapist to demonstrate that there has been no exploitation or injury to the former client or to the client's immediate family.

1.7 Marriage and family therapists do not use their professional relationships with clients to further their own interests.

3.4 Marriage and family therapists do not provide services that create a conflict of interest that may impair work performance or clinical judgment.

3.5 Marriage and family therapists, as presenters, teachers, supervisors, consultants and researchers, are dedicated to high standards of scholarship, present accurate information, and disclose potential conflicts of interest.

3.8 Marriage and family therapists do not engage in sexual or other forms of harassment of clients, students, trainees, supervisees, employees, colleagues, or research subjects.

3.9 Marriage and family therapists do not engage in the exploitation of clients, students, trainees, supervisees, employees, colleagues, or research subjects.

3.10 Marriage and family therapists do not give to or receive from clients (a) gifts of substantial value or (b) gifts that impair the integrity or efficacy of the therapeutic relationship.

4.1 Marriage and family therapists are aware of their influential positions with respect to students and supervisees, and they avoid exploiting the trust and dependency of such persons. Therapists, therefore, make every effort to avoid conditions and multiple relationships that could impair professional objectivity or increase the risk of exploitation. When the risk of impairment or exploitation exists due to conditions or multiple roles, therapists take appropriate precautions.

4.2 Marriage and family therapists do not provide therapy to current students or supervisees.

4.3 Marriage and family therapists do not engage in sexual intimacy with students or supervisees during the evaluative or training relationship between the therapist and student or supervisee. Should a supervisor engage in sexual activity with a former supervisee, the burden of proof shifts to the supervisor to demonstrate that there has been no exploitation or injury to the supervisee.

4.6 Marriage and family therapists avoid accepting as supervisees or students those individuals with whom a prior or existing relationship could compromise the therapist's objectivity. When such situations cannot be avoided, therapists take appropriate precautions to maintain objectivity. Examples of such relationships include, but are not limited to, those individuals with whom the therapist has a current or prior sexual, close personal, immediate familial, or therapeutic relationship.

NATIONAL ASSOCIATION OF SOCIAL WORKERS (NASW), *CODE OF ETHICS* (2008)

1.06 Conflicts of Interest

(a) Social workers should be alert to and avoid conflicts of interest that interfere with the exercise of professional discretion and impartial judgment. Social workers should inform clients when a real or potential conflict of interest arises and take reasonable steps to resolve the issue in a manner that makes the clients' interests primary and protects clients' interests to the greatest extent possible. In some cases, protecting clients' interests may require termination of the professional relationship with proper referral of the client.

(b) Social workers should not take unfair advantage of any professional relationship or exploit others to further their personal, religious, political, or business interests.

(c) Social workers should not engage in dual or multiple relationships with clients or former clients in which there is a risk of exploitation or potential harm to the client. In instances when dual or multiple relationships are unavoidable, social workers should take steps to protect clients and are responsible for setting clear, appropriate, and culturally sensitive boundaries. (Dual or multiple relationships occur when social workers relate to clients in more than one relationship, whether professional, social, or business. Dual or multiple relationships can occur simultaneously or consecutively.)

(d) When social workers provide services to two or more people who have a relationship with each other (for example, couples, family members), social workers should clarify with all parties which individuals will be considered clients and the nature of social workers' professional obligations to the various individuals who are receiving services. Social workers who anticipate a conflict of interest among the individuals receiving services or who anticipate having to perform in potentially conflicting roles (for example, when a social worker is asked to testify in a child custody dispute or divorce proceedings involving clients) should clarify their role with the parties involved and take appropriate action to minimize any conflict of interest.

1.09 Sexual Relationships

(a) Social workers should under no circumstances engage in sexual activities or sexual contact with current clients, whether such contact is consensual or forced.

(b) Social workers should not engage in sexual activities or sexual contact with clients' relatives or other individuals with whom clients maintain a close personal relationship when there is a risk of exploitation or potential harm to the client. Sexual activity or sexual contact with clients' relatives or other individuals with whom clients maintain a personal relationship has the potential to be harmful to the client and may make it difficult for the social worker and client to maintain appropriate professional boundaries. Social workers—not their clients, their clients' relatives, or other individuals with whom the client maintains a personal relationship—assume the full burden for setting clear, appropriate, and culturally sensitive boundaries.

(c) Social workers should not engage in sexual activities or sexual contact with former clients because of the potential for harm to the client. If social workers engage in conduct contrary to this prohibition or claim that an exception to this prohibition is warranted because of extraordinary circumstances, it is social workers—not their clients—who assume the full burden of demonstrating that the former client has not been exploited, coerced, or manipulated, intentionally or unintentionally.

(d) Social workers should not provide clinical services to individuals with whom they have had a prior sexual relationship. Providing clinical services to a former sexual partner has the potential to be harmful to the individual and is likely to make it difficult for the social worker and individual to maintain appropriate professional boundaries.

1.10 Physical Contact

Social workers should not engage in physical contact with clients when there is a possibility of psychological harm to the client as a result of the contact (such as cradling or caressing clients). Social workers who engage in appropriate physical contact with clients are responsible for setting clear, appropriate, and culturally sensitive boundaries that govern such physical contact.

1.11 Sexual Harassment

Social workers should not sexually harass clients. Sexual harassment includes sexual advances, sexual solicitation, requests for sexual favors, and other verbal or physical conduct of a sexual nature.

1.13 Payment for Services

(b) Social workers should avoid accepting goods or services from clients as payment for professional services. Bartering arrangements, particularly involving services, create the potential for conflicts of interest, exploitation, and inappropriate boundaries in social workers' relationships with clients. Social workers should explore and may participate in bartering only in very limited circumstances when it can be demonstrated that such arrangements are an accepted practice among professionals in the local community, considered to be essential for the provision of services, negotiated without coercion, and entered into at the client's initiative and with the client's informed consent. Social workers who accept goods or services from clients as payment for professional services assume the full burden of demonstrating that this arrangement will not be detrimental to the client or the professional relationship.

1.16 Termination of Services

(d) Social workers should not terminate services to pursue a social, financial, or sexual relationship with a client.

2.07 Sexual Relationships

(a) Social workers who function as supervisors or educators should not engage in sexual activities or contact with supervisees, students, trainees, or other colleagues over whom they exercise professional authority.

(b) Social workers should avoid engaging in sexual relationships with colleagues when there is potential for a conflict of interest. Social workers who become involved in, or anticipate becoming involved in, a sexual relationship with a colleague have a duty to transfer professional responsibilities, when necessary, to avoid a conflict of interest.

2.08 Sexual Harassment

Social workers should not sexually harass supervisees, students, trainees, or colleagues. Sexual harassment includes sexual advances, sexual solicitation, requests for sexual favors, and other verbal or physical conduct of a sexual nature.

3.01 Supervision and Consultation

(c) Social workers should not engage in any dual or multiple relationships with supervisees in which there is a risk of exploitation of or potential harm to the supervisee.

3.02 Education and Training

(d) Social workers who function as educators or field instructors for students should not engage in any dual or multiple relationships with students in which there is a risk of exploitation or potential harm to the student. Social work educators and field instructors are responsible for setting clear, appropriate, and culturally sensitive boundaries.

4.03 Private Conduct

Social workers should not permit their private conduct to interfere with their ability to fulfill their professional responsibilities.

4.07 Solicitations

(a) Social workers should not engage in uninvited solicitation of potential clients who, because of their circumstances, are vulnerable to undue influence, manipulation, or coercion.

(b) Social workers should not engage in solicitation of testimonial endorsements (including solicitation of consent to use a client's prior statement as a testimonial endorsement) from current clients or from other people who, because of their particular circumstances, are vulnerable to undue influence.

5.02 Evaluation and Research

(o) Social workers engaged in evaluation or research should be alert to and avoid conflicts of interest and dual relationships with participants, should inform participants when a real or potential conflict of interest arises, and should take steps to resolve the issue in a manner that makes participants' interests primary.

AMERICAN COUNSELING ASSOCIATION, *CODE OF ETHICS* (2005)

A.5.a. Current Clients

Sexual or romantic counselor-client interactions or relationships with current clients, their romantic partners, or their family members are prohibited.

A.5.b. Former Clients

Sexual or romantic counselor-client interactions or relationships with former clients, their romantic partners, or their family members are prohibited for a period of 5 years following the last professional contact. Counselors, before engaging in sexual or romantic interactions or relationships with clients, their romantic partners, or client family members after 5 years following the last professional contact, demonstrate forethought and document (in written form) whether the interactions or relationship can be viewed as exploitive in some way and/or whether there is still potential to harm the former client; in cases of potential exploitation and/or harm, the counselor avoids entering such an interaction or relationship.

A.5.c. Nonprofessional Interactions or Relationships (Other Than Sexual or Romantic Interactions or Relationships)

Counselor-client nonprofessional relationships with clients, former clients, their romantic partners, or their family members should be avoided, except when the interaction is potentially beneficial to the client.

A.5.d. Potentially Beneficial Interactions

When a counselor-client nonprofessional interaction with a client or former client may be potentially beneficial to the client or former client, the counselor must document in case records, prior to the interaction (when feasible), the rationale for such an interaction, the potential benefit, and anticipated consequences for the client or former client and other individuals significantly involved with the client or former client. Such interactions should be initiated with appropriate client consent. Where unintentional harm occurs to the client or former client, or to an individual significantly involved with the client or former client, due to the nonprofessional interaction, the counselor must show evidence of an attempt to remedy such harm. Examples of potentially beneficial interactions include, but are not limited to, attending a formal ceremony (e.g., a wedding/commitment ceremony or graduation); purchasing a service or product provided by a client or former client (excepting unrestricted bartering); hospital visits to an ill family member; mutual membership in a professional association, organization, or community.

A.5.e. Role Changes in the Professional Relationship

When a counselor changes a role from the original or most recent contracted relationship, he or she obtains informed consent from the client and explains the right of the client to refuse services related to the change. Examples of role changes include (1) changing from individual to relationship or family counseling, or vice versa; (2) changing from a nonforensic evaluative role to a therapeutic role, or vice versa; (3) changing from a counselor to a researcher role (i.e., enlisting clients as research participants), or vice versa; and (4) changing from a counselor to a mediator role, or vice versa. Clients must be fully informed of any anticipated consequences (e.g., financial, legal, personal, or therapeutic) of counselor role changes.

A.7. Multiple Clients

When a counselor agrees to provide counseling services to two or more persons who have a relationship, the counselor clarifies at the outset which person or persons are clients and the nature of the relationships the counselor will have with each involved person. If it becomes apparent that the counselor may be called upon to perform potentially conflicting roles, the counselor will clarify, adjust, or withdraw from roles appropriately.

A.10.d. Bartering

Counselors may barter only if the relationship is not exploitive or harmful and does not place the counselor in an unfair advantage, if the client requests it, and if such arrangements are an accepted practice among professionals in the community. Counselors consider the cultural implications of bartering and discuss relevant concerns with clients and document such agreements in a clear written contract.

A.10.e. Receiving Gifts

Counselors understand the challenges of accepting gifts from clients and recognize that in some cultures, small gifts are a token of respect and showing gratitude. When determining whether or not to accept a gift from clients, counselors take into account the therapeutic relationship, the monetary value of the gift, a client's motivation for giving the gift, and the counselor's motivation for wanting or declining the gift.

C.6.a. Sexual Harassment

Counselors do not engage in or condone sexual harassment. Sexual harassment is defined as sexual solicitation, physical advances, or verbal or nonverbal conduct that is sexual in nature, that occurs in connection with professional activities or roles, and that either (1) is unwelcome, is offensive, or creates a hostile workplace or learning environment, and counselors know or are told this; or (2) is sufficiently severe or intense to be perceived as harassment to a reasonable person in the context in which the behavior occurred. Sexual harassment can consist of a single intense or severe act or multiple persistent or pervasive acts.

F.3.a. Relationship Boundaries with Supervisees

Counseling supervisors clearly define and maintain ethical professional, personal, and social relationships with their supervisees. Counseling supervisors avoid nonprofessional relationships with current supervisees. If supervisors must assume other professional roles (e.g., clinical and administrative supervisor, instructor) with supervisees, they work to minimize potential conflicts and explain to supervisees the expectations and responsibilities associated with each role. They do not engage in any form of nonprofessional interaction that may compromise the supervisory relationship.

F.3.b. Sexual Relationships

Sexual or romantic interactions or relationships with current supervisees are prohibited.

F.3.c. Sexual Harassment

Counseling supervisors do not condone or subject supervisees to sexual harassment.

F.3.d. Close Relatives and Friends

Counseling supervisors avoid accepting close relatives, romantic partners, or friends as supervisees.

F.3.e. Potentially Beneficial Relationships

Counseling supervisors are aware of the power differential in their relationships with supervisees. If they believe nonprofessional relationships with a supervisee may be potentially beneficial to the supervisee, they take precautions similar to those taken by counselors when working with clients. Examples of potentially beneficial interactions or relationships include attending a formal ceremony; hospital visits; providing support during a stressful event; or mutual membership in a professional association, organization, or community. Counseling supervisors engage in open discussions with supervisees when they consider entering into relationships with them outside of their roles as clinical and/or administrative supervisors. Before engaging in nonprofessional relationships, supervisors discuss with supervisees and document the rationale for such interactions, potential benefits or drawbacks, and anticipated consequences for the supervisee. Supervisors clarify the specific nature and limitations of the additional role(s) they will have with the supervisee.

F.5.c. Counseling for Supervisees

If supervisees request counseling, supervisors provide them with acceptable referrals. Counselors do not provide counseling services to supervisees. Supervisors address interpersonal competencies in terms of the impact of these issues on clients, the supervisory relationship, and professional functioning.

F. 10. Roles and Relationships between Counselor Educators and Students

F.10.a. Sexual or Romantic Relationships

Sexual or romantic interactions or relationships with current students are prohibited.

F.10.b. Sexual Harassment

Counselor educators do not condone or subject students to sexual harassment.

F.10.c. Relationships with Former Students

Counselor educators are aware of the power differential in the relationship between faculty and students. Faculty members foster open discussions with former students when considering engaging in a social, sexual, or other intimate relationship. Faculty members discuss with the former student how their former relationship may affect the change in relationship.

F.10.d. Nonprofessional Relationships

Counselor educators avoid nonprofessional or ongoing professional relationships with students in which there is a risk of potential harm to the student or that may compromise the training experience or grades assigned. In addition, counselor educators do not accept any form of professional services, fees, commissions, reimbursement, or remuneration from a site for student or supervisee placement.

F.10.e. Counseling Services

Counselor educators do not serve as counselors to current students unless this is a brief role associated with a training experience.

F.10.f. Potentially Beneficial Relationships

Counselor educators are aware of the power differential in the relationship between faculty and students. If they believe a nonprofessional relationship with a student may be potentially beneficial to the student, they take precautions similar to those taken by counselors when working with clients. Examples of potentially beneficial interactions or relationships include, but are not limited to, attending a formal ceremony; hospital visits; providing support during a stressful event; or mutual membership in a professional association, organization, or community. Counselor educators engage in open discussions with students when they consider entering into relationships with students outside of their roles as teachers and supervisors. They discuss with students the rationale for such interactions, the potential benefits and drawbacks, and the anticipated consequences for the student. Educators clarify the specific nature and limitations of the additional role(s) they will have with the student prior to engaging in a nonprofessional relationship. Nonprofessional relationships with students should be time-limited and initiated with student consent.

G.3. Relationships with Research Participants (When Research Involves Intensive or Extended Interactions)

G.3.a. Nonprofessional Relationships

Nonprofessional relationships with research participants should be avoided.

G.3.b. Relationships with Research Participants

Sexual or romantic counselor-research participant interactions or relationships with current research participants are prohibited.

G.3.c. Sexual Harassment and Research Participants

Researchers do not condone or subject research participants to sexual harassment.

G.3.d. Potentially Beneficial Interactions

When a nonprofessional interaction between the researcher and the research participant may be potentially beneficial, the researcher must document, prior to the interaction (when feasible), the rationale for such an interaction, the potential benefit, and anticipated consequences for the research participant. Such interactions should be initiated with appropriate consent of the research participant. Where unintentional harm occurs to the research participant due to the nonprofessional interaction, the researcher must show evidence of an attempt to remedy such harm.

AMERICAN PSYCHOLOGICAL ASSOCIATION, *ETHICAL PRINCIPLES OF PSYCHOLOGISTS AND CODE OF CONDUCT* (2010)

3.02 Sexual Harassment

Psychologists do not engage in sexual harassment. Sexual harassment is sexual solicitation, physical advances, or verbal or nonverbal conduct that is sexual in nature, that occurs in connection with the psychologist's activities or roles as a psychologist, and that either (1) is unwelcome, is offensive, or creates a hostile workplace or educational environment, and the psychologist knows or is told this or (2) is sufficiently severe or intense to be abusive to a reasonable person in the context. Sexual harassment can consist of a single intense or severe act or of multiple persistent or pervasive acts.

3.05 Multiple Relationships

(a) A multiple relationship occurs when a psychologist is in a professional role with a person and (1) at the same time is in another role with the same person, (2) at the same time is in a relationship with a person closely associated with or related to the person with whom the psychologist has the professional relationship, or (3) promises to enter into another relationship in the future with the person or a person closely associated with or related to the person.

A psychologist refrains from entering into a multiple relationship if the multiple relationship could reasonably be expected to impair the psychologist's objectivity, competence, or effectiveness in performing his or her functions as a psychologist, or otherwise risks exploitation or harm to the person with whom the professional relationship exists.

Multiple relationships that would not reasonably be expected to cause impairment or risk exploitation or harm are not unethical.

(b) If a psychologist finds that, due to unforeseen factors, a potentially harmful multiple relationship has arisen, the psychologist takes reasonable steps to resolve it with due regard for the best interests of the affected person and maximal compliance with the Ethics Code.

(c) When psychologists are required by law, institutional policy, or extraordinary circumstances to serve in more than one role in judicial or administrative proceedings, at the outset they clarify role expectations and the extent of confidentiality and thereafter as changes occur.

3.06 Conflict of Interest

Psychologists refrain from taking on a professional role when personal, scientific, professional, legal, financial, or other interests or relationships could reasonably be expected to (1) impair their objectivity, competence, or effectiveness in performing their functions as psychologists or (2) expose the person or organization with whom the professional relationship exists to harm or exploitation.

3.07 Third-Party Requests for Services

When psychologists agree to provide services to a person or entity at the request of a third party, psychologists attempt to clarify at the outset of the service the nature of the relationship with all individuals or organizations involved. This clarification includes the role of the psychologist (e.g., therapist, consultant, diagnostician, or expert witness), an identification of who is the client, the probable uses of the services provided or the information obtained, and the fact that there may be limits to confidentiality.

3.08 Exploitative Relationships

Psychologists do not exploit persons over whom they have supervisory, evaluative, or other authority such as clients/patients, students, supervisees, research participants, and employees.

5.05 Testimonials

Psychologists do not solicit testimonials from current therapy clients/patients or other persons who because of their particular circumstances are vulnerable to undue influence.

5.06 In-Person Solicitation

Psychologists do not engage, directly or through agents, in uninvited in-person solicitation of business from actual or potential therapy clients/patients or other persons who because of their particular circumstances are vulnerable to undue influence. However, this prohibition does not preclude (1) attempting to implement appropriate collateral contacts for the purpose of benefiting an already engaged therapy client/patient or (2) providing disaster or community outreach services.

6.05 Barter with Clients/Patients

Barter is the acceptance of goods, services, or other nonmonetary remuneration from clients/patients in return for psychological services. Psychologists may barter only if (1) it is not clinically contraindicated, and (2) the resulting arrangement is not exploitative.

7.07 Sexual Relationships with Students and Supervisees

Psychologists do not engage in sexual relationships with students or supervisees who are in their department, agency, or training center or over whom psychologists have or are likely to have evaluative authority.

10.02 Therapy Involving Couples or Families

(a) When psychologists agree to provide services to several persons who have a relationship (such as spouses, significant others, or parents and children), they take reasonable steps to clarify at the outset (1) which of the individuals are clients/patients and (2) the relationship the psychologist will have with each person. This clarification includes the psychologist's role and the probable uses of the services provided or the information obtained.

(b) If it becomes apparent that psychologists may be called on to perform potentially conflicting roles (such as family therapist and then witness for one party in divorce proceedings), psychologists take reasonable steps to clarify and modify, or withdraw from, roles appropriately.

10.06 Sexual Intimacies with Relatives or Significant Others of Current Therapy Clients/Patients

Psychologists do not engage in sexual intimacies with individuals they know to be close relatives, guardians, or significant others of current clients/patients. Psychologists do not terminate therapy to circumvent this standard.

10.07 Therapy with Former Sexual Partners

Psychologists do not accept as therapy clients/patients persons with whom they have engaged in sexual intimacies.

10.08 Sexual Intimacies with Former Therapy Clients/Patients

(a) Psychologists do not engage in sexual intimacies with former clients/patients for at least two years after cessation or termination of therapy.

(b) Psychologists do not engage in sexual intimacies with former clients/patients even after a two-year interval except in the most unusual circumstances. Psychologists who engage in such activity after the two years following cessation or termination of therapy and of having no sexual contact with the former client/patient bear the burden of demonstrating that there has been no exploitation, in light of all relevant factors, including (1) the amount of time that has passed since therapy terminated; (2) the nature, duration, and intensity of the therapy; (3) the circumstances of termination; (4) the client's/patient's personal history; (5) the client's/patient's current mental status; (6) the likelihood of adverse impact on the client/patient; and (7) any statements or actions made by the therapist during the course of therapy suggesting or inviting the possibility of a post-termination sexual or romantic relationship with the client/patient.

AMERICAN PSYCHIATRIC ASSOCIATION, *THE PRINCIPLES OF MEDICAL ETHICS WITH ANNOTATIONS ESPECIALLY APPLICABLE TO PSYCHIATRY* (2009)

Section 1

A physician shall be dedicated to providing competent medical service with compassion and respect for human dignity and rights.

1. A psychiatrist shall not gratify his/her own needs by exploiting the patient. The psychiatrist shall be ever vigilant about the impact that his or her conduct has upon the boundaries of the doctor-patient relationship, and thus upon the well being of the patient. These requirements become particularly important because of the essentially private, highly personal, and sometimes intensely emotional nature of the relationship established with the psychiatrist.

Section 2

A physician shall uphold the standards of professionalism, be honest in all professional interactions and strive to report physicians deficient in character or competence, or engaging in fraud or deception to appropriate entities.

1. The requirement that the physician conduct himself/herself with propriety in his/her profession and in all the actions of his/her life is especially important in the case of the psychiatrist because the patient tends to model his/her behavior after that of his/her psychiatrist by identification. Further, the necessary intensity of the treatment relationship may tend to activate sexual and other needs and fantasies on the part of both patient and psychiatrist, while weakening the objectivity necessary for control. Additionally, the inherent inequality in the doctor-patient relationship may lead to exploitation of the patient. Sexual activity with a current or former patient is unethical.

2. The psychiatrist should diligently guard against exploiting information furnished by the patient and should not use the unique position of power afforded him/her by the psychotherapeutic situation to influence the patient in any way not directly relevant to the treatment goals.

Section 4

A physician shall respect the rights of patients, colleagues, and other health professionals, and shall safeguard patient confidences and privacy within the constraints of the law.

14. Sexual involvement between a faculty member or supervisor and a trainee or student, in those situations in which an abuse of power can occur, often takes advantage of inequalities in the working relationship and may be unethical because:

a. Any treatment of a patient being supervised may be deleteriously affected.

b. It may damage the trust relationship between teacher and student.

c. Teachers are important professional role models for their trainees and affect their trainees' future professional behavior.

REFERENCES

Aisner, A. 2008. "Ex-therapist Faces Prison for Assaulting Patients." *Ann Arbor News*, January 28. http://blog.mlive.com/annarbornews/2008/01/extherapist_faces_prison_for_a.html.

Akamatsu, T. J. 1988. "Intimate Relationships with Former Clients: National Survey of Attitudes and Behavior among Practitioners." *Professional Psychology: Research and Practice* 19:454–58.

Alcoholics Anonymous World Services. 1984. *This Is A.A.: An Introduction to the A.A. Recovery Program* [brochure]. New York: Author.

Amdur, R. and E. A. Bankert. 2010. *Institutional Review Board: Member Handbook.* Sudbury, Mass.: Jones & Bartlett.

American Association for Marriage and Family Therapy. 2001. *AAMFT Code of Ethics.* Washington, D.C.: American Association for Marriage and Family Therapy.

American Counseling Association. 2005. *ACA Code of Ethics.* Alexandria, Va.: American Counseling Association.

American Psychological Association. 2010. *Ethical Principles of Psychologists and Code of Conduct.* Washington, D.C.: American Psychological Association.

Anderson, S. C. and D. L. Mandell. 1989. "The Use of Self-disclosure by Professional Social Workers." *Social Casework* 70:259–67.

Anderson, S. K. and K. S. Kitchener. 1998. "Nonsexual Psychotherapy Relationships: A Conceptual Framework." *Professional Psychology: Research and Practice* 29:91–99.

Appelbaum, P. S. and L. Jorgenson. 1991. "Psychotherapist-Patient Sexual Contact after Termination of Treatment: An Analysis and a Proposal." *American Journal of Psychiatry* 148:1466–73.

Austin, K. M., M. E. Moline, and G. T. Williams. 1990. *Confronting Malpractice: Legal and Ethical Dilemmas in Psychotherapy.* Newbury Park, Calif.: Sage.

Baer, B. E. and N. L. Murdock. 1995. "Nonerotic Dual Relationships between Therapist and Clients: The Effect of Sex, Theoretical Orientation, and Interpersonal Boundaries." *Ethics and Behavior* 5:131–45.

Barglow, P. 2005. "Self-disclosure in Psychotherapy." *American Journal of Psychotherapy* 59:83–99.

Barker, R. L. 1999. *The Social Work Dictionary*. 4th ed. Washington, D.C.: National Association of Social Workers.

Barker, R. L. and D. M. Branson. 2000. *Forensic Social Work*. 2d ed. Binghamton, N.Y.: Haworth.

Barnett, J. and W. B. Johnson. 2008. *Ethics Desk Reference for Psychologists*. Washington, D.C.: American Psychological Association Books.

Barnett, J. E. and B. A. Yutrzenka. 1995. "Nonsexual Dual Relationships in Professional Practice, with Special Applications to Rural and Military Communities." *Independent Practitioner* 14:243–48.

Barr, D. 1997. "Clinical Social Worker, Disciplined by State, Sued over Patient Relations." *(Harrisonburg, Va.) Daily News-Record*, November 14, 19.

Barrett, M. S. and J. S. Berman. 2001. "Is Psychotherapy More Effective When Therapists Disclose Information about Themselves?" *Journal of Consulting and Clinical Psychology* 69:597–603.

Barry, V. 1986. *Moral Issues in Business*. 3d ed. Belmont, Calif.: Wadsworth.

Barsky, A. E. 2009. *Ethics and Values in Social Work*. New York: Oxford University Press.

Berliner, A. K. 1989. "Misconduct in Social Work Practice." *Social Work* 34:69–72.

Bernard, J. L. and C. S. Jara. 1986. "The Failure of Clinical Psychology Students to Apply Understood Ethical Principles." *Professional Psychology: Research and Practice* 17:316–21.

Bernsen, A., B. G. Tabachnick, and K. S. Pope. 1994. "National Survey of Social Workers' Sexual Attraction to Their Clients: Results, Implications, and Comparison to Psychologists." *Ethics and Behavior* 4:369–88.

Bernstein, T. L. and B. E. Hartsell. 2008. *The Portable Ethicist for Mental Health Professionals*. 2d ed. New York: Wiley.

Bersoff, D. N., ed. 2008. *Ethical Conflicts in Psychology*. 4th ed. Washington, D.C.: American Psychological Association.

Besharov, D. J. 1985. *The Vulnerable Social Worker: Liability for Serving Children and Families*. Silver Spring, Md.: National Association of Social Workers.

Bissell, L. and P. W. Haberman. 1984. *Alcoholism in the Professions*. New York: Oxford University Press.

Blackshaw, S. L. and J. B. Miller. 1994. Letter to the editor. *American Journal of Psychiatry* 151:293.

Bloom, M., J. Fischer, and J. Orme. 2009. *Evaluating Practice: Guidelines for the Accountable Professional*, 6th ed. Boston: Allyn & Bacon.

Bograd, M. 1993. "The Duel over Dual Relationships." *California Therapist* 5:7–16.

Bohmer, C. 2000. *The Wages of Seeking Help: Sexual Exploitation by Professionals*. Westport, Conn.: Praeger.

Bonosky, N. 1995. "Boundary Violations in Social Work Supervision: Clinical, Educational, and Legal Implications." *Clinical Supervisor* 13:79–95.

Borys, D. S. and K. S. Pope. 1989. "Dual Relationships between Therapist and Client: A National Study of Psychologists, Psychiatrists, and Social Workers." *Professional Psychology: Research and Practice* 20:283–93.

Bouhoutsos, J. C. 1985. "Therapist-Client Sexual Involvement: A Challenge for Mental Health Professionals." *Professional Psychology: Research and Practice* 14:185–96.

Bouhoutsos, J. C., J. Holroyd, H. Lerman, B. Forer, and M. Greenberg. 1983. "Sexual Intimacy between Psychotherapists and Patients." *Professional Psychology: Research and Practice* 14:185–96.

Brenner, E., D. Kindler, and M. Freundlich. 2010. "Dual Relationships in Child Welfare Practice: A Framework for Ethical Decision Making." *Children & Youth Services Review* 32:1437–45.

Bridges, N. A. 2001. "Therapist's Self-disclosure: Expanding the Comfort Zone." *Psychotherapy* 38:21–30.

Brodsky, A. M. 1986. "The Distressed Psychologist: Sexual Intimacies and Exploitation." In Kilburg, Nathan, and Thoreson, *Professionals in Distress*, 153–71.

Brown, L. S. 1984. "The Lesbian Therapist in Private Practice and Her Community." *Psychotherapy in Private Practice* 2(4):9–16.

Brownlee, K. 1992. "Constructivist Family Therapy: A Promising Method for Rural Settings." *Human Services in the Rural Environment* 16:18–23.

Brownlee, K. 1996. "The Ethics of Nonsexual Dual Relationships: A Dilemma for the Rural Mental Health Professional." *Community Mental Health Journal* 32:497–503.

Bruni, F. 1998. "Jury Finds Psychiatrist Was Negligent in Pedophile Case." *New York Times*, October 9, B4.

Bullis, R. K. 1995. *Clinical Social Worker Misconduct.* Chicago: Nelson-Hall.

Cahn, S. and P. Markie. 2008. *Ethics: History, Theory, and Contemporary Issues.* 4th ed. New York: Oxford University Press.

Calfee, B. E. 1997. "Lawsuit Prevention Techniques." In *Hatherleigh Guide to Ethics in Therapy*, 109–25.

Campbell, C. D. and M. C. Gordon. 2003. "Acknowledging the Inevitable: Understanding Multiple Relationships in Rural Practice." *Professional Psychology: Research and Practice* 34:430–34.

Celenza, A. 2007. *Sexual Boundary Violations: Therapeutic, Supervisory, and Academic Contexts.* Lanham, Md.: Aronson.

Chapman, C. 1997. "Dual Relationships in Substance Abuse Treatment." *Alcoholism Treatment Quarterly* 15:73–79.

Coleman, E. and S. Schaefer. 1986. "Boundaries of Sex and Intimacy between Client and Counselor." *Journal of Counseling and Development* 64:341–44.

Commission on Employment and Economic Support. National Association of Social Workers. 1987. *Impaired Social Worker Program Resource Book*. Silver Spring, Md.: National Association of Social Workers.

Committee on Women in Psychology. American Psychological Association. 1989. "If Sex Enters into the Psychotherapy Relationship." *Professional Psychology: Research and Practice* 20:112–15.

Congress, E. P. 1996. "Dual Relationships in Academia: Dilemmas for Social Work Educators." *Journal of Social Work Education* 32:329–38.

———. 1999. *Social Work Values and Ethics*. Belmont, Calif.: Brooks/Cole.

Corcoran, K. and J. Fischer. 2000. *Couples, Families, and Children*. Vol. 1 of *Measures for Clinical Practice: A Sourcebook*. New York: Free Press.

Corey, G., M. Corey, and P. Callanan. 2010. *Issues and Ethics in the Helping Professions*. 10th ed. Belmont, Calif.: Brooks/Cole.

Corey, G. and B. Herlihy. 1997. "Dual/Multiple Relationships: Toward a Consensus of Thinking." In *Hatherleigh Guide to Ethics in Therapy*, 183–94.

Cornell, W. F. 2007. "The Intricate Intimacies of Psychotherapy and Questions of Self-disclosure." *European Journal of Psychotherapy and Counseling* 9:51–61.

"Counselor Begins Sexual Relationship with Client." 1991. *Mental Health Law News* 6(4):1.

"Counselor, Counseling Center Mishandle Transference Phenomenon." 1997. *Mental Health Law News* 12(9):6.

"Court Upholds Law Used to Convict Therapist for Sexual Misconduct." 1998. *Mental Health Law News* 13(3):2

"Court Upholds Revocation of Psychologist's License Because He Had Sex with Patient." 1998. *Mental Health Law News* 13(2):6.

Cranford, R. E. and A. E. Doudera, eds. 1984. *Institutional Ethics Committees and Health Care Decision Making*. Ann Arbor, Mich.: Health Administration Press.

Daley, M. and M. Doughty. 2006. "Ethics Complaints in Social Work Practice: A Rural-Urban Comparison." *Journal of Social Work Values & Ethics* 3(1). www.socialworker.com/jswve/content/view/28/44/.

Davidson, V. 1991. "Touching Patients: Implications of the Handshake, the Hug, and the Embrace." *Psychodynamic Letter* 1(3):5–7.

DeJulio, L. M. and C. S. Berkman. 2003. "Nonsexual Multiple Relationships: Attitudes and Behaviors of Social Workers." *Ethics and Behavior* 13:57–74.

Deutsch, C. 1985. "A Survey of Therapists' Personal Problems and Treatment." *Professional Psychology: Research and Practice* 16:305–15.

Donagan, A. 1977. *The Theory of Morality*. Chicago: University of Chicago Press.

Dorland's Medical Dictionary. 1974. 25th ed. Philadelphia: Saunders.

Downey, D. L. 2001. "Therapeutic Touch in Psychotherapy." *Psychotherapy* 36(1):35–38.

Doyle, K. 1997. "Substance Abuse Counselors in Recovery: Implications for the Ethical Issue of Dual Relationships." *Journal of Counseling and Development* 75:428–32.

Dryden, W. 1990. "Self-disclosure in Rational-Emotive Therapy." In Stricker and Fisher, *Self-disclosure in the Therapeutic Relationship*, 61–74.

Durana, C. 1998. "The Use of Touch in Psychotherapy: Ethical and Clinical Guidelines." *Psychotherapy* 35:269–80.

Ebert, B. W. 1997. "Dual-Relationship Prohibitions: A Concept Whose Time Never Should Have Come." *Applied and Preventive Psychology* 6:137–56.

Elliott, R. L., G. Wolber, and W. Ferriss. 1997. "A Survey of Hospital Staff Attitudes toward Ethically Problematic Relationships with Patients." *Administration and Policy in Mental Health* 24:443–49.

Epstein, R. 1994. *Keeping Boundaries: Maintaining Safety and Integrity in the Psychotherapeutic Process.* Washington, D.C.: American Psychiatric Press.

Epstein, R. S. and R. I. Simon. 1990. "The Exploitation Index: An Early Warning Indicator of Boundary Violations in Psychotherapy." *Bulletin of the Menninger Clinic* 54:450–65.

Farber, B. A., ed. 1983. *Stress and Burnout in the Human Service Professions.* New York: Pergamon.

——. 2006. *Self-disclosure in Psychotherapy: Patient, Therapist, and Supervisory Perspectives.* New York: Guilford.

Farber, B. A. and L. Heifetz. 1981. "The Satisfactions and Stresses of Psychotherapeutic Work: A Factor Analysis Study." *Professional Psychology* 12:621–30.

Faulkner, K. K. and T. A. Faulkner. 1997. "Managing Multiple Relationships in Rural Communities: Neutrality and Boundary Violations." *Clinical Psychology: Science and Practice* 4:225–34.

Feldman-Summers, S. and G. Jones. 1984. "Psychological Impacts of Sexual Contact between Therapists or Other Health Care Practitioners and Their Clients." *Journal of Consulting and Clinical Psychology* 52:1054–61.

Fenby, B. L. 1978. "Social Work in a Rural Setting." *Social Work* 23:162–63.

Fleishman, J. L. and B. L. Payne. 1980. *Ethical Dilemmas and the Education of Policymakers.* Hastings-on-Hudson, N.Y.: Hastings Center.

Frankena, W. K. 1973. *Ethics.* 2d ed. Englewood Cliffs, N.J.: Prentice-Hall.

Freud, S. 1963. "Further Recommendations in the Technique of Psycho-analysis: Observations on Transference-love." 1915. In P. Rieff, ed., *Freud: Therapy and Technique*, 167–80. New York: Collier.

Freudenberger, H. J. 1986. "Chemical Abuse among Psychologists: Symptoms, Causes, and Treatment Issues." In Kilburg, Nathan, and Thoreson, *Professionals in Distress.* 135–52.

Gabbard, G. O., ed. 1989. *Sexual Exploitation in Professional Relationships.* Washington, D.C.: American Psychiatric Press.

———. 1990. *Psychodynamic Psychiatry in Clinical Practice.* Washington, D.C.: American Psychiatric Press.

———. 1996. "Lessons to Be Learned from the Study of Boundary Violations." *American Journal of Psychotherapy* 50:311–21.

Gabriel, L. 2005. *Speaking the Unspeakable: The Ethics of Dual Relationships in Counseling and Psychotherapy.* New York: Routledge.

Gaines, R. 2003. "Therapist Self-disclosure with Children, Adolescents, and Their Parents." *Journal of Clinical Psychology: In Session* 59:589–98.

Gartrell, N., J. Herman, S. Olarte, M. Feldstein, and R. Localio. 1986. "Psychiatrist-Patient Sexual Contact: Results of a National Survey." *American Journal of Psychiatry* 143(9):1126–31.

———. "Reporting Practices of Psychiatrists Who Knew of Sexual Misconduct by Colleagues." *American Journal of Orthopsychiatry* 57:287–95.

Gates, K. and K. Speare. 1990. "Overlapping Relationships in the Rural Community." In H. Lerner and N. Porter, eds., *Feminist Ethics in Psychotherapy*, 97–101. New York: Springer.

Gechtman, L. 1989. "Sexual Contact between Social Workers and Their Clients." In Gabbard, *Sexual Exploitation in Professional Relationships*, 27–38.

Gechtman, L. and J. C. Bouhoutsos. 1985. "Sexual Intimacy between Social Workers and Clients." Paper presented at the annual meeting of the Society for Clinical Social Workers, University City, Calif.

Gerson, A. and D. D. Fox. 1999. "Boundary Violations: The Gray Area." *American Journal of Forensic Psychology* 17(2):57–61.

Gifis, S. H. 1991. *Law Dictionary.* 3d ed. Hauppauge, N.Y.: Barron's.

Glass, L. L. 2003. "The Gray Areas of Boundary Crossings and Violations." *American Journal of Psychotherapy* 57:429–44.

Goisman, R. M. and T. G. Gutheil. 1992. "Risk Management in the Practice of Behavior Therapy: Boundaries and Behavior." *American Journal of Psychotherapy* 46(4):532–43.

Goldfried, M. R., L. A. Burckell, and C. Eubanks-Carter. 2003. "Therapist Self-disclosure in Cognitive-Behavioral Therapy." *Journal of Clinical Psychology* 59:555–68.

Goldstein, E. G. 1997. "To Tell or Not to Tell: The Disclosure of Events in the Therapist's Life to the Patient." *Clinical Social Work Journal* 25:41–58.

Gorovitz, S., ed. 1971. *Mill: Utilitarianism.* Indianapolis: Bobbs-Merrill.

Gottlieb, M. C. 1993. "Avoiding Exploitive Dual Relationships: A Decision-Making Model." *Psychotherapy* 30:41–48.

Gray, M. and S. Webb, eds. 2010. *Ethics and Value Perspectives in Social Work.* Hampshire, U.K.: Palgrave Macmillan.

Grosskurth, P. 1986. *Melanie Klein: Her World and Her Work.* New York: Alfred A. Knopf.

Grossman, M. 1973. "The Psychiatrist and the Subpoena." *Bulletin of the American Academy of Psychiatry and the Law* 1:245–53.

Gutheil, T. G. 1989. "Borderline Personality Disorder, Boundary Violations, and Patient-Therapist Sex: Medicolegal Pitfalls." *American Journal of Psychiatry* 146:597–602.

——. 2005. "Boundary Issues and Personality Disorders." *Journal of Psychiatric Practice* 11:88–96.

Gutheil, T. G. and A. Brodsky. 2008. *Preventing Boundary Violations in Clinical Practice*. New York: Guilford.

Gutheil, T. G. and G. O. Gabbard. 1993. "The Concept of Boundaries in Clinical Practice: Theoretical and Risk-Management Dimensions." *American Journal of Psychiatry* 150:188–96.

Gutheil, T. G. and R. I. Simon. 1995. "Between the Chair and the Door: Boundary Issues in the Therapeutic 'Transition Zone.'" *Harvard Review of Psychiatry* 2:336–40.

——. 2002. "Non-sexual Boundary Crossings and Boundary Violations: The Ethical Dimension." *Psychiatric Clinics of North America* 25:585–92.

——. 2005. "E-mails, Extra-Therapeutic Contact, and Early Boundary Problems: The Internet as a 'Slippery Slope.'" *Psychiatric Annals* 35:952–60.

Guthmann, D. and K. A. Sandberg. 2002. "Dual Relationships in the Deaf Community: When Dual Relationships Are Unavoidable and Essential." In A. A. Lazarus and O. Zur, eds., *Dual Relationships and Psychotherapy*, 287–97. New York: Springer.

Guy, J. D., P. L. Poelstra, and M. Stark. 1989. "Personal Distress and Therapeutic Effectiveness: National Survey of Psychologists Practicing Psychotherapy." *Professional Psychology: Research and Practice* 20:48–50.

Haas, L. J. and J. L. Malouf. 1989. *Keeping Up the Good Work: A Practitioner's Guide to Mental Health Ethics*. Sarasota, Fla.: Professional Resource Exchange.

The Hatherleigh Guide to Ethics in Therapy. New York: Hatherleigh.

Hedges, L. E., R. Hilton, V. W. Hilton, and O. B. Caudill Jr., eds. 1997. *Therapists at Risk: Perils of the Intimacy of the Therapeutic Relationship*. Northvale, N.J.: Aronson.

Helbok, C. M. 2003. "The Practice of Psychology in Rural Communities: Potential Ethical Dilemmas." *Ethics and Behavior* 13:367–84.

Helbok, C. M., R. P. Marinelli, and R. T. Walls. 2006. "National Survey of Ethical Practices across Rural and Urban Communities." *Professional Psychology: Research and Practice* 37:36–44.

Herlihy, B. and G. Corey. 2006. *Boundary Issues in Counseling: Multiple Roles and Responsibilities*. 2d ed. Alexandria, Va.: American Association for Counseling and Development.

Hester, D. 2007. *Ethics by Committee: A Textbook on Consultation, Organization, and Education for Hospital Ethics Committees.* Lanham, Md.: Rowman & Littlefield.

Hill, C. E. and S. Knox. 2002. "Self-disclosure." In J. C. Norcross, ed., *Psychotherapy Relationships That Work: Therapist Contributions and Responsiveness to Patients,* 255–65. New York: Oxford University Press.

Hill, M. 1999. "Barter: Ethical Considerations in Psychotherapy." *Women and Therapy* 22(3):81–91.

Hines, A. H., D. N. Adler, A. S. Chang, and J. R. Rundell. 1998. "Dual Agency, Dual Relationships, Boundary Crossings, and Associated Boundary Violations: A Survey of Military and Civilian Psychiatrists." *Military Medicine* 163:826–33.

Hunter, M. and J. Struve. 1998. *The Ethical Use of Touch in Psychotherapy.* Thousand Oaks, Calif.: Sage.

"Improper Sexual Contact Blamed for Further Psychological Problems." 1997. *Mental Health Law News* 12(6):4.

Jayaratne, S. and W. A. Chess. 1984. "Job Satisfaction, Burnout, and Turnover: A National Study." *Social Work* 29:448–55.

Jayaratne, S., T. Croxton, and D. Mattison. 1997. "Social Work Professional Standards: An Exploratory Study." *Social Work* 42:187–99.

Johnson, M. and G. L. Stone. 1986. "Social Workers and Burnout." *Journal of Social Work Research* 10:67–80.

Johnson, W. B. 2008. "Top Ethical Challenges for Military Psychologists." *Military Psychology* 20:49–62.

Johnson, W. B. and G. P. Koocher, eds. 2011. *Ethical Conundrums, Quandaries and Predicaments in Mental Health Practice: A Casebook from the Files of Experts.* New York: Oxford University Press.

Johnson, W. B., J. Ralph, and S. J. Johnson. 2005. "Managing Multiple Roles in Embedded Environments: The Case of Aircraft Carrier Psychology." *Professional Psychology: Research and Practice* 36:73–81.

Johnston, S. and B. A. Farber. 1996. "The Maintenance of Boundaries in Psychotherapeutic Practice" *Psychotherapy: Theory, Research, Practice, and Training* 33:391–402.

Jones, G.. and A. Stokes. 2009. *Online Counseling: A Handbook for Practitioners.* New York: Palgrave Macmillan.

Jonsen, A. R. 1984. "A Guide to Guidelines." *American Society of Law and Medicine: Ethics Committee Newsletter* 2:4.

Jorgenson, L. M. 1995. "Rehabilitating Sexually Exploitative Therapists: A Risk-Management Perspective." *Psychiatric Annals* 25:118–22.

Kagle, J. D. and P. N. Giebelhausen. 1994. "Dual Relationships and Professional Boundaries." *Social Work* 39:213–20.

Kagle, J. D. and S. Kopels. 2008. *Social Work Records.* 3d ed. Prospect Heights, Ill.: Waveland Press.

Kardener, S. H., M. Fuller, and I. N. Mensh. 1976. "Characteristics of Erotic Practitioners." *American Journal of Psychiatry* 133:1324–25.

Kertay, L. and S. L. Reviere. 1993. "The Use of Touch in Psychotherapy: Theoretical and Ethical Considerations." *Psychotherapy* 30:32–40.

Kessler, L. E. and C. A. Waehler. 2005. "Addressing Multiple Relationships between Clients and Therapists in Lesbian, Gay, Bisexual, and Transgender Communities." *Professional Psychology: Research and Practice* 36:66–72.

Kilburg, R. R., F. W. Kaslow, and G. R. VandenBos. 1988. "Professionals in Distress." *Hospital and Community Psychiatry* 39:723–25.

Kilburg, R. R., P. E. Nathan, and R. W. Thoreson, eds. 1986. *Professionals in Distress: Issues, Syndromes, and Solutions in Psychology.* Washington, D.C.: American Psychological Association.

Kitchener, K. S. 1988. "Dual Role Relationships: What Makes Them So Problematic?" *Journal of Counseling and Development* 67:217–21.

Knox, S., S. A. Hess, E. N. Williams, and C. E. Hill. 2003. "Here's a Little Something for You: How Therapists Respond to Clients' Gifts." *Journal of Counseling Psychology* 50:199–210.

Knox, S. and C. E. Hill. 2003. "Therapist Self-disclosure: Research-Based Suggestions for Practitioners." *Journal of Clinical Psychology: In Session* 59:529–40.

Koeske, G. F. and R. D. Koeske. 1989. "Work Load and Burnout: Can Social Support and Perceived Accomplishment Help?" *Social Work* 34:243–48.

Kolmes, K. 2011. "My Private Practice Social Media Policy." www.drkkolmes.com /docs/socmed.pdf.

Koocher, G. P. and P. Keith-Spiegel. 2008. *Ethics in Psychology and the Mental Health Professions.* 3d ed. New York: Oxford University Press.

Krassner, D. 2004. "Gifts from Physicians to Patients: An Ethical Dilemma." *Psychiatric Services* 55:505–6.

Kraus, R., G. Stricker, and C. Speyer, eds. 2011. *Online Counseling: A Handbook for Mental Health Professionals,* 2d ed. London: Elsevier.

Kutchins, H. 1991. "The Fiduciary Relationship: The Legal Basis for Social Workers' Responsibilities to Clients." *Social Work* 36:106–13.

Laliotis, D. A. and J. H. Grayson. 1985. "Psychologist Heal Thyself: What Is Available for the Impaired Psychologist." *American Psychologist* 40:84–96.

Lamb, D. H., S. J. Catanzaro, and A. S. Moorman. 2004. "A Preliminary Look at How Psychologists Identify, Evaluate, and Proceed When Faced with Possible Multiple Relationship Dilemmas." *Professional Psychology: Research and Practice* 35:248–54.

Lamb, D. H., N. R. Presser, K. S. Pfost, M. C. Baum, V. R. Jackson, and P. A. Jarvis. 1987. "Confronting Professional Impairment during the Internship: Identification, Due Process, and Remediation." *Professional Psychology: Research and Practice* 18:597–603.

Lane, R. and J. Hull. 1990. "Self-disclosure and Classical Psychoanalysis." In Stricker and Fisher, *Self-disclosure in the Therapeutic Relationship*, 31–46.

Lazarus, A. A. and O. Zur. 2002. *Dual Relationships and Psychotherapy*. New York: Springer.

Lipton, S. D. 1977. "The Advantages of Freud's Technique as Shown in His Analysis of the Rat Man." *International Journal of Psychoanalysis* 58:255–73.

Little, M. I. 1990. *Psychotic Anxieties and Containment: A Personal Record of an Analysis with Winnicott*. Northvale, N.J.: Aronson.

Loewenberg, F., R. Dolgoff, and D. Harrington. 2008. *Ethical Decisions for Social Work Practice*. 8th ed. Belmont, Calif.: Brooks/Cole.

Luepker, E. T. 1999. "Effects of Practitioners' Sexual Misconduct: A Follow-up Study." *Journal of the American Academy of Psychiatry and the Law* 27:51–63.

——. 2002. *Record Keeping in Psychotherapy and Counseling*. New York: Routledge.

McCrady, B. S. 1989. "The Distressed or Impaired Professional: From Retribution to Rehabilitation." *Journal of Drug Issues* 19:337–49.

Madden, R. G. 1998. *Legal Issues in Social Work, Counseling, and Mental Health*. Thousand Oaks, Calif.: Sage.

Maroda, K. J. 1994. *The Power of Countertransference: Innovations in Analytic Technique*. Northvale, N.J.: Aronson.

Maslach, C. 2003. *Burnout: The Cost of Caring*. Los Altos, Calif.: Malor.

Milam, J. R. and K. Ketcham. 1981. *Under the Influence: A Guide to the Myths and Realities of Alcoholism*. Seattle: Madrona.

Millon, T., C. Millon, and M. Antoni. 1986. "Sources of Emotional and Mental Disorder among Psychologists: A Career Development Perspective." In Kilburg, Nathan, and Thoreson, *Professionals in Distress*, 119–34.

Mittendorf, S. and J. Schroeder. 2004. "Boundaries in Social Work: The Ethical Dilemma of Social Worker-Client Sexual Relationships." *Journal of Social Work Values & Ethics* 1(1). www.socialworker.com/jswve/content/view/11/30/.

Moleski, S. M. and M. S. Kiselica. 2005. "Dual Relationships: A Continuum Ranging from Destructive to Therapeutic." *Journal of Counseling and Development* 83:3–11.

Moline, M., G. T. Williams, and K. M. Austin. 1998. *Documenting Psychotherapy: Essentials for Mental Health Practitioners*. Thousand Oaks, Calif.: Sage.

Myers, W. A. 1994. Letter to the editor. *American Journal of Psychiatry* 151:293–94.

Nagy, T. 2010. *Essential Ethics for Psychologists*. Washington, D.C.: American Psychological Association.

National Association of Social Workers. 2008. *Code of Ethics*. Washington, D.C.: National Association of Social Workers.

Nickel, M. 2004. "Professional Boundaries: The Dilemma of Dual and Multiple Relationships in Rural Clinical Practice." *Counseling and Clinical Psychology Journal* 1:17–22.

Nugent, W., J. Sieppert, and W. Hudson. 2001. *Practice Evaluation for the 21st Century.* Belmont, Calif.: Brooks/Cole.

Olarte, S. W. 1997. "Sexual Boundary Violations." In *Hatherleigh Guide to Ethics in Therapy,* 195–209.

"Patient's Claims against Psychiatrist Dismissed." 1998. *Mental Health Law News* 13(12):2.

Pearson, M. M. and E. A. Strecker. 1960. "Physicians as Psychiatric Patients: Private Practice Experience." *American Journal of Psychiatry* 116:915–19.

Penfold, P. S. 1998. *Sexual Abuse by Health Professionals: A Personal Search for Meaning and Healing.* Toronto: University of Toronto Press.

Peterson, M. R. 1992. *At Personal Risk: Boundary Violations in Professional-Client Relationships.* New York: W. W. Norton.

——. 1996. "Common Problem Areas and Their Causes Resulting in Disciplinary Action." In L. J. Bass et al., eds., *Professional Conduct and Discipline in Psychology,* 71–89. Washington, D.C.: American Psychological Association.

Plaut, S. M. 1997. "Boundary Violations in Professional-Client Relationships: Overview and Guidelines for Prevention." *Sexual and Marital Therapy* 12:77–94.

Polowy, C. I. and C. Gorenberg. 1997. *"Client Confidentiality and Privileged Communication: Office of General Counsel Law Notes.* Washington, D.C.: National Association of Social Workers.

Pope, G. G. 1990. "Abuse of Psychotherapy: Psychotherapist-Patient Intimacy." *Psychotherapy and Psychosomatics* 53:191–98.

Pope, K. S. 1986. "New Trends in Malpractice Cases and Changes in APA's Liability Insurance." *Independent Practitioner* 6:23–6.

——. 1988. "How Clients Are Harmed by Sexual Contact with Mental Health Professionals: The Syndrome and Its Prevalence." *Journal of Counseling and Development* 67:222–26.

——. 1989. "Sexual Intimacies between Psychologists and their Students and Supervisees: Research, Standards, and Professional Liability." *Independent Practitioner* 9:33–41.

——. 1991. "Dual Relationships in Psychotherapy." *Ethics and Behavior* 1:21–34.

——. 1994. *Sexual Involvement with Therapists: Patient Assessment, Subsequent Therapy, Forensics.* Washington, D.C.: American Psychological Association.

Pope, K. S. and J. Bouhoutsos. 1986. *Sexual Intimacy between Therapists and Patients.* New York: Praeger.

Pope, K. S. and M. Vasquez. 2010. *Ethics in Psychotherapy and Counseling: A Practical Guide,* 4th ed. Hoboken, N.J.: John Wiley.

Pope, K .S., P. Keith-Spiegel, and B. G. Tabachnick. 1986. "Sexual Attraction to Clients: The Human Therapist and the (Sometimes) Inhuman Training System." *American Psychologist* 41:147–58.

Pope, K. S., B. G. Tabachnick, and P. Keith-Spiegel. 1988. "Good and Bad Practice in Psychotherapy: National Survey of Beliefs of Psychologists." *Professional Psychology: Research and Practice* 19:547–52.

Popper, K. 1966. *The Open Society and Its Enemies*. 5th ed. London: Routledge and Kegan Paul.

Post, L., J. Blustein, and N. Dubler. 2006. *Handbook for Health Care Ethics Committees*. Baltimore: Johns Hopkins University Press.

Prochaska, J. O. and J. C. Norcross. 1983. "Psychotherapists' Perspectives on Treating Themselves and Their Clients for Psychic Distress." *Professional Psychology: Research and Practice* 14:642–55.

"Psychiatrist Censured for Engaging in Commercial Transactions with Clients." 1996. *Mental Health Law News* 11(3):6.

"Psychologist Encourages Sexual Misconduct between Patient and Psychiatrist." 1989. *Mental Health Law News* 4(3):2.

Reamer, F. G. 1987. "Ethics Committees in Social Work." *Social Work* 32:188–92.

——. 1990. *Ethical Dilemmas in Social Service*. 2d ed. New York: Columbia University Press.

——. 1992. "The Impaired Social Worker." *Social Work* 37:165–70.

——. 1994. "Social Work Values and Ethics." In F. G. Reamer, ed., *The Foundations of Social Work Knowledge*, 195–230. New York: Columbia University Press.

——. 1995a. "Ethics Consultation in Social Work." *Social Thought* 18:3–16.

——. 1995b. "Malpractice and Liability Claims against Social Workers: First Facts." *Social Work* 40:595–601.

——. 1997. "Ethical Issues for Social Work Practice." In M. Reisch and E. Gambrill, eds., *Social Work in the Twenty-first Century*, 340–49. Thousand Oaks, Calif.: Pine Forge/Sage.

——. 2001a. *Ethics Education in Social Work*. Alexandria, Va.: Council on Social Work Education.

——. 2001b. *The Social Work Ethics Audit: A Risk Management Tool*. Washington, D.C.: NASW Press.

——. 2003a. "Boundary Issues in Social Work: Managing Dual Relationships." *Social Work* 48:121–33.

——. 2003b. *Social Work Malpractice and Liability: Strategies for Prevention*. 2d ed. New York: Columbia University Press.

——. 2005. "Documentation in Social Work: Evolving Ethical and Risk Management Standards." *Social Work* 50:325–34.

——. 2006a. *Ethical Standards in Social Work: A Review of the NASW Code of Ethics*. 2d ed. Washington, D.C.: NASW Press.

——. 2006b. "Nontraditional and Unorthodox Interventions in Social Work: Ethical and Legal Implications." *Families in Society* 87:191–7.

——. 2006c. *Social Work Values and Ethics*. 3d ed. New York: Columbia University Press.

——. 2008a. "Ethical Standards in Social Work: The NASW Code of Ethics." In
  T. Mizrahi and L. E. Davis, eds., *Encyclopedia of Social Work*, 4:391–97. 20th ed.
  New York and Washington: Oxford University Press and NASW Press.

——. 2008b. "Ethics and Values." In Mizrahi and Davis, *Encyclopedia of Social
  Work*, 2:143–51.

——. 2008c. "Social Workers' Management of Error: Ethical and Risk Management Issues." *Families in Society* 89:61–68.

——. 2009a. "Ethical Issues in Social Work." In A. R. Roberts, ed., *Social Workers'
  Desk Reference*, 115–20. New York: Oxford University Press.

——. 2009b. "The Impaired Social Work Professional." In Roberts, *Social Workers'
  Desk Reference*, 163–68.

——. 2009c. "Risk Management in Social Work." In Roberts, *Social Workers' Desk
  Reference*, 121–27.

——. 2009d. *The Social Work Ethics Casebook: Cases and Commentary*. Washington, D.C.: NASW Press.

Reamer, F. G. and M. Abramson. 1982. *The Teaching of Social Work Ethics*. Hastings-on-Hudson, N.Y.: Hastings Center.

Reamer, F. G. and D. H. Siegel. 2008. *Teens in Crisis: How the Industry Serving
  Struggling Teens Helps and Hurts Our Kids*. New York: Columbia University
  Press.

Reaves, R. R. 1986. "Legal Liability and Psychologists." In Kilburg, Nathan, and
  Thoreson, *Professionals in Distress*, 173–84.

"'Rebirthing' Therapists Get Prison Terms." 2011. *ABC News*, June 18. http://abcnews
  .go.com/US/story?id=93074&page=1.

Reupert, A. 2007. "Social Worker's Use of Self." *Clinical Social Work Journal*
  35:107–16.

Roberts, J. R. 2005. "Transparency and Self-disclosure in Family Therapy: Dangers
  and Possibilities." *Family Process* 44:45–63.

Ross, W. D. 1930. *The Right and the Good*. Oxford: Clarendon.

St. Germaine, J. 1993. "Dual Relationships: What's Wrong with Them?" *American
  Counselor* 2:25–30.

——. 1996. "Dual Relationships and Certified Alcohol and Drug Counselors: A
  National Study of Ethical Beliefs and Behaviors." *Alcoholism Treatment Quarterly* 14:29–44.

Samuel, S. E. and G. E. Gorton. 2001. "Sexual Exploitation: An Extreme of Professional Deception." *American Journal of Forensic Psychiatry* 22:63–81.

Schank, A. J. and T. M. Skovholt. 1997. "Dual Relationship Dilemmas of Rural and
  Small-Community Psychologists." *Professional Psychology: Research and Practice* 28:44–49.

——. 2006. *Ethical Practice in Small Communities: Challenges and Rewards for
  Psychologists*. Washington, D.C.: American Psychological Association.

Schoener, G. R. 1995. "Assessment of Professionals Who Have Engaged in Boundary Violations." *Psychiatric Annals* 25:95–99.

Schoener, G. R. and J. C. Gonsiorek. 1989. "Assessment and Development of Rehabilitation Plans for the Therapist." In Schoener et al., *Psychotherapists' Sexual Involvement with Clients*, 401–20.

Schoener, G. R., J. H. Milgrom, J. C. Gonsiorek, E. T. Luepker, and R. M. Conroe, eds. 1989. *Psychotherapists' Sexual Involvement with Clients: Intervention and Prevention*. Minneapolis: Walk-In Counseling Center.

Schon, D. 1983. *The Reflective Practitioner: How Professionals Think in Action*. New York: Basic Books.

Schutz, B. M. 1982. *Legal Liability in Psychotherapy*. San Francisco: Jossey-Bass.

Sell, J. M., M. C. Gottlieb, and L. Schoenfeld. 1986. "Ethical Considerations of Social/Romantic Relationships with Present and Former Clients." *Professional Psychology: Research and Practice* 17:504–8.

Senger, H. L. 1994. Letter to the editor. *American Journal of Psychiatry* 151:294.

Sidell, N. 2011. *Social Work Documentation*. Washington, D.C.: NASW Press.

Simon, R. I. 1991. "Psychological Injury Caused by Boundary Violation Precursors to Therapist-Patient Sex." *Psychiatric Annals* 21:614–19.

——. 1992. "Treatment Boundary Violations: Clinical, Ethical, and Legal Considerations." *Bulletin of the American Academy of Psychiatry and the Law* 20:269–88.

——. 1995. "The Natural History of Therapist Sexual Misconduct: Identification and Prevention." *Psychiatric Annals* 25:90–94.

——. 1999. "Therapist-Patient Sex: From Boundary Violations to Sexual Misconduct." *Forensic Psychiatry* 22:31–47.

Smart, J. J. C. 1971. "Extreme and Restricted Utilitarianism." In Gorovitz, *Mill: Utilitarianism*, 195–203.

Smith, D. and M. Fitzpatrick. 1995. "Patient-Therapist Boundary Issues: An Integrative Review of Theory and Research." *Professional Psychology: Research and Practice* 26:499–506.

Smolar, A. M. 2002. "Reflections on Gifts in the Therapeutic Setting: The Gift from Patient to Therapist." *American Journal of Psychotherapy* 56:27–45.

——. 2003. "When We Give More: Reflections on Intangible Gifts from Therapist to Patient." *American Journal of Psychotherapy* 57:300–23.

"Social Worker Engages in Sexual Relationship with Patient." 1999. *Mental Health Law News* 14(5):2.

Sonnenstuhl, W. J. 1989. "Reaching the Impaired Professional: Applying Findings from Organizational and Occupational Research." *Journal of Drug Issues* 19:533–39.

Staal, M. A. and R. E. King. 2000. "Managing a Multiple Relationship Environment: The Ethics of Military Psychology." *Professional Psychology: Research and Practice* 31:698–705.

Stake, J. E. and J. Oliver. 1991. "Sexual Contact and Touching between Therapist and Client: A Survey of Psychologists' Attitudes and Behavior." *Professional Psychology: Research and Practice* 22:297–307.

Stone, A. A. 1984. *Law, Psychiatry, and Morality.* Washington, D.C.: American Psychiatric Press.

Strasburger, L. H., L. Jorgenson, and R. Randles. 1995. "Criminalization of Psychotherapist-Patient Sex." In D. N. Bersoff, ed., *Ethical Conflicts in Psychology,* 229–33. Washington, D.C.: American Psychological Association.

Stricker, G. and M. Fisher, eds. 1990. *Self-disclosure in the Therapeutic Relationship.* New York: Plenum.

Strom-Gottfried, K. J. 1999. "Professional Boundaries: An Analysis of Violations by Social Workers." *Families in Society* 80:439–49.

Sussman, M. B. 1995. A *Perilous Calling: The Hazards of Psychotherapy Practice.* New York: Wiley.

Syme, G. 2003. *Dual Relationships in Counselling and Psychotherapy.* London: Sage.

Teel, K. 1975. "The Physician's Dilemma: A Doctor's View: What the Law Should Be." *Baylor Law Review* 27:6–9.

"Therapist Marries Patient with Multiple Personalities: Showcases Her While Treating Condition." 1996. *Mental Health Law News* 11(12):2.

Thoreson, R. W., M. Miller, and C. J. Krauskopf. 1989. "The Distressed Psychologist: Prevalence and Treatment Considerations." *Professional Psychology: Research and Practice* 20:153–58.

Thoreson, R. W., P. E. Nathan, J. K. Skoria, and R. R. Kilburg. 1983. "The Alcoholic Psychologist: Issues, Problems, and Implications for the Profession." *Professional Psychology: Research and Practice* 14:670–84.

Trice, H. M. and J. M. Beyer. 1984. "Work-Related Outcomes of the Constructive Confrontation Strategy in a Job-Based Alcoholism Program." *Journal of Studies on Alcohol* 45:393–404.

Twemlow, S. W. and G. O. Gabbard. 1989. "The Love-Sick Therapist." In Gabbard, *Sexual Exploitation in Professional Relationships,* 71–87.

Vaillant, G. E., J. R. Brighton, and C. McArthur. 1970. "Physicians' Use of Mood-Altering Drugs: A 20-year Follow-up Report." *New England Journal of Medicine* 282:365–70.

VandenBos, G. R. and R. F. Duthie. 1986. "Confronting and Supporting Colleagues in Distress." In Kilburg, Nathan, and Thoreson, *Professionals in Distress,* 211–31.

Vonk, E., T. Tripodi, and I. Epstein. 2007. *Research Techniques for Clinical Social Workers.* New York: Columbia University Press.

Wilcoxon, A., T. Remley, and S. Gladding. 2011. *Ethical, Legal, and Professional Issues in the Practice of Marriage and Family Therapy.* 5th ed. Upper Saddle River, N.J.: Prentice-Hall.

Willison, B. G. and R. L. Masson. 1986. "The Role of Touch in Therapy: An Adjunct to Communication." *Journal of Counseling and Development* 64:497–500.

Wilson, S. J. 1978. *Confidentiality in Social Work: Issues and Principles.* New York: Free Press.

Winnicott, D. W. 1949. "Hate in the Countertransference." *International Journal of Psychoanalysis* 30:69–74.

"Woman Blames Psychological Problems on Psychologist's Sexual Relationship with Her." 1997. *Mental Health Law News* 12(8):2.

"Woman Claims Improper Sexual Conduct by Psychologist." 1996. *Mental Health Law News* 11(2):3.

Wood, B. J., S. Klein, H. J. Cross, C. J. Lammers, and J. K. Elliott. 1985. "Impaired Practitioners: Psychologists' Opinions about Prevalence, and Proposals for Intervention." *Professional Psychology: Research and Practice* 16:843–50.

Woody, R. H. 1998. "Bartering for Psychological Services." *Professional Psychology: Research and Practice* 29:174–78.

Younggren, J. N. and M. C. Gottlieb. 2004. "Managing Risk When Contemplating Multiple Relationships." *Professional Psychology: Research and Practice* 35:255–60.

Zur, O. 2007. *Boundaries in Psychotherapy: Ethical and Clinical Explorations.* Washington, D.C.: American Psychological Association.

INDEX

act utilitarianism, 28. *See also* rule
  utilitarianism; utilitarianism
actual duty (Ross), 26
advice, receipt of from clients, 135–138
affectionate communications, 114–116
Akamatsu, T., 76
Alcoholics Anonymous, 180–82
altruism, as source of boundary issues, 18
American Association for Marriage and
  Family Therapy, *Code of Ethics*, 7, 15,
  41, 75–76
American Counseling Association, *Code
  of Ethics*, 15, 41, 76, 127–128
American Distance Counseling
  Association, 209
American Medical Association, *Principles
  of Medical Ethics with Annotations
  Especially Applicable to Psychiatry*, 7
American Psychological Association,
  *Ethical Principles of Psychologists and
  Code of Conduct*, 13, 33, 75–76, 119,
  127, 195
appearance of impropriety, concept of, 8
Association for Counseling and Therapy
  Online, 209
avatar therapy, as source of boundary
  issues, 10, 106

Barry, V., 198–99
barter, use of with clients, 14–15, 124–130
Bentham, J., 27
Berkman, C., 99, 108, 126, 139, 142, 145, 147

Blackshaw, S., 71
Bograd, M., 100
Borys, D., 56
Bouhoutsos, J., 37, 63
boundary crossing, 6, 7–8
boundary issues, defined, 2, 3; typology,
  11–19
boundary violation, 6
Brodsky, A., 44, 47–48, 94–95, 112, 122,
  135, 142
Brownlee, K., 186
business relationships with clients,
  130–135

Calfee, B, 65–66
Celenza, A., 48–49, 55, 62–63, 64–65, 85
codes of ethics, 28–29
Commission on Employment and
  Economic Support (National
  Association of Social Workers), 36
community-based contact with clients,
  117–122
conflicts of interest, concept of, 6–7,
  148–154, 193–201
Congress, E., 84
constructive confrontation, concept of
  (Sonnenstuhl), 72
consultation, role of, in ethical decision-
  making, 30–32
Council on Mental Health (American
  Medical Association), 34
Corey, G., 5